The
California Dante,
in addition to the intro-
duction, facing text, and verse
translation volume dedicated to
each *cantica* of *The Divine Comedy*,
will present, under the General Edi-
torship of Allen Mandelbaum, a separate volume of commentary for each of the
cantiche. These three commentary volumes
will constitute the California Lectura Dantis;
in these volumes, which will call on Ameri-
can, Italian, English, German, and other in-
ternational scholar-critics, each contributor
will present his or her reading, in essay
form, of one or of several cantos. The
thirty-three—or in the case of *Inferno*,
thirty-four—canto readings in each
volume will be supplemented
by a comprehensive index-
glossary and synoptic
appendices.

DANTE ALIGHIERI

The Divine Comedy of

Dante Alighieri

A Verse Translation

with Introductions & Commentary by

Allen Mandelbaum

Drawings by Barry Moser

University of California Press

Berkeley · Los Angeles · London

This translation of the PURGATORIO *is inscribed to
Irma Brandeis and Helaine Newstead—
as* l'altro Guido *had it:*
CHÉ 'N TUTTE GUISE VI DEGGIO LAUDARE

UNIVERSITY OF CALIFORNIA PRESS
Berkeley and Los Angeles, California
University of California Press, Ltd.
London, England

English translation copyright © 1982 by Allen Mandelbaum

Drawings copyright © 1982 by Barry Moser

ISBN 0-520-04516-5
Library of Congress Catalogue Number 73-94441

PRINTED IN THE UNITED STATES OF AMERICA

PURGATORIO

Part One: Introduction,

Italian Text & Translation,

and Thirty-Four Drawings

INTRODUCTION

For the Virgil of Dante's *Purgatorio*, "love is the seed in you of every virtue/ and of all acts deserving punishment" (XVII, 104–105). To find one same source for all good and all evil is to insist on the need for the education of desire. The descent through Hell and ascent of the seven terraces of the Mount of Purgatory are the tale of that education of Dante's hungering, longing, thirsting, will. After those terraces, at the threshold of the Earthly Paradise, Virgil can assure him: "Today your hungerings will find their peace/ . . . My son, you've seen the temporary fire/ and the eternal fire; you have reached/ the place past which my powers cannot see./ I've brought you here through intellect and art;/ from now on, let your pleasure be your guide;/ you're past the steep and past the narrow paths. . . ./ Await no further word or sign from me:/ your will is free, erect, and whole—to act/ against that will would be to err: therefore/ I crown and miter you over yourself" (XXVII, 115–142).

This tale forms part of what Thomas Carlyle called Dante's "unfathomable heart-song." But in the *Purgatorio*, the song is sung by a careful cartographer and passionately precise watcher of the skies, one who contains time and space in the calculated space and time of his own lines: "Reader, I am not squandering more rhymes/ in order to describe their forms; since I/ must spend elsewhere, I can't be lavish here" (XXIV, 97–99); and then, "If, reader, I had ampler space in which/ to write, I'd sing—though incompletely—that/ sweet draught for which my thirst was limitless;/ but since all of the pages pre-disposed/ for this, the second canticle, are full,/ the curb of art will not let me continue" (XXXIII, 136–141).

The space of Dante's island Mountain of Purgatory is in the southern hemisphere of Earth, directly opposite the northern hemisphere's Jerusalem. In that southern hemisphere, the hemisphere of water, it is the only body of land. Souls who will undergo purgation before their entry into Paradise disembark on the shore of the solitary island. Behind them lies their sea-voyage from the mouth of the Tiber, which "always is the place of gathering/ for those who do not sink to Acheron" (II, 104–105), under the care of a "helmsman sent from Heaven," in a "boat so light, so quick/ that nowhere did the water swallow it" (II, 40–41). Ahead of Dante there lies the writing of the *Purgatorio*, also—by way of likeness—a sea-voyage: "To course across more kindly waters now/ my talent's little vessel lifts her sails,/ leaving behind herself a sea so cruel" (I, 1–3).

The lower slopes of the island are a waiting place, the Ante-Purgatory (II–IX), where those who delayed their repentance until the end of life must wait longest before they are allowed to enter Purgatory.

Purgatory proper, occupying eighteen cantos of *Purgatorio*, is entered by a gate at the top of a three-step stairway (IX, 76–145) and consists of seven terraces. These are level indentations in the tall mountain; they are joined to each other by stairways carved through the rifted rock, with the ascent growing easier as one moves upward. Each of the terraces punishes a sin; and the hierarchy of sins places the most grievous sins on the lower terraces. In ascending order, the seven terraces punish — remedially — pride, envy, wrath, sloth, avarice (coupled with its counter-sin, prodigality), gluttony, and lust.

The Earthly Paradise occupies the summit of the island mountain and the last, and rather autonomous, six cantos of *Purgatorio* (XXVIII–XXXIII). (Indeed, this mountain may also be called the Mountain of Earthly Paradise, the mountain foreshadowed by the "mountain of delight" that Dante cannot climb in Canto I of the *Inferno*—and it is probably the same peak Ulysses sees at the end of Canto XXVI of the *Inferno*, the summit in sight of which Ulysses, unaided by grace, shipwrecks.)

Time is charted with equal care: Dante the voyager moves through these three regions of Purgatory in an ascent that most paraphrasts explain as lasting from the morning of Easter Sunday, April 10, 1300, to noon of Wednesday, April 13. Where the *Inferno* begins at night in the "shadowed forest," with the entry into Hell, or, more precisely, to the Ante-Inferno, on the evening of Good Friday (*Inf.* II, 1–3), *Purgatorio* begins shortly before dawn, the entry to Purgatory proper, two hours after dawn, and to the Earthly Paradise at dawn.

But Dante climbs only by day. The first night is spent in that portion of the Ante-Purgatory called the Valley of the Rulers, where men of state who, in life, delayed their repentance through negligence wait (IX); the second night is spent on the fourth terrace, the terrace of sloth, at the end of his climb through the terraces of the four weightier sins, at the threshold of the fifth terrace (XVIII, 143 to XIX, 36). The third night is spent, after Dante's passage through fire on the seventh terrace (this is the "temporary fire," as Hell's fire is the "eternal fire" of XXVII, 127–128), the terrace of the lustful, at the threshold of the Earthly Paradise (XXVII). On each of these equidistant nights, Dante dreams: first the dream of the Eagle (IX, 13–32); then the dream of the Siren and the nameless "alert and saintly" woman, (XIX, 7–33); and finally the dream of Leah, exemplar of the active life, and Rachel, exemplar of the meditative life (XXVII, 91–114).

The movements of heavenly bodies, somewhat clairvoyantly referred to by Virgil but never directly present in Hell, punctuate *Purgatorio* throughout. References play between the southern skies of Purgatory, present *there* for Dante, and our skies, the skies of the northern hemisphere, present to us and to Dante returned from his voyage. Here, in our world, Jerusalem marks the center, and the mouth of the Ganges marks the eastern limit; while the western limit is marked by the Straits of Gibraltar or, in its stead, either Gades (our Cadiz) or the River Ebro. Reading the hands of his Earth clock, Dante can amplify the hour of sunset in Purgatory thus: "Just as, there where its Maker shed His blood,/ the sun shed its first rays, and Ebro lay/ beneath high Libra, and the ninth hour's rays/ were scorching Ganges' waves; so here, the sun/ stood at the point of day's departure . . ." (XXVII, 1–5).

The planets (of which the sun, for Dante, is one), the constellations, the hours—all participate in these recordings.

Sometimes Dante's recordings are direct, even when allegorical, as in the vision of the four stars that symbolize the four "natural" virtues (prudence, justice, fortitude, and temperance). There his most memorable juxtaposition of Purgatorial skies and our skies concludes his first scanning of Purgatory's skies (I, 13–27):

> *The gentle hue of oriental sapphire*
> *in which the sky's serenity was steeped—*
> *its aspect pure as far as the horizon—*
> * brought back my joy in seeing just as soon*
> *as I had left behind the air of death*
> *that had afflicted both my sight and breast.*
> * The lovely planet that is patroness*
> *of love made all the eastern heavens glad,*
> *veiling the Pisces in the train she led.*
> * Then I turned to the right, setting my mind*
> *upon the other pole, and saw four stars*
> *not seen before except by the first people.*
> * Heaven appeared to revel in their flames:*
> *o northern hemisphere, because you were*
> *denied that sight, you are a widower!*

Sometimes he is obsessively periphrastic; at a pole far from plain style (and Dante experiments with *all* styles), he lets us know that it is 3 p.m., the beginning of vespers, "there" in Purgatory by a likeness that measures the morning span between 6 a.m. and 9 a.m.: "As many as the hours in which the sphere/ that's always playing like a child appears/ from daybreak to the end of the third hour,/ so many were the hours of light still left/ before the course of day had reached sunset;/ vespers was there; and where we are, midnight" (XV, 1–6).

And at times Dante records the skies not through the movements of stellar bodies but through the motions of the soul, as in the six lines for which Paget Toynbee, in 1900, could total up sixteen translations into English independent of translations forming part of full translations of the *Purgatorio* or the *Comedy*: "It was the hour that turns seafarers' longings/ homeward—the hour that makes their hearts grow tender/ upon the day they bid sweet friends farewell;/ the hour that pierces the new traveler/ with love when he has heard, far off, the bell/ that seems to mourn the dying of the day" (VIII, 1–6).

The heavens serve not only to measure time there; Dante will also use our skies here as likenesses of what he saw there, most indelibly in reinforcing his first vision of Beatrice in the *Comedy* (XXX, 22–39):

> *I have at times seen all the eastern sky*
> *becoming rose as day began and seen,*
> *adorned in lovely blue, the rest of heaven;*
> *   and seen the sun's face rise so veiled that it*
> *was tempered by the mist and could permit*
> *the eye to look at length upon it; so,*
> *   within a cloud of flowers that were cast*
> *by the angelic hands and then rose up*
> *and then fell back, outside and in the chariot,*
> *   a woman showed herself to me; above*
> *a white veil, she was crowned with olive boughs;*
> *her cape was green; her dress beneath, flame-red.*
> *   Within her presence, I had once been used*
> *to feeling—trembling—wonder, dissolution;*
> *but that was long ago. Still, though my soul,*
> *   now she was veiled, could not see her directly,*
> *by way of hidden force that she could move,*
> *I felt the mighty power of old love.*

This tight construct of space and time serves as container for a *cantica* less dispersive and digressive than the *Inferno*, with its crowded population and its percussiveness.

Of course, even in *Purgatorio*, Dante can, with *Infern*-al velocity, in thirty lines, examine the nature of attentiveness, refute the Platonic doctrine of the plurality of souls, offer us the vision of a farmer preventing thieves from entering his field, conjure hard ascents and descents in four Italian hilly terrains, and define Virgil as "the guide who gave me hope and was my light" (IV, 1–30).

And he can dart, in his dance of likenesses, from "a fledgling stork" to the "iron of the arrow" touching the "bowstring," to "leavings left on the table"—a likeness of the blood the veins have not drunk up—to seeing the fetus as a "sea-sponge," to invoking "the sun's heat that, when combined/ with sap that flows from vines, is then made wine," to summoning

"the saturated air," which, reflecting "the rays the sun has
sent,/ takes rainbow colors as its ornament," and then to
conjuring the flame that follows after "the fire whenever
fire moves" (with the poet's own pace not unlike the flame's)
—justifying, as much as does the combustible thread of ex-
position along which these flames run, the conclusion: "This
is the cause of your astonishment" (xxv, 10–108). The end of
the previous canto is not much less various (xxiv, 94–154), as
Dante's likenesses move from a horseman who "sometimes
gallops out,/ leaving behind his troop of riders, so/ that he
may gain the honor of the first/ clash," to "little, eager, empty-
headed children/ who beg—but he of whom they beg does
not/ reply, but to provoke their longing, he/ holds high, and
does not hide, the thing they want," to seeing himself as "a
scared young animal," to the red glow of "glass or metal . . .
seen within a furnace," to the "breeze of May that—herald-
ing/ the dawning of the day—when it is steeped/ in flowers
and in grass, stirs fragrantly," in a passage that ends by bless-
ing those "whose hungering is always in just measure" but
belies that "just measure" with Dante's own measureless
hungering for metaphor.

But, generally, the similes of *Purgatorio* share the tighter
"curb of art" and sense of rite that rein the actions, rhetoric,
spacings, and timings of *Purgatorio*: a gravity, a concentration,
that relies on prefatory announcement and alerting, on formal greetings and valedictions, on strategies of stylization
and sacralization.

The line of rite begins in the first canto, with its formal pre-
announcement by Cato: "Go then; but first/ wind a smooth
rush around his waist and bathe/ his face to wash away all of
Hell's stains" (i, 94–96), and then its emblematic etching of a
shore where only pliant rushes can grow (i, 100–105):

> This solitary island, all around
> its very base, there where the breakers pound,
> bears rushes on its soft and muddy ground.
>   There is no other plant that lives below:
> no plant with leaves or plant that, as it grows,
> hardens—and breaks beneath the waves' harsh blows.

That line of rite continues in the angelic apparition of Canto II, the first of a series (Cantos VIII, IX, XII, XVII, XIX); in the formal entry to Purgatory with its three steps and seven P's (for *peccato*, sin) traced on Dante's forehead; in the astonished shades' repeated recognitions of Dante's having a material body; in the sequence of dreams noted above (Cantos IX, XIX, XXVII), each dream preceded, in the sentence announcing it, by the time of its occurrence, pre-dawn; in the embeddings, within this verbal artifact, of artifacts that include the wall reliefs and pavement reliefs of the first terrace; in the double rivering of Dante, first with Lethe, the classic river of forgetfulness, erasing the memory of misdoing, then Eunoe, the river of recall, Dante's invention, restoring memory of the good we have done; in the retinue of Beatrice, with her seven handmaids, four for the "natural" virtues, three for the theological; and in the vast processional in the Earthly Paradise.

That line will be reinforced by two complementary aspects of *Purgatorio*: its more frequent intervals of solitude or shared solitude—of Dante or of what he sees (Cato, Sordello, Matilda) —and the choral sense that makes its terraces, as Francesco D'Ovidio had it, a "colossal monastery," with its hymns and psalms, rapid Biblical and liturgical inserts, its Latin and paraphrases of Latin joined by citation and translations (and a mistranslation) of Virgil, and, twice, by Dante's own Latin inserts.

Rite will also find support in rhetorical symmetries, as in the sequence of thirteen tercets (XII, 25–63) in which four tercets beginning with "I saw" are followed by four beginning with exclamatory "O"'s and four beginning with "it showed," with that sequence followed by a summative thirteenth tercet, where the lines begin, respectively, "I saw," "o," and "it showed": "I saw Troy turned to caverns and to ashes; / o Ilium, your effigy in stone—/ it showed you there so squalid, so cast down!" (XII, 61–63).

However sardonically placed it is, even Dante's designation of his long polemic against Italy and Florence as "digression" (VI, 128), his only use of the word in all the *Comedy*, involves some self-conscious sense of transgression and reinforces our sense of art as rite in *Purgatorio*.

For similes that—unlike the staccato, nervous examples cited above—participate in the formal ritual climate, witness the doves (II, 124–132), the sheep moving out of the fold (III, 79–87), even the elaborated street-scene of the dice-players (VI, 1–12), and the corbels (X, 130–135), and the likeness that embraces Virgil and Statius as herdsmen and Dante as goat (XXVII, 76–87):

> Like goats that, when they grazed, were swift and tameless
> along the mountain peaks, but now are sated,
> and rest and ruminate—while the sun blazes—
> untroubled, in the shadows, silently,
> watched over by the herdsman as he leans
> upon his staff and oversees their peace;
> or like the herdsman in the open fields,
> spending the night beside his quiet flock,
> watching to see that no beast drives them off;
> such were all three of us at that point—they
> were like the herdsmen, I was like the goat;
> upon each side of us, high rock walls rose.

If *Purgatorio* is more circumscribed than *Inferno*, it is because of the "immense desire" that it abets and must contain (IV, 29). Dante's constant intellectual and visual curiosity now has "natural thirst," the thirst to know and to know that which grace alone can offer, as its source: "The natural thirst that never can be quenched/ except by water that gives grace —the draught/ the simple woman of Samaria sought—/ tormented me" (XXI, 1–4).

Dante drives and is driven beyond the melancholia of Virgil's injunction, Virgil's questioning of questing, his reasoning's self-delimiting sadness, its awareness that it can describe *what* is but cannot supply the *why* (III, 37–45):

> "Confine yourselves, o humans, to the quia;
> had you been able to see all, there would
> have been no need for Mary to give birth.
> You saw the fruitless longing of those men
> who would—if reason could—have been content,
> those whose desire eternally laments:
> I speak of Aristotle and of Plato—

and many others." Here he bent his head
and said no more, remaining with his sorrow.

Dante's need to array thirsts and hungerings and longings is as "limitless" as his thirst for the waters of Eunoe in the final canto (xxxiii, 138–139). When Dante receives an answer, he continues: "I am more hungry now for satisfaction" (xv, 58). His soul tastes "that food which, even as/ it quenches hunger, spurs the appetite" (xxxi, 129–130). He is "still goaded by new thirst" (xviii, 4). Reluctantly, he draws his "unquenchable sponge out of the water" (xx, 3). "A thousand longings burning more than flames" compel his eyes (xxxi, 118). Guido Guinizzelli burns for an answer "in fire and thirst" and lets Dante know that Guinizelli's fellow shades thirst for that answer "more than/ an Indian or Ethiopian/ thirsts for cool water" (xxvi, 18–22). When Dante asks the Muses for recompense ("O Virgins, sacrosanct, if I have ever,/ for your sake, suffered vigils, cold, and hunger,/ great need makes me entreat my recompense": xxix, 37–39), the hunger seems not only the hunger of indigent exile but the hungering and thirsting of this work.

That force of longing is, of course, only abetted by the nearness now, in Purgatory, of Beatrice, by the ten years of thirst between her death in 1290 and the date of the fictive voyage, and the even longer span between her death and Dante's writing of the *Purgatorio* (xxxii, 1–9):

> *My eyes were so insistent, so intent*
> *on finding satisfaction for their ten-*
> *year thirst that every other sense was spent.*
> *And to each side, my eyes were walled in by*
> *indifference to all else (with its old net,*
> *the holy smile so drew them to itself),*
> *when I was forced to turn my eyes leftward*
> *by those three goddesses because I heard*
> *them warning me: "You stare too fixedly."*

It is this uncontainable desire that presses against the container. So, too, do the ways of envisioning that *Purgatorio* spans. If what Dante sees here is less varied than what he saw in the *Inferno*, his modes of vision are much more various. He sees with the sensual waking eye (both seeing directly and seeing

mimetic artifacts), with the "intellect's sharp eyes" (xviii, 16),
with the "shut . . . eyes" of dream (xviii, 144–145); and in
"ecstatic vision" (xv, 86), he sees images that are impressed
upon—or have "rained" into—his "fantasy" and "imagination" (xvii, 13–45). Dante comments on these latter modes
as if he were providing us with one aspect of the poetics of his
larger fiction through his anatomy of these partial envisionings of fantasy (these "not false errors": xv, 117): "At this, my
mind withdrew to the within,/ to what imagining might
bring; no thing/ that came from the without could enter in"
(xvii, 22–24). Another direction, another aspect of Dante's
poetics, his emphasis on mimetic credibility, is reinforced by
the firmness with which he asserts the accuracy of the wall
reliefs and pavement reliefs he sees on the first terrace, "carv-
ings/ so accurate—not only Polycletus/ but even Nature, there,
would feel defeated" (x, 31–33): "What master of the brush or
of the stylus/ had there portrayed such masses, such outlines/
as would astonish all discerning minds?/ The dead seemed
dead and the alive, alive:/ I saw, head bent, treading those
effigies,/ as well as those who'd seen those scenes directly"
(xii, 64–69).

Dante will also examine attentively the points of passage
between waking vision, sharp thought, random thought,
reverie, dream, and fantasy, and the paralimnions of each
state (even as he had examined the shoreline of Purgatory):
"I was so drawn from random thought/ to thought that, wandering in mind, I shut/ my eyes, transforming thought on
thought to dream" (xviii, 144–145); "And when this image
shattered of itself,/ just like a bubble that has lost the water/
beneath which it was formed . . ." (xvii, 31–34); and, "Even as
sleep is shattered when new light/ strikes suddenly against
closed eyes and, once/ it's shattered, gleams before it dies
completely,/ so my imagination fell away" (xvii, 40–43).

In this last passage, "new light" almost becomes an emblem
of Dante's own light, a light that is both more abruptly shat-
tering and more darting than the light of Virgil's *Aeneid*:
whatever limits Dante sets for himself in the *Purgatorio*, his is
a more restless light than Virgil's—a modern light, the light
of the "immense desire" that made the need for *Purgatorio*'s
"curb of art" so imperative.

In a journey as long as the *Comedy*, with its 14,233 lines and more than 650 similes, our memory not only commits paraphrase; it also misremembers, and dismembers the text through specific but highly selective recall, even as Dante himself—as Gianfranco Contini reminds us—recalls configurations of sound but uses those configurations in drastically altered contexts. Few readers of the *Inferno* will not tally up Francesca, Farinata, Pier della Vigna, Brunetto Latini, Ulysses. Sometimes these tesserae in the mosaic of memory are not personages but extended similes. Sometimes they are bits as swift as "the lightning-flash" of the lizard in *Inf.* xxv, or the plunging fish of *Purg.* xxvi. In edifying the *Purgatorio*, the mosaic of memory draws heavily on the rituals and repetitions noted above, and on the map of space and time that Dante is so careful to trace for the reader-voyager. But groupings of personages found in three divisions of the mountain, Ante-Purgatory, Purgatory proper, and the Earthly Paradise, can also serve as tesserae. (In the case of *Purgatorio*, memory can more easily contain the complete array of characters who speak; even hasty scrutinists can intuit the presence of fewer figures in the round than the *Inferno* presents, and Thomas Bergin's demographic comparison of the three *cantiche* documents their intuition.)

In *Inferno* there was only one principal figure from antiquity other than Virgil: Ulysses, whose insatiable curiosity makes him a kind of counter-figure of Dante. In *Purgatorio*, Statius, another poet of antiquity, will join Virgil as a figure complementing, not countering, Dante. And antiquity also provides the guardian of Purgatory's shores: Cato of Utica (95–46 B.C.).

Pagan and, after Caesar's victories at Pharsalus in 48 B.C. and Thapsus in 46 B.C., a suicide at Utica in Africa, the intractable republican would have been a possible candidate for Limbo, where his widow Marcia is to be found, or for the Wood of the Suicides (*Inf.* xiii). But Dante had already, in his *Convivio*, glorified "the most holy breast of Cato" (iv, v, 16), and had asked and answered: "And what earthly man was was more worthy of signifying God than Cato? Certainly no one" (iv, xxviii, 15). And in his *Monarchy* (very possibly composed after the *Purgatorio*), Dante speaks of "the ineffable sacrifice of the most intransigent champion of liberty, Marcus Cato . . . who showed how great liberty is by preferring to die rather than to live without it" (II, v, 15). Behind this image of Cato there lie Book IX of Lucan's *Pharsalia* and Cicero's *De officiis*; but it is a daring appropriator who, though he himself is a Christian and a pro-Imperial poet, mobilizes a pagan and an adversary of Caesar for the guardianship of Purgatory.

Cato hardly belongs to any Purgatorial lodge—of either ancients or moderns. Unlike the shades he superintends, he does not need the prayers of those still alive, and the cords that link Forese Donati to his widow Nella (XXIII, 85–93) are hardly present for Cato in relation to his Marcia (I, 85–90).

But with Casella in Canto II, we meet inhabitants of Purgatory who are more collegial and choral than Cato is. Casella, like Belacqua in Canto IV, Nino Visconti in Canto VIII, and Forese Donati in Cantos XXIII–XXIV, is a friend of Dante. And, as a musician, he joins Sordello (who appears in Cantos VI–VII–VIII not only as courtier but as fellow-Mantuan of Virgil and fellow-poet—in the "mother tongues"—of Dante) in the series of *Purgatorio*'s artists that will also include the miniaturist Oderisi of Gubbio (XI, 73–142) and the poets Bonagiunta da Lucca (XXIV, 19–21 and 34–63), Guido Guinizzelli (XXVI, 16–24 and 72–135), Arnaut Daniel (XXVI, 136–148), and Statius himself—as well as others who are referred to, evoked.

Casella's affection and gentle, enrapturing singing of a setting for one of Dante's own poems had been preceded by Cato's austerity and is interrupted by Cato's austerity (II, 118–123).

From the music of Casella, we move, in Canto III, to the violent death and dispersed bones of the excommunicate Manfred, the last great hope of the Imperial forces against the Papacy in the 13th century, a hope shattered when Manfred, illegitimate son of Frederick II, was defeated at Benevento in 1266. With the alternations characteristic of these opening cantos, Manfred's bones bathed by rain give way to the languor of Belacqua, whose laziness is not without humor. He asks: "And have you fathomed how/ the sun can drive his chariot on your left?" (IV, 119–120), addressing his question to his friend Dante, who had, with such fanatic energy, wondered why the sun was at his left as he faced east. In turn, the listless Belacqua is followed, in the next canto, by three shades who underwent violent deaths.

The death of Jacopo del Cassero (1260–1298), a distinguished warrior and politician, at the hands of Ezzo d'Este's killers was so well-known to Dante's contemporaries that Dante does not even need to name him (v, 64–84).

Buonconte da Montefeltro (born c. 1250), son of Guido da Montefeltro (*Inf.* XXVII), was the leader of the Ghibellines of Arezzo in the battle of Campaldino, fought against the forces of Florence, a battle in which Dante himself probably took part. Buonconte died in that encounter on June 11, 1289, and his body was never found. But where his father, in *Inferno*, was, at the point of death, snatched from St. Francis by a devil, the soul of the son is saved from the devil by an angel. The devil's revenge on Buonconte's body counters the cloudless skies of Purgatory with an inexorable storm-scene in our world (v, 85–129).

Pia, possibly of the Tolomei family of Siena, was killed—hurled down from the balcony of her house—by her husband, Nello, chief magistrate of Volterra and Lucca, who outlived Dante. She concentrates her tragedy in three lines, but not before she has voiced her own compassion for the weariness of any living body undertaking a journey as arduous as Dante's: "Pray, after your returning to the world,/ when, after your long journeying, you've rested/ . . . may you remember me, who am La Pia;/ Siena made—Maremma unmade—me:/ he who, when we were wed, gave me his pledge/ and then, as nuptial ring, his gem, knows that" (v, 130–136).

After these three (and others who suffered violent deaths but do not speak—or better, who importune Dante but without his referring their words to us), it is the quiet enclave of the Valley of the Rulers that occupies the rest of Ante-Purgatory. We and Dante are introduced to the valley and its inhabitants (identified in the headnote to Canto VII) by Sordello (c. 1200–1269), the most famous of the Italian troubadours, who wrote in Provençal and served as courtier in Italy, Provence, and then again—under Charles of Anjou—in Italy. It is Sordello's greeting of his fellow-Mantuan, Virgil, in Canto VI, 71–75 that spurs Dante's polemical "digression" against Italy and Florence, well-placed in this canto of Sordello, a poet whose own achievements in political and didactic poetry were notable. Sordello's review of the presences in the valley (VII, 91–136) is complemented in the next canto by the direct encounter with a political figure whom Dante knew well, the Guelph Nino Visconti—grandson of the Ugolino of Canto XXXIII of the *Inferno*—who died in 1296, after serving as animator of Guelph Genoa, Florence, and Lucca against Pisa. (Visconti's only daughter, Giovanna, died in poverty in Florence before 1339; in 1300, his widow married Galeazzo Visconti, lord of Milan, who then fell on hard times. The serpent was emblem of the Milanese Visconti, the rooster of the Pisan Visconti: VIII, 67–81.) In that same canto Dante encounters Currado Malaspina, who died in 1294, but whose family offered their hospitality (here repaid) to the exiled Dante in 1306.

In Purgatory proper, Canto X has no new presences; and the next nine cantos assign speaking roles—or amply refer—to nine modern Italian penitents: the Tuscan Aldobrandesco (who died in 1259), lord of Campagnatico and a powerful enemy of Siena, who died in battle near Campagnatico or was killed in bed by assassins hired by the Sienese (XI, 49–72); Oderisi of Gubbio (died c. 1299), the famous miniaturist, whose place in the terrace of pride is not divorced from Dante's awareness of his own desire for artistic eminence (XI, 73–142); Provenzan Salvani of Siena (c. 1220–1269), a Ghibelline leader, who humbled himself to beg funds for the ransom of a friend who had been captured by Charles of Anjou (XI, 121–142); Sapia of Siena, an aunt of Provenzan (XIII, 100–154); one Ghibelline of Romagna, Guido del Duca (who died after 1249), and one Guelph, Rinieri da Calboli (who died in 1296), joint presences in Canto XIV; Marco Lombardo, a figure of the second half of the 13th century, known for his wisdom primarily from literary sources, not least this Canto XVI; the Abbot of St. Zeno, an abbot of Verona who has never been well identified outside this Canto XVIII; and in Canto XIX, Pope Adrian V, Ottobono Fieschi (born between 1210 and 1215), member of a powerful Genoese family, who was pope for 38 days in 1276, when he died (and since there is little warrant for applying Dante's account to Adrian V but much for its relevance to Adrian IV, pope from 1154 to 1159, Umberto Bosco sees some confusion here in Dante). In Canto xx, Hugh (II) Capet, king of France from 987 to 996 (whom Dante confounds with Hugh II's father, Hugh the Great, as the founder of the dynasty of France), excoriates his successors.

On the remaining terraces of Purgatory (Cantos xxi–xxvii), all the speaking roles other than Virgil's and Dante's are assigned to poets—from three literatures, Latin, Italian, and Provençal—and to an old friend of Dante, Forese Donati, who, though not essentially a poet, had exchanged epistolary poems with Dante.

Statius (c. 45–96 A.D.), to whom Dante, following medieval confusions, assigns Toulouse as birthplace rather than Naples, was the poet of the *Thebaid*, the tale of Thebes from the struggle between Eteocles and Polynices to Theseus' expedition against Creon; and of the *Achilleid*, which was to recount all the tale of Achilles, but was interrupted in the middle of Book II by Statius' death. (Dante probably did not know the *Silvae* of Statius.) With or without previous medieval sources before him, Dante "recruits" Statius to Christianity; and with warrant in Statius' own work, he finds a surrogate and passionate complement for his—Dante's—own adoration of Virgil (xxi, 94–136 and xxii, 64–73). Statius completes the company of poets of antiquity to whom Dante had himself joined in Limbo, in Canto iv of the *Inferno*. The poets of Limbo had included Homer, Virgil, Horace, Ovid, Lucan; and now, Juvenal as well as others are mentioned "retroactively" by Virgil (xxii, 13–14 and 97–108). But the "effective" company to which Dante adds himself has Virgil, Ovid, Lucan, and Statius as its poets. However warm his relations to his Romance predecessors are, it is antiquity he hopes to join or asserts he has joined (even as the vision of the otherworld granted to Dante allows him to join Aeneas and Paul "in a manner most unusual for moderns": xvi, 41–42).

For those Romance predecessors, it is three colloquies in *Purgatorio* that are central. The first is in Canto xxiv (34–63) with Bonagiunta (Orbiciani) da Lucca (c. 1220–death date uncertain), a poet instrumental in introducing the mode of the

Sicilian poets to central Italy. The poets whom he sees as having been overarched by the "sweet [or suasive] new manner"
of Dante and others are: the "Notary," that is, Jacopo da Len-
tini, poet and notary at the court of Frederick II, doyen of the
Sicilian school, who died c. 1250; and Guittone d'Arezzo, who
died in Florence in 1294, the head of the school that may be
seen as having worked in modes less harmonious and subtle
than those of Cavalcanti and the earlier Dante.

The second colloquy with a Romance poet (xxvi) has as its
poet-interlocutor Guido Guinizzelli (probably to be identified with a Guido who was exiled from Bologna in 1274 and
died by 1276). Seen by Cavalcanti and Dante as forerunner
of their manner, Guinizzelli here also comes down hard
on Guittone d' Arezzo (or, better, one may say that Dante,
using both Bonagiunta and Guinizzelli, seems to come down
strangely—or understandably—too hard on Guittone, a pre-
decessor to whom both he and Guinizzelli are much indebted).
He also reappraises, among the Provençal poets, Giraut de
Bornelh (in fact born near Limoges rather than in it: xxvi,
120), who lived between the last half of the twelfth century
and the beginning of the thirteenth; for where Dante, in his
De vulgari eloquentia, had praised Giraut, it is now Arnaut
Daniel whom he has Guinizzelli praise as *"il miglior fabbro"*,
"a better/ artisan of the mother tongue—surpassing/ all those
who wrote their poems of love or prose/ romances" (xxvi,
116–119).

Arnaut, Dante's third Romance interlocutor, born in the
same region as Giraut, was active as poet between 1180 and
1210. However much Guinizzelli may have been used by
Dante for "local" anti-Guittone purposes, there is significant
freedom from chauvinism in allowing Italian no special privilege among the modern maternal tongues, in assigning the
premier post among all writers in the modern tongues to a
Provençal (who here, in *Purgatorio*, speaks in Provençal: xxvi,
140–147).

This leaves one Florentine friend requiring a brief note: Forese Donati (xxiii and xxiv). Forese is seen here chiefly as in-
timate friend of Dante; but his exchange of sonnets with Dante was so intemperate and scurrilous that Dante, recalling

that and obviously much more in their years of friendship together, can only feel shame (XXIII, 115–117). But certainly the energies of invective, venom, and execration share place with the energy of love in Dante's descent and ascent.

The remorse of both Forese (who died in 1296)—distant relative of Dante's wife, Gemma Donati—and Dante, and Forese's tenderness with respect to his widow Nella (XXIII, 85–93) and sister Piccarda (XXIV, 10–16), whom we shall meet in Canto III of *Paradiso*, are followed by his prophecy of the death of his brother, Corso Donati. Corso (c. 1250–1308), one of the most arrogant and violent protagonists of Florentine politics, did not participate directly in the bloody brawl of May Day, 1300, between the White Guelphs ("the party of the woods" of *Inf.* VI, 60–72, and Dante's own party) and the Black Guelphs (Corso's party), but he was the principal conspirator in the Black cabal that followed that brawl. He had conspired from a distance and was condemned to death in contumacy. With the entry of Charles de Valois into Florence in 1301, the exiled Blacks—abetted, as always, by Boniface VIII—regained control of Florence. By April, 1302, more than six hundred Whites were exiled, among them Dante himself. Corso was the chief power in the city after that, and the figure most hated by the banished Whites. But it was the hatred of those within Florence that finally overthrew him in 1308. In flight, he was caught by Catalan mercenaries and may indeed have been killed in the way Dante describes, dragged at the tail of a horse (XXIV, 82–87).

In the Earthly Paradise, Virgil talks no more. Only his smile speaks in XXVIII, 147, and only his eyes speak in XXIX, 55–57. His words concluding Canto XXVII were indeed his valediction, as Dante will see when he turns around to share with Virgil the awesome wonder of re-encountering Beatrice, only to find that Virgil has vanished (XXX, 43–54, where the "ancient mother" is, of course, Eve):

> I turned around and to my left—just as
> a little child, afraid or in distress,
> will hurry to its mother—anxiously,
>   to say to Virgil: "I am left with less
> than one drop of my blood that does not tremble:

I recognize the signs of the old flame."
 But Virgil had deprived us of himself,
Virgil, the gentlest father, Virgil, he
to whom I gave my self for my salvation;
 and even all our ancient mother lost
was not enough to keep my cheeks, though washed
with dew, from darkening again with tears.

The chief speaker of the Earthly Paradise is Beatrice, the "soul more worthy than I am" of Virgil's account in *Inf.* I, 122. Born in 1266, the year after Dante's birth, Beatrice is loved by Dante from his boyhood and celebrated by Dante—after her death in 1290—in his *Vita Nuova.* If that is already a saint's life, with Beatrice as implicit incarnation of the divine way of the power of grace, the *Vita Nuova* did not yet contain polemic against the way of self-sufficient reason, a way "distant from the divine" (xxxiii, 85–90); nor was the *Vita Nuova* subject to political imperatives, which here make Beatrice prophesy "a time in which, dispatched by God, a Five/ Hundred and Ten and Five will slay the whore/ together with that giant who sins with her" (xxxiii, 43–45—and see below for the giant and the whore), where the Roman numerals for five-hundred and ten and five yield D.X.V., probably to be transposed to D.V.X. (leader), and possibly to be identified with a secular political figure, Henry VII— the last Imperial hope of Dante—who descended into Italy in 1311 but died suddenly, at Buonconvento, in 1313.

But it is Beatrice's companion whom Dante meets first in the Earthly Paradise, though he and we learn her name, Matilda, only toward the very end of *Purgatorio* (xxxiii, 119). Identifying Matilda with an historical personage is an attempt that, however assiduously pursued, remains problematic. And no allegorical accounting for her matches the haunting sense of her initial presence under the aegis of namelessness (xxviii, 34–42 and 52–55):

 I halted, and I set my eyes upon
the farther bank, to look at the abundant
variety of newly-flowered boughs;
 and there, just like a thing that, in appearing
most suddenly, repels all other thoughts,

so great is the astonishment it brings,
I saw a solitary woman moving,
singing, and gathering up flower on flower—
the flowers that colored all of her pathway.

and

As, when she turns, a woman, dancing, keeps
her soles close to the ground and to each other
and scarcely lets one foot precede the other,
so did she turn. . . . .

The limited population of the Earthly Paradise allows life-space for a procession of emblematic presences, moving behind a standard made up of seven candelabra, or—some would have it—one candelabrum with seven candles. For this procession, one can more easily use the equation words "is" and "are" and "may be" and "represent." In Canto XXIX, 43–150, the seven candelabra may be the seven churches of Asia, with the seven pennants as the seven gifts of the Holy Ghost. The twenty-four elders represent the twenty-four books of the Old Testament; the four animals, the books of the four Evangelists; the chariot, the Church; the griffin—with the head of a lion and body and wings of an eagle—Christ, with his two natures; and of the seven women, the three to the right of the chariot are the three theological virtues (faith, hope, and charity, dressed in white, green, and red) and the four to the left, the four cardinal virtues (prudence, justice, fortitude, and temperance, with prudence having three eyes —to see past, present, and future). The final seven elders represent: the Acts of the Apostles, whose author was St. Luke, a physician; the Epistles of St. Paul, who had urged the faithful to wear "God's armor" and take up "the sword of the spirit, which is the word of God" (Ephesians 6: 11 ff.); the four Epistles of Peter, John, James, and Jude; and Revelation, with an elder "as if in sleep," that is, visionary, and "keen," that is, prophetic.

In Canto XXXII, still other emblematic actors are involved in a tableau of Church history: the eagle, emblem of the Roman Empire, persecutor of the Church from Nero to Diocletian; the fox, emblem of heresy; the dragon, for whom the Anti-Christ is only one of many readings; the giant, prob- ably the dynasty of France; and the whore, the corrupted Church.

In the Earthly Paradise, Virgil vanishes and Statius is silent; and though other emblematic members of the sacred procession do hymn or sing or chant, the only emblems that speak are the seven handmaids. Indeed, through all six cantos of the Earthly Paradise, only women—Beatrice, Matilda, and the handmaids—speak to Dante. Nine female presences—though eight of them dance—do not always reinforce mystery, and certainly not in some of the harsh rebukes leveled by Beatrice; but they certainly do so in the first apparition of Matilda and in the approach to Eunoe, where "the seven ladies halted at the edge/ of a dense shadow such as mountains cast/ beneath green leaves and black boughs, on cold banks" (XXXIII, 109–111).

Often, in the *Comedy*, Dante's lucidities and relentless analysis and cartography might remind us of an anecdote about Aeschylus, who, when accused of revealing the mysteries, may—like other distracted scribes—have won his acquittal by replying: "I said the first thing that occurred to me—I did not know it was a secret." But some of the rites of Purgatory, not least the final immersion in Eunoe, do mime the mystery of Augustine's *"pacem quietis, pacem sabbati, pacem sine vespera,"* "peace of quiet, sabbath peace, peace that knows no twilight." Here, at least, for the most restless of poets, there is provisional rest before the ascent through Paradise.

Prior to that ascent, Dante sums up and transcends all the many changes rung on the word "new" by the thirteenth-century Italian poets who preceded him and by his own use of "new" in the title of his *Vita Nuova* (just as in his transmutation of Dido's line into his own awareness of Beatrice—"I recognize the signs of the old flame" in XXX, 48—he had offered a summative epigraph for his many uses of *"antico,"* "old"): "Remade, as new trees are/ renewed when they bring forth new boughs, I was/ pure and prepared to climb unto the stars" (XXXIII, 143–145).

xxviii PURGATORIO Most of this *Purgatorio* translation was completed in Orta San Giulio and Boulder, Colorado. I thank Luigi Alberti, Luciana Lamperti, and Carlo Carena, who live, above Orta, in the house that honors the *"cantor de' buccolici carmi,"* for the blessings their presence has brought to me over many years; and Margherita Bogat, whose love of Orta has been *ardor* and *seme* and *favilla.* I am grateful to many colleagues and students who, in Boulder and Denver and on Bellyache Ridge, complemented the skies of Colorado, which indeed *"a li occhi miei ricominciò diletto"* when translating *Inferno* lay behind me. Ruth Hein, as always, edited copy with needling, fruitful care; my son Jonathan lent me his precious skills at a crucial time in revisions, and Ellen E. Martin worked probingly and unstintingly in the preparation of the final drafts. Paul Mariani, Bruce Bassoff, and James Hans were constant sources—not least, through their own work—of the spirit that engenders. Michael Bixler shared his craft and serenity with Barry Moser, Chet Grycz, and me. Laury Magnus—unfailing, invaluable—took soundings and governed the ungovernable sea of rough drafts like a *"celestial nocchier[e]."* Barry Moser, through the fourth volume on which we have worked together, has been both penetrating *fabbro* and buoyant friend, ever *"disposto a salire"* to the next volume.

The Graduate Center Allen Mandelbaum
of the City University of New York
September, 1981

PURGATORIO

PURGATORIO

CANTO I

To course across more kindly waters now
my talent's little vessel lifts her sails,
leaving behind herself a sea so cruel;
    and what I sing will be that second kingdom,   4
in which the human soul is cleansed of sin,
becoming worthy of ascent to Heaven.
    But here, since I am yours, o holy Muses,   7
may this poem rise again from Hell's dead realm;
and may Calliope rise somewhat here,
    accompanying my singing with that music   10
whose power struck the poor Pierides
so forcefully that they despaired of pardon.
    The gentle hue of oriental sapphire   13
in which the sky's serenity was steeped—
its aspect pure as far as the horizon—
    brought back my joy in seeing just as soon   16
as I had left behind the air of death
that had afflicted both my sight and breast.
    The lovely planet that is patroness   19
of love made all the eastern heavens glad,
veiling the Pisces in the train she led.
    Then I turned to the right, setting my mind   22
upon the other pole, and saw four stars
not seen before except by the first people.
    Heaven appeared to revel in their flames: 25
o northern hemisphere, because you were
denied that sight, you are a widower!
    After my eyes took leave of those four stars,   28
turning a little toward the other pole,
from which the Wain had disappeared by now,
    I saw a solitary patriarch   31
near me—his aspect worthy of such reverence
that even son to father owes no more.

Proem and Invocation. The skies of the Southern Pole before
dawn. The four stars. Cato of Utica, custodian of the island
Mountain of Purgatory. Cato's queries and Virgil's reply.
Instructions by Cato. Virgil bathing Dante's face and, on the
shore, girding him with a rush.

Per correr miglior acque alza le vele
omai la navicella del mio ingegno,
che lascia dietro a sé mar sì crudele;

   e canterò di quel secondo regno   4
dove l'umano spirito si purga
e di salire al ciel diventa degno.

   Ma qui la morta poesì resurga,   7
o sante Muse, poi che vostro sono;
e qui Calïopè alquanto surga,

   seguitando il mio canto con quel suono   10
di cui le Piche misere sentiro
lo colpo tal, che disperar perdono.

   Dolce color d'orïental zaffiro,   13
che s'accoglieva nel sereno aspetto
del mezzo, puro infino al primo giro,

   a li occhi miei ricominciò diletto,   16
tosto ch'io usci' fuor de l'aura morta
che m'avea contristati li occhi e 'l petto.

   Lo bel pianeto che d'amar conforta   19
faceva tutto rider l'orïente,
velando i Pesci ch'erano in sua scorta.

   I' mi volsi a man destra, e puosi mente   22
a l'altro polo, e vidi quattro stelle
non viste mai fuor ch'a la prima gente.

   Goder pareva 'l ciel di lor fiammelle: 25
oh settentrïonal vedovo sito,
poi che privato se' di mirar quelle!

   Com' io da loro sguardo fui partito,   28
un poco me volgendo a l'altro polo,
là onde 'l Carro già era sparito,

   vidi presso di me un veglio solo,   31
degno di tanta reverenza in vista,
che più non dee a padre alcun figliuolo.

His beard was long and mixed with white, as were   34
the hairs upon his head; and his hair spread
down to his chest in a divided tress.

The rays of the four holy stars so framed   37
his face with light that in my sight he seemed
like one who is confronted by the sun.

"Who are you—who, against the hidden river,   40
were able to escape the eternal prison?"
he said, moving those venerable plumes.

"Who was your guide? What served you both as lantern   43
when, from the deep night that will always keep
the hellish valley dark, you were set free?

The laws of the abyss—have they been broken?   46
Or has a new, a changed decree in Heaven
let you, though damned, approach my rocky slopes?"

My guide took hold of me decisively;   49
by way of words and hands and other signs,
he made my knees and brow show reverence.

Then he replied: "I do not come through my   52
own self. There was a lady sent from Heaven;
her pleas led me to help and guide this man.

But since your will would have a far more full   55
and accurate account of our condition,
my will cannot withhold what you request.

This man had yet to see his final evening;   58
but, through his folly, little time was left
before he did—he was so close to it.

As I have told you, I was sent to him   61
for his deliverance; the only road
I could have taken was the road I took.

I showed him all the people of perdition;   64
now I intend to show to him those spirits
who, in your care, are bent on expiation.

To tell you how I led him would take long;   67
it is a power descending from above
that helps me guide him here, to see and hear you.

Now may it please you to approve his coming;   70
he goes in search of liberty—so precious,
as he who gives his life for it must know.

You know it—who, in Utica, found death   73
for freedom was not bitter, when you left
the garb that will be bright on the great day.

Lunga la barba e di pel bianco mista 34
portava, a' suoi capelli simigliante,
de' quai cadeva al petto doppia lista.

Li raggi de le quattro luci sante 37
fregiavan sì la sua faccia di lume,
ch'i' 'l vedea come 'l sol fosse davante.

"Chi siete voi che contro al cieco fiume 40
fuggita avete la pregione etterna?"
diss' el, movendo quelle oneste piume.

"Chi v'ha guidati, o che vi fu lucerna, 43
uscendo fuor de la profonda notte
che sempre nera fa la valle inferna?

Son le leggi d'abisso così rotte? 46
o è mutato in ciel novo consiglio,
che, dannati, venite a le mie grotte?"

Lo duca mio allor mi diè di piglio, 49
e con parole e con mani e con cenni
reverenti mi fé le gambe e 'l ciglio.

Poscia rispuose lui: "Da me non venni: 52
donna scese del ciel, per li cui prieghi
de la mia compagnia costui sovvenni.

Ma da ch'è tuo voler che più si spieghi 55
di nostra condizion com' ell' è vera,
esser non puote il mio che a te si nieghi.

Questi non vide mai l'ultima sera; 58
ma per la sua follia le fu sì presso,
che molto poco tempo a volger era.

Sì com' io dissi, fui mandato ad esso 61
per lui campare; e non lì era altra via
che questa per la quale i' mi son messo.

Mostrata ho lui tutta la gente ria; 64
e ora intendo mostrar quelli spirti
che purgan sé sotto la tua balìa.

Com' io l'ho tratto, saria lungo a dirti; 67
de l'alto scende virtù che m'aiuta
conducerlo a vederti e a udirti.

Or ti piaccia gradir la sua venuta: 70
libertà va cercando, ch'è sì cara,
come sa chi per lei vita rifiuta.

Tu 'l sai, ché non ti fu per lei amara 73
in Utica la morte, ove lasciasti
la vesta ch'al gran dì sarà sì chiara.

Eternal edicts are not broken for us; 76
this man's alive, and I'm not bound by Minos;
but I am from the circle where the chaste

eyes of your Marcia are; and she still prays 79
to you, o holy breast, to keep her as
your own: for her love, then, incline to us.

Allow our journey through your seven realms. 82
I shall thank her for kindness you bestow—
if you would let your name be named below."

"While I was there, within the other world, 85
Marcia so pleased my eyes," he then replied,
"each kindness she required, I satisfied.

Now that she dwells beyond the evil river, 88
she has no power to move me any longer,
such was the law decreed when I was freed.

But if a lady come from Heaven speeds 91
and helps you, as you say, there is no need
of flattery; it is enough, indeed,

to ask me for her sake. Go then; but first 94
wind a smooth rush around his waist and bathe
his face, to wash away all of Hell's stains;

for it would not be seemly to approach 97
with eyes still dimmed by any mists, the first
custodian angel, one from Paradise.

This solitary island, all around 100
its very base, there where the breakers pound,
bears rushes on its soft and muddy ground.

There is no other plant that lives below: 103
no plant with leaves or plant that, as it grows,
hardens—and breaks beneath the waves' harsh blows.

That done, do not return by this same pass; 106
the sun, which rises now, will show you how
this hillside can be climbed more easily."

With that he vanished; and without a word, 109
I rose and drew in closer to my guide,
and it was on him that I set my eyes.

And he began: "Son, follow in my steps; 112
let us go back; this is the point at which
the plain slopes down to reach its lowest bounds."

Daybreak was vanquishing the dark's last hour, 115
which fled before it; in the distance, I
could recognize the trembling of the sea.

Non son li editti etterni per noi guasti,   76
ché questi vive e Minòs me non lega;
ma son del cerchio ove son li occhi casti

di Marzia tua, che 'n vista ancor ti priega,   79
o santo petto, che per tua la tegni:
per lo suo amore adunque a noi ti piega.

Lasciane andar per li tuoi sette regni;   82
grazie riporterò di te a lei,
se d'esser mentovato là giù degni."

"Marzïa piacque tanto a li occhi miei   85
mentre ch'i' fu' di là," diss' elli allora,
"che quante grazie volse da me, fei.

Or che di là dal mal fiume dimora,   88
più muover non mi può, per quella legge
che fatta fu quando me n'usci' fora.

Ma se donna del ciel ti move e regge,   91
come tu di', non c'è mestier lusinghe:
bastisi ben che per lei mi richegge.

Va dunque, e fa che tu costui ricinghe   94
d'un giunco schietto e che li lavi 'l viso,
sì ch'ogne sucidume quindi stinghe;

ché non si converria, l'occhio sorpriso   97
d'alcuna nebbia, andar dinanzi al primo
ministro, ch'è di quei di paradiso.

Questa isoletta intorno ad imo ad imo,   100
là giù colà dove la batte l'onda,
porta di giunchi sovra 'l molle limo:

null' altra pianta che facesse fronda   103
o indurasse, vi puote aver vita,
però ch'a le percosse non seconda.

Poscia non sia di qua vostra reddita;   106
lo sol vi mosterrà, che surge omai,
prendere il monte a più lieve salita."

Così sparì; e io sù mi levai   109
sanza parlare, e tutto mi ritrassi
al duca mio, e li occhi a lui drizzai.

El cominciò: "Figliuol, segui i miei passi: 112
volgianci in dietro, ché di qua dichina
questa pianura a' suoi termini bassi."

L'alba vinceva l'ora mattutina   115
che fuggia innanzi, sì che di lontano
conobbi il tremolar de la marina.

We made our way across the lonely plain,   118
like one returning to a lost pathway,
who, till he finds it, seems to move in vain.

When we had reached the point where dew contends   121
with sun and, under sea winds, in the shade,
wins out because it won't evaporate,

my master gently placed both of his hands—   124
outspread—upon the grass; therefore, aware
of what his gesture and intention were,

I reached and offered him my tear-stained cheeks;   127
and on my cheeks, he totally revealed
the color that Inferno had concealed.

Then we arrived at the deserted shore,   130
which never yet had seen its waters coursed
by any man who journeyed back again.

There, just as pleased another, he girt me.   133
O wonder! Where he plucked the humble plant
that he had chosen, there that plant sprang up

again, identical, immediately.   136

Noi andavam per lo solingo piano
com' om che torna a la perduta strada,
che 'nfino ad essa li pare ire in vano.

   Quando noi fummo là 've la rugiada   121
pugna col sole, per essere in parte
dove, ad orezza, poco si dirada,

   ambo le mani in su l'erbetta sparte   124
soavemente 'l mio maestro pose:
ond' io, che fui accorto di sua arte,

   porsi ver' lui le guance lagrimose;   127
ivi mi fece tutto discoverto
quel color che l'inferno mi nascose.

   Venimmo poi in sul lito diserto,   130
che mai non vide navicar sue acque
omo, che di tornar sia poscia esperto.

   Quivi mi cinse sì com' altrui piacque: 133
oh maraviglia! ché qual elli scelse
l'umile pianta, cotal si rinacque

   subitamente là onde l'avelse.   136

CATO

II·27

CANTO II

By now the sun was crossing the horizon
of the meridian whose highest point
covers Jerusalem; and from the Ganges,
    night, circling opposite the sun, was moving   4
together with the Scales that, when the length
of dark defeats the day, desert night's hands;
    so that, above the shore that I had reached,   7
the fair Aurora's white and scarlet cheeks
were, as Aurora aged, becoming orange.
    We still were by the sea, like those who think   10
about the journey they will undertake,
who go in heart but in the body stay.
    And just as Mars, when it is overcome   13
by the invading mists of dawn, glows red
above the waters' plain, low in the west,
    so there appeared to me—and may I see it   16
again—a light that crossed the sea: so swift,
there is no flight of bird to equal it.
    When, for a moment, I'd withdrawn my eyes   19
that I might ask a question of my guide,
I saw that light again, larger, more bright.
    Then, to each side of it, I saw a whiteness,   22
though I did not know what that whiteness was;
below, another whiteness slowly showed.
    My master did not say a word before   25
the whitenesses first seen appeared as wings;
but then, when he had recognized the helmsman,
    he cried: "Bend, bend your knees: behold the angel   28
of God, and join your hands; from this point on,
this is the kind of minister you'll meet.
    See how much scorn he has for human means;   31
he'd have no other sail than his own wings
and use no oar between such distant shores.

Ante-Purgatory. Dawn on the shore of the island mountain. CANTO II 13
*The sudden light upon the sea. The helmsman angel and the boat
full of arriving souls. The encounter with Casella, Dante's friend.
Casella's singing. Cato's rebuke. The simile of the doves.*

Già era 'l sole a l'orizzonte giunto
lo cui meridïan cerchio coverchia
Ierusalèm col suo più alto punto;

   e la notte, che opposita a lui cerchia,   4
uscia di Gange fuor con le Bilance,
che le caggion di man quando soverchia;

   sì che le bianche e le vermiglie guance,   7
là dov' i' era, de la bella Aurora
per troppa etate divenivan rance.

   Noi eravam lunghesso mare ancora,   10
come gente che pensa a suo cammino,
che va col cuore e col corpo dimora.

   Ed ecco, qual, sorpreso dal mattino,   13
per li grossi vapor Marte rosseggia
giù nel ponente sovra 'l suol marino,

   cotal m'apparve, s'io ancor lo veggia,   16
un lume per lo mar venir sì ratto,
che 'l muover suo nessun volar pareggia.

   Dal qual com' io un poco ebbi ritratto   19
l'occhio per domandar lo duca mio,
rividil più lucente e maggior fatto.

   Poi d'ogne lato ad esso m'appario   22
un non sapeva che bianco, e di sotto
a poco a poco un altro a lui uscìo.

   Lo mio maestro ancor non facea motto,   25
mentre che i primi bianchi apparver ali;
allor che ben conobbe il galeotto,

   gridò: "Fa, fa che le ginocchia cali.   28
Ecco l'angel di Dio: piega le mani;
omai vedrai di sì fatti officiali.

   Vedi che sdegna li argomenti umani,   31
sì che remo non vuol, né altro velo
che l'ali sue, tra liti sì lontani.

See how he holds his wings, pointing to Heaven,   34
piercing the air with his eternal pinions,
which do not change as mortal plumage does."
    Then he—that bird divine—as he drew closer   37
and closer to us, seemed to gain in brightness,
so that my eyes could not endure his nearness,
    and I was forced to lower them; and he   40
came on to shore with boat so light, so quick
that nowhere did the water swallow it.
    The helmsman sent from Heaven, at the stern,   43
seemed to have blessedness inscribed upon him;
more than a hundred spirits sat within.
    "*In exitu Isräel de Aegypto,*"   46
with what is written after of that psalm,
all of those spirits sang as with one voice.
    Then over them he made the holy cross   49
as sign; they flung themselves down on the shore,
and he moved off as he had come—swiftly.
    The crowd that he had left along the beach   52
seemed not to know the place; they looked about
like those whose eyes try out things new to them.
    Upon all sides the sun shot forth the day;   55
and from mid-heaven its incisive arrows
already had chased Capricorn away,
    when those who'd just arrived lifted their heads   58
toward us and said: "Do show us, if you know,
the way by which we can ascend this slope."
    And Virgil answered: "You may be convinced   61
that we are quite familiar with this shore;
but we are strangers here, just as you are;
    we came but now, a little while before you,   64
though by another path, so difficult
and dense that this ascent seems sport to us."
    The souls who, noticing my breathing, sensed   67
that I was still a living being, then,
out of astonishment, turned pale; and just
    as people crowd around a messenger   70
who bears an olive branch, to hear his news,
and no one hesitates to join that crush,
    so here those happy spirits—all of them—   73
stared hard at my face, just as if they had
forgotten to proceed to their perfection.

Vedi come l'ha dritte verso 'l cielo,   34
trattando l'aere con l'etterne penne,
che non si mutan come mortal pelo."

    Poi, come più e più verso noi venne   37
l'uccel divino, più chiaro appariva;
per che l'occhio da presso nol sostenne,

    ma chinail giuso; e quei sen venne a riva   40
con un vasello snelletto e leggero,
tanto che l'acqua nulla ne 'nghiottiva.

    Da poppa stava il celestial nocchiero,   43
tal che parea beato per iscripto;
e più di cento spirti entro sediero.

    "*In exitu Israël de Aegypto*"   46
cantavan tutti insieme ad una voce
con quanto di quel salmo è poscia scripto.

    Poi fece il segno lor di santa croce;   49
ond' ei si gittar tutti in su la piaggia:
ed el sen gì, come venne, veloce.

    La turba che rimase lì, selvaggia   52
parea del loco, rimirando intorno
come colui che nove cose assaggia.

    Da tutte parti saettava il giorno   55
lo sol, ch'avea con le saette conte
di mezzo 'l ciel cacciato Capricorno,

    quando la nova gente alzò la fronte   58
ver' noi, dicendo a noi: "Se voi sapete,
mostratene la via di gire al monte."

    E Virgilio rispuose: "Voi credete   61
forse che siamo esperti d'esto loco;
ma noi siam peregrin come voi siete.

    Dianzi venimmo, innanzi a voi un poco,   64
per altra via, che fu sì aspra e forte,
che lo salire omai ne parrà gioco."

    L'anime, che si fuor di me accorte,   67
per lo spirare, ch'i' era ancor vivo,
maravigliando diventaro smorte.

    E come a messagger che porta ulivo   70
tragge la gente per udir novelle,
e di calcar nessun si mostra schivo,

    così al viso mio s'affisar quelle   73
anime fortunate tutte quante,
quasi oblïando d'ire a farsi belle.

I saw one of those spirits moving forward   76
in order to embrace me—his affection
so great that I was moved to mime his welcome.

    O shades—in all except appearance—empty!   79
Three times I clasped my hands behind him and
as often brought them back against my chest.

    Dismay, I think, was painted on my face;   82
at this, that shadow smiled as he withdrew;
and I, still seeking him, again advanced.

    Gently, he said that I could now stand back;   85
then I knew who he was, and I beseeched
him to remain awhile and talk with me.

    He answered: "As I loved you when I was   88
within my mortal flesh, so, freed, I love you:
therefore I stay. But you, why do you journey?"

    "My own Casella, to return again   91
to where I am, I journey thus; but why,"
I said, "were you deprived of so much time?"

    And he: "No injury is done to me   94
if he who takes up whom—and when—he pleases
has kept me from this crossing many times,

    for his own will derives from a just will.   97
And yet, for three months now, he has accepted,
most tranquilly, all those who would embark.

    Therefore, I, who had turned then to the shore   100
at which the Tiber's waters mix with salt,
was gathered in by his benevolence.

    Straight to that river mouth, he set his wings: 103
that always is the place of gathering
for those who do not sink to Acheron."

    And I: "If there's no new law that denies   106
you memory or practice of the songs
of love that used to quiet all my longings,

    then may it please you with those songs to solace   109
my soul somewhat; for—having journeyed here
together with my body—it is weary."

    "Love that discourses to me in my mind"   112
he then began to sing—and sang so sweetly
that I still hear that sweetness sound in me.

    My master, I, and all that company   115
around the singer seemed so satisfied,
as if no other thing might touch our minds.

Io vidi una di lor trarresi avante   76
per abbracciarmi, con sì grande affetto,
che mosse me a far lo somigliante.

  Ohi ombre vane, fuor che ne l'aspetto!   79
tre volte dietro a lei le mani avvinsi,
e tante mi tornai con esse al petto.

  Di maraviglia, credo, mi dipinsi;   82
per che l'ombra sorrise e si ritrasse,
e io, seguendo lei, oltre mi pinsi.

  Soavemente disse ch'io posasse;   85
allor conobbi chi era, e pregai
che, per parlarmi, un poco s'arrestasse.

  Rispuosemi: "Così com' io t'amai   88
nel mortal corpo, così t'amo sciolta:
però m'arresto; ma tu perché vai?"

  "Casella mio, per tornar altra volta   91
là dov' io son, fo io questo vïaggio,"
diss' io; "ma a te com' è tanta ora tolta?"

  Ed elli a me: "Nessun m'è fatto oltraggio,   94
se quei che leva quando e cui li piace,
più volte m'ha negato esto passaggio;

  ché di giusto voler lo suo si face: 97
veramente da tre mesi elli ha tolto
chi ha voluto intrar, con tutta pace.

  Ond' io, ch'era ora a la marina vòlto   100
dove l'acqua di Tevero s'insala,
benignamente fu' da lui ricolto.

  A quella foce ha elli or dritta l'ala,   103
però che sempre quivi si ricoglie
qual verso Acheronte non si cala."

  E io: "Se nuova legge non ti toglie   106
memoria o uso a l'amoroso canto
che mi solea quetar tutte mie voglie,

  di ciò ti piaccia consolare alquanto   109
l'anima mia, che, con la sua persona
venendo qui, è affannata tanto!"

  Amor che ne la mente mi ragiona   112
cominciò elli allor sì dolcemente,
che la dolcezza ancor dentro mi suona.

  Lo mio maestro e io e quella gente   115
ch'eran con lui parevan sì contenti,
come a nessun toccasse altro la mente.

We all were motionless and fixed upon   118
the notes, when all at once the grave old man
cried out: "What have we here, you laggard spirits?

What negligence, what lingering is this?   121
Quick, to the mountain to cast off the slough
that will not let you see God show Himself!"

Even as doves, assembled where they feed,   124
quietly gathering their grain or weeds,
forgetful of their customary strut,

will, if some thing appears that makes them fear,   127
immediately leave their food behind
because they are assailed by greater care;

so did I see that new-come company—   130
they left the song behind, turned toward the slope,
like those who go and yet do not know where.

And we were no less hasty in departure.   133

Noi eravam tutti fissi e attenti   118
a le sue note; ed ecco il veglio onesto
gridando: "Che è ciò, spiriti lenti?

   qual negligenza, quale stare è questo?   121
Correte al monte a spogliarvi lo scoglio
ch'esser non lascia a voi Dio manifesto."

   Come quando, cogliendo biado o loglio,   124
li colombi adunati a la pastura,
queti, sanza mostrar l'usato orgoglio,

   se cosa appare ond' elli abbian paura,   127
subitamente lasciano star l'esca,
perch' assaliti son da maggior cura;

   così vid' io quella masnada fresca   130
lasciar lo canto, e fuggir ver' la costa,
com' om che va, né sa dove rïesca;

   né la nostra partita fu men tosta.   133

CANTO III

But while their sudden flight was scattering
those souls across the plain and toward the mountain
where we are racked by rightful punishments,
I drew in closer to my true companion.   4
For how could I have run ahead without him?
Who could have helped me as I climbed the mountain?
He seemed like one who's stung by self-reproof;   7
o pure and noble conscience, you in whom
each petty fault becomes a harsh rebuke!
And when his feet had left off hurrying—   10
for haste denies all acts their dignity—
my mind, which was—before—too focused, grew
more curious and widened its attention;   13
I set my vision toward the slope that rises
most steeply, up to heaven from the sea.
Behind my back the sun was flaming red;   16
but there, ahead of me, its light was shattered
because its rays were resting on my body.
And when I saw the ground was dark in front   19
of me and me alone, afraid that I
had been abandoned, I turned to my side;
and he, my only comfort, as he turned   22
around, began: "Why must you still mistrust?
Don't you believe that I am with—and guide—you?
The body from within which I cast shadows   25
is buried where it now is evening: taken
from Brindisi, it now belongs to Naples.
Thus, if no shadow falls in front of me,   28
do not be more amazed than when you see
the heavens not impede each other's rays.
The Power has disposed such bodiless   31
bodies to suffer torments, heat and cold;
how this is done, He would not have us know.

Ante-Purgatory. From the shore to the base of the mountain.
Dante's fear when his shadow—and no other—appears.
Reassurance by Virgil and explanation of the nature of shades.
Consideration of the way to ascend the Mountain of Purgatory.
The meeting with the souls of the Late-Repentant who were also
Excommunicates. Manfred.

Avvegna che la subitana fuga
dispergesse color per la campagna,
rivolti al monte ove ragion ne fruga,

i' mi ristrinsi a la fida compagna: 4
e come sare' io sanza lui corso?
chi m'avria tratto su per la montagna?

El mi parea da sé stesso rimorso: 7
o dignitosa coscïenza e netta,
come t'è picciol fallo amaro morso!

Quando li piedi suoi lasciar la fretta,   10
che l'onestade ad ogn' atto dismaga,
la mente mia, che prima era ristretta,

lo 'ntento rallargò, sì come vaga,   13
e diedi 'l viso mio incontr' al poggio
che 'nverso 'l ciel più alto si dislaga.

Lo sol, che dietro fiammeggiava roggio,   16
rotto m'era dinanzi a la figura,
ch'avëa in me de' suoi raggi l'appoggio.

Io mi volsi dallato con paura   19
d'essere abbandonato, quand' io vidi
solo dinanzi a me la terra oscura;

e 'l mio conforto: "Perché pur diffidi?"   22
a dir mi cominciò tutto rivolto;
"non credi tu me teco e ch'io ti guidi?

Vespero è già colà dov'è sepolto   25
lo corpo dentro al quale io facea ombra;
Napoli l'ha, e da Brandizio è tolto.

Ora, se innanzi a me nulla s'aombra,   28
non ti maravigliar più che d'i cieli
che l'uno a l'altro raggio non ingombra.

A sofferir tormenti, caldi e geli   31
simili corpi la Virtù dispone
che, come fa, non vuol ch'a noi si sveli.

Foolish is he who hopes our intellect   34
can reach the end of that unending road
only one Substance in three Persons follows.

Confine yourselves, o humans, to the *quia*;   37
had you been able to see all, there would
have been no need for Mary to give birth.

You saw the fruitless longing of those men   40
who would—if reason could—have been content,
those whose desire eternally laments:

I speak of Aristotle and of Plato—   43
and many others." Here he bent his head,
and said no more, remaining with his sorrow.

By this time we had reached the mountain's base,   46
discovering a wall of rock so sheer
that even agile legs are useless there.

The loneliest, most jagged promontory   49
that lies between Turbìa and Lerici,
compared with it, provides stairs wide and easy.

"Now who knows where, along this mountainside,"   52
my master, halting, asked, "one finds a rise
where even he who has no wings can climb?"

While he, his eyes upon the ground, consulted   55
his mind, considering what road to take,
and I looked up around the wall of rock,

along the left a band of souls appeared   58
to me to be approaching us—but so
unhurriedly, their movements did not show.

"Lift up your eyes," I told my master; "here   61
are those who can advise us how to go,
if you can find no counsel in yourself."

At this, he looked at them and, less distressed,   64
replied: "Let us go there; their steps are slow;
and you, my gentle son, hold fast to hope."

The distance from that company to us—   67
I mean when we had gone a thousand paces—
was still as far as a fine hurler's toss,

when they all huddled toward the hard rock wall   70
and, once they'd crowded there, refused to budge,
even as men, when apprehensive, halt.

"O chosen souls, you who have ended well,"   73
Virgil began, "by virtue of that peace
which I believe awaits you all, please tell

Matto è chi spera che nostra ragione 34
possa trascorrer la infinita via
che tiene una sustanza in tre persone.

State contenti, umana gente, al *quia*; 37
ché, se potuto aveste veder tutto,
mestier non era parturir Maria;

e disïar vedeste sanza frutto 40
tai che sarebbe lor disio quetato,
ch'etternalmente è dato lor per lutto:

io dico d'Aristotile e di Plato 43
e di molt' altri"; e qui chinò la fronte,
e più non disse, e rimase turbato.

Noi divenimmo intanto a piè del monte; 46
quivi trovammo la roccia sì erta,
che 'ndarno vi sarien le gambe pronte.

Tra Lerice e Turbìa la più diserta, 49
la più rotta ruina è una scala,
verso di quella, agevole e aperta.

"Or chi sa da qual man la costa cala," 52
disse 'l maestro mio fermando 'l passo,
"sì che possa salir chi va sanz' ala?"

E mentre ch'e' tenendo 'l viso basso 55
essaminava del cammin la mente,
e io mirava suso intorno al sasso,

da man sinistra m'apparì una gente 58
d'anime, che movieno i piè ver' noi,
e non pareva, sì venïan lente.

"Leva," diss' io, "maestro, li occhi tuoi: 61
ecco di qua chi ne darà consiglio,
se tu da te medesmo aver nol puoi."

Guardò allora, e con libero piglio 64
rispuose: "Andiamo in là, ch'ei vegnon piano;
e tu ferma la spene, dolce figlio."

Ancora era quel popol di lontano, 67
i' dico dopo i nostri mille passi,
quanto un buon gittator trarria con mano,

quando si strinser tutti ai duri massi 70
de l'alta ripa, e stetter fermi e stretti
com' a guardar, chi va dubbiando, stassi.

"O ben finiti, o già spiriti eletti," 73
Virgilio incominciò, "per quella pace
ch'i' credo che per voi tutti s'aspetti,

us where the slope inclines and can be climbed;   76
for he who best discerns the worth of time
is most distressed whenever time is lost."

   Even as sheep that move, first one, then two,   79
then three, out of the fold—the others also
stand, eyes and muzzles lowered, timidly;

   and what the first sheep does, the others do,   82
and if it halts, they huddle close behind,
simple and quiet and not knowing why:

   so, then, I saw those spirits in the front   85
of that flock favored by good fortune move—
their looks were modest; seemly, slow, their walk.

   As soon as these souls saw, upon my right,   88
along the ground, a gap in the sun's light,
where shadow stretched from me to the rock wall,

   they stopped and then drew back somewhat; and all   91
who came behind them—though they did not know
why those ahead had halted—also slowed.

   "Without your asking, I shall tell you plainly   94
that you are looking at a human body;
that's why the sunlight on the ground is broken.

   Don't be astonished; rest assured that he   97
would not attempt to cross this wall without
a force that Heaven sent him as support."

   These were my master's words. That worthy band   100
replied: "Come back, and move in our direction,"
and gestured—with backhanded motions—right.

   And one of them began: "Whoever you   103
may be, as you move forward, turn and see:
consider if—beyond—you've ever seen me."

   I turned to look at him attentively: 106
he was fair-haired and handsome and his aspect
was noble—but one eyebrow had been cleft

   by a swordstroke. When I had humbly noted   109
that I had never seen him, he said: "Look
now"—showing me a wound high on his chest.

   Then, as he smiled, he told me: "I am Manfred,   112
the grandson of the Empress Constance; thus,
I pray that, when you reach the world again,

   you may go to my lovely daughter, mother   115
of kings of Sicily and Aragon—
tell her the truth, lest she's heard something other.

ditene dove la montagna giace,   76
sì che possibil sia l'andare in suso;
ché perder tempo a chi più sa più spiace."

  Come le pecorelle escon del chiuso   79
a una, a due, a tre, e l'altre stanno
timidette atterrando l'occhio e 'l muso;

  e ciò che fa la prima, e l'altre fanno,   82
addossandosi a lei, s'ella s'arresta,
semplici e quete, e lo 'mperché non sanno;

  sì vid' io muovere a venir la testa   85
di quella mandra fortunata allotta,
pudica in faccia e ne l'andare onesta.

  Come color dinanzi vider rotta   88
la luce in terra dal mio destro canto,
sì che l'ombra era da me a la grotta,

  restaro, e trasser sé in dietro alquanto,   91
e tutti li altri che venieno appresso,
non sappiendo 'l perché, fenno altrettanto.

  "Sanza vostra domanda io vi confesso   94
che questo è corpo uman che voi vedete;
per che 'l lume del sole in terra è fesso.

  Non vi maravigliate, ma credete   97
che non sanza virtù che da ciel vegna
cerchi di soverchiar questa parete."

  Così 'l maestro; e quella gente degna   100
"Tornate," disse, "intrate innanzi dunque,"
coi dossi de le man faccendo insegna.

  E un di loro incominciò: "Chiunque   103
tu se', così andando, volgi 'l viso:
pon mente se di là mi vedesti unque."

  Io mi volsi ver' lui e guardail fiso: 106
biondo era e bello e di gentile aspetto,
ma l'un de' cigli un colpo avea diviso.

  Quand' io mi fui umilmente disdetto   109
d'averlo visto mai, el disse: "Or vedi";
e mostrommi una piaga a sommo 'l petto.

  Poi sorridendo disse: "Io son Manfredi,   112
nepote di Costanza imperadrice;
ond' io priego che, quando tu riedi,

  vadi a mia bella figlia, genitrice   115
de l'onor di Cicilia e d'Aragona,
e dichi 'l vero a lei, s'altro si dice.

After my body had been shattered by   118
two fatal blows, in tears, I then consigned
myself to Him who willingly forgives.

My sins were ghastly, but the Infinite   121
Goodness has arms so wide that It accepts
all those who would return, imploring It.

And if Cosenza's pastor, who was sent   124
to hunt me down—alive or dead—by Clement,
had understood this facet of God's mercy,

my body's bones would still be there—beneath   127
the custody of the great heap of stones—
near Benevento, at the bridgehead; now

rain bathes my bones, the wind has driven them   130
beyond the Kingdom, near the Verde's banks,
where he transported them with tapers spent.

Despite the Church's curse, there is no one   133
so lost that the eternal love cannot
return—as long as hope shows something green.

But it is true that anyone who dies   136
in contumacy of the Holy Church,
though he repented at the end, must wait

along this shore for thirty times the span   139
he spent in his presumptuousness, unless
that edict is abridged through fitting prayers.

Now see if you, by making known to my   142
kind Constance where you saw my soul and why
delay's decreed for me, can make me happy;

those here–through those beyond–advance more quickly."

Poscia ch'io ebbi rotta la persona   118
di due punte mortali, io mi rendei,
piangendo, a quei che volontier perdona.

   Orribil furon li peccati miei;   121
ma la bontà infinita ha sì gran braccia,
che prende ciò che si rivolge a lei.

   Se 'l pastor di Cosenza, che a la caccia   124
di me fu messo per Clemente allora,
avesse in Dio ben letta questa faccia,

   l'ossa del corpo mio sarieno ancora   127
in co del ponte presso a Benevento,
sotto la guardia de la grave mora.

   Or le bagna la pioggia e move il vento   130
di fuor dal regno, quasi lungo 'l Verde,
dov' e' le trasmutò a lume spento.

   Per lor maladizion sì non si perde,   133
che non possa tornar, l'etterno amore,
mentre che la speranza ha fior del verde.

   Vero è che quale in contumacia more   136
di Santa Chiesa, ancor ch'al fin si penta,
star li convien da questa ripa in fore,

   per ognun tempo ch'elli è stato, trenta,   139
in sua presunzïon, se tal decreto
più corto per buon prieghi non diventa.

   Vedi oggimai se tu mi puoi far lieto,   142
revelando a la mia buona Costanza
come m'hai visto, e anco esto divieto;

   ché qui per quei di là molto s'avanza.''   145

MANFRED

BELACQUA

CANTO IV

When any of our faculties retains
a strong impression of delight or pain,
the soul will wholly concentrate on that,
    neglecting any other power it has   4
(and this refutes the error that maintains
that—one above the other—several souls
    can flame in us); and thus, when something seen   7
or heard secures the soul in stringent grip,
time moves and yet we do not notice it.
    The power that perceives the course of time   10
is not the power that captures all the mind;
the former has no force—the latter binds.
    And I confirmed this by experience,   13
hearing that spirit in my wonderment;
for though the sun had fully climbed fifty
    degrees, I had not noticed it, when he   16
came to the point at which in unison
those souls cried out to us: "Here's what you want."
    The farmer, when the grape is darkening,   19
will often stuff a wider opening
with just a little forkful of his thorns,
    than was the gap through which my guide and I,   22
who followed after, climbed, we two alone,
after that company of souls had gone.
    San Leo can be climbed, one can descend   25
to Noli and ascend Cacume and
Bismantova with feet alone, but here
    I had to fly: I mean with rapid wings   28
and pinions of immense desire, behind
the guide who gave me hope and was my light.
    We made our upward way through rifted rock;   31
along each side the edges pressed on us;
the ground beneath required feet and hands.

Quando per dilettanze o ver per doglie,
che alcuna virtù nostra comprenda,
l'anima bene ad essa si raccoglie,

    par ch'a nulla potenza più intenda;   4
e questo è contra quello error che crede
ch'un'anima sovr' altra in noi s'accenda.

    E però, quando s'ode cosa o vede   7
che tegna forte a sé l'anima volta,
vassene 'l tempo e l'uom non se n'avvede;

    ch'altra potenza è quella che l'ascolta,   10
e altra è quella c'ha l'anima intera:
questa è quasi legata e quella è sciolta.

    Di ciò ebb' io esperïenza vera,   13
udendo quello spirto e ammirando;
ché ben cinquanta gradi salito era

    lo sole, e io non m'era accorto, quando   16
venimmo ove quell' anime ad una
gridaro a noi: "Qui è vostro dimando."

    Maggiore aperta molte volte impruna   19
con una forcatella di sue spine
l'uom de la villa quando l'uva imbruna,

    che non era la calla onde salìne   22
lo duca mio, e io appresso, soli,
come da noi la schiera si partìne.

    Vassi in Sanleo e discendesi in Noli,   25
montasi su in Bismantova e 'n Cacume
con esso i piè; ma qui convien ch'om voli;

    dico con l'ale snelle e con le piume   28
del gran disio, di retro a quel condotto
che speranza mi dava e facea lume.

    Noi salavam per entro 'l sasso rotto,   31
e d'ogne lato ne stringea lo stremo,
e piedi e man volea il suol di sotto.

When we had reached the upper rim of that   34
steep bank, emerging on the open slope,
I said: "My master, what way shall we take?"

And he to me: "Don't squander any steps;   37
keep climbing up the mountain after me
until we find some expert company."

The summit was so high, my sight fell short;   40
the slope was far more steep than the line drawn
from middle-quadrant to the center point.

I was exhausted when I made this plea: 43
"O gentle father, turn around and see—
I will be left alone unless you halt."

"My son," he said, "draw yourself up to there,"   46
while pointing to a somewhat higher terrace,
which circles all the slope along that side.

His words incited me; my body tried;   49
on hands and knees I scrambled after him
until the terrace lay beneath my feet.

There we sat down together, facing east,   52
in the direction from which we had come:
what joy—to look back at a path we've climbed!

My eyes were first set on the shores below,   55
and then I raised them toward the sun; I was
amazed to find it fall upon our left.

And when the poet saw that I was struck   58
with wonder as I watched the chariot
of light passing between the north and us,

he said to me: "Suppose Castor and Pollux   61
were in conjunction with that mirror there,
which takes the light and guides it north and south,

then you would see the reddish zodiac   64
still closer to the Bears as it revolves—
unless it has abandoned its old track.

If you would realize how that should be,   67
then concentrate, imagining this mountain
so placed upon this earth that both Mount Zion

and it, although in different hemispheres,   70
share one horizon; therefore, you can see,
putting your mind to it attentively,

how that same path which Phaethon drove so poorly   73
must pass this mountain on the north, whereas
it skirts Mount Zion on the southern side."

Poi che noi fummo in su l'orlo suppremo   34
de l'alta ripa, a la scoperta piaggia,
"Maestro mio," diss' io, "che via faremo?"

    Ed elli a me: "Nessun tuo passo caggia;   37
pur su al monte dietro a me acquista,
fin che n'appaia alcuna scorta saggia."

    Lo sommo er' alto che vincea la vista,   40
e la costa superba più assai
che da mezzo quadrante a centro lista.

    Io era lasso, quando cominciai: 43
"O dolce padre, volgiti, e rimira
com' io rimango sol, se non restai."

    "Figliuol mio," disse, "infin quivi ti tira,"   46
additandomi un balzo poco in sùe
che da quel lato il poggio tutto gira.

    Sì mi spronaron le parole sue,   49
ch'i' mi sforzai carpando appresso lui,
tanto che 'l cinghio sotto i piè mi fue.

    A seder ci ponemmo ivi ambedui   52
vòlti a levante ond' eravam saliti,
che suole a riguardar giovare altrui.

    Li occhi prima drizzai ai bassi liti;   55
poscia li alzai al sole, e ammirava
che da sinistra n'eravam feriti.

    Ben s'avvide il poeta ch'io stava   58
stupido tutto al carro de la luce,
ove tra noi e Aquilone intrava.

    Ond' elli a me: "Se Castore e Poluce   61
fossero in compagnia di quello specchio
che sù e giù del suo lume conduce,

    tu vedresti il Zodïaco rubecchio   64
ancora a l'Orse più stretto rotare,
se non uscisse fuor del cammin vecchio.

    Come ciò sia, se 'l vuoi poter pensare,   67
dentro raccolto, imagina Sïòn
con questo monte in su la terra stare

    sì, ch'amendue hanno un solo orizzòn   70
e diversi emisperi; onde la strada
che mal non seppe carreggiar Fetòn,

    vedrai come a costui convien che vada   73
da l'un, quando a colui da l'altro fianco,
se lo 'ntelletto tuo ben chiaro bada."

I said: "My master, surely I have never— 76
since my intelligence seemed lacking—seen
as clearly as I now can comprehend,

that the mid-circle of the heavens' motion 79
(one of the sciences calls it Equator),
which always lies between the sun and winter,

as you explained, lies as far north of here 82
as it lies southward of the site from which
the Hebrews, looking toward the tropics, saw it.

But if it please you, I should willingly 85
learn just how far it is we still must journey:
the slope climbs higher than my eyes can follow."

And he to me: "This mountain's of such sort 88
that climbing it is hardest at the start;
but as we rise, the slope grows less unkind.

Therefore, when this slope seems to you so gentle 91
that climbing farther up will be as restful
as traveling downstream by boat, you will

be where this pathway ends, and there you can 94
expect to put your weariness to rest.
I say no more, and this I know as truth."

And when his words were done, another voice 97
nearby was heard to say: "Perhaps you will
have need to sit before you reach that point!"

Hearing that voice, both of us turned around, 100
and to the left we saw a massive boulder,
which neither he nor I—before—had noticed.

We made our way toward it and toward the people 103
who lounged behind that boulder in the shade,
as men beset by listlessness will rest.

And one of them, who seemed to me exhausted, 106
was sitting with his arms around his knees;
between his knees, he kept his head bent down.

"O my sweet lord," I said, "look carefully 109
at one who shows himself more languid than
he would have been were laziness his sister!"

Then that shade turned toward us attentively, 112
lifting his face, but just along his thigh,
and said: "Climb, then, if you're so vigorous!"

Then I knew who he was, and the distress 115
that still was quickening my breath somewhat
did not prevent my going to him; and

"Certo, maestro mio," diss'io, "unquanco
non vid' io chiaro sì com' io discerno
là dove mio ingegno parea manco,

che 'l mezzo cerchio del moto superno,   79
che si chiama Equatore in alcun' arte,
e che sempre riman tra 'l sole e 'l verno,

per la ragion che di', quinci si parte   82
verso settentrïon, quanto li Ebrei
vedevan lui verso la calda parte.

Ma se a te piace, volontier saprei   85
quanto avemo ad andar; ché 'l poggio sale
più che salir non posson li occhi miei."

Ed elli a me: "Questa montagna è tale,   88
che sempre al cominciar di sotte è grave;
e quant' om più va sù, e men fa male.

Però, quand' ella ti parrà soave   91
tanto, che sù andar ti fia leggero
com' a seconda giù andar per nave,

allor sarai al fin d'esto sentiero;   94
quivi di riposar l'affanno aspetta.
Più non rispondo, e questo so per vero."

E com' elli ebbe sua parola detta,   97
una voce di presso sonò: "Forse
che di sedere in pria avrai distretta!"

Al suon di lei ciascun di noi si torse,   100
e vedemmo a mancina un gran petrone,
del qual né io né ei prima s'accorse.

Là ci traemmo; e ivi eran persone   103
che si stavano a l'ombra dietro al sasso
come l'uom per negghienza a star si pone.

E un di lor, che mi sembiava lasso,   106
sedeva e abbracciava le ginocchia,
tenendo 'l viso giù tra esse basso.

"O dolce segnor mio," diss'io, "adocchia   109
colui che mostra sé più negligente
che se pigrizia fosse sua serocchia."

Allor si volse a noi e puose mente,   112
movendo 'l viso pur su per la coscia,
e disse: "Or va tu sù, che se' valente!"

Conobbi allor chi era, e quella angoscia   115
che m'avacciava un poco ancor la lena,
non m'impedì l'andare a lui; e poscia

when I had reached him, scarcely lifting up   118
his head, he said: "And have you fathomed how
the sun can drive his chariot on your left?"

The slowness of his movements, his brief words   121
had stirred my lips a little toward a smile;
then I began: "From this time on, Belacqua,

I need not grieve for you; but tell me, why   124
do you sit here? Do you expect a guide?
Or have you fallen into your old ways?"

And he: "O brother, what's the use of climbing?   127
God's angel, he who guards the gate, would not
let me pass through to meet my punishment.

Outside that gate the skies must circle round   130
as many times as they did when I lived—
since I delayed good sighs until the end—

unless, before then, I am helped by prayer   133
that rises from a heart that lives in grace;
what use are other prayers—ignored by Heaven?"

And now the poet climbed ahead, before me,   136
and said: "It's time; see the meridian
touched by the sun; elsewhere, along the Ocean,

night now has set its foot upon Morocco."   139

ch'a lui fu' giunto, alzò la testa a pena, 118
dicendo: "Hai ben veduto come 'l sole
da l'omero sinistro il carro mena?"

Li atti suoi pigri e le corte parole 121
mosser le labbra mie un poco a riso;
poi cominciai: "Belacqua, a me non dole

di te omai; ma dimmi: perché assiso 124
quiritto se'? attendi tu iscorta,
o pur lo modo usato t'ha' ripriso?"

Ed elli: "O frate, andar in sù che porta? 127
ché non mi lascerebbe ire a' martìri
l'angel di Dio che siede in su la porta.

Prima convien che tanto il ciel m'aggiri 130
di fuor da essa, quanto fece in vita,
per ch'io 'ndugiai al fine i buon sospiri,

se orazïone in prima non m'aita 133
che surga sù di cuor che in grazia viva;
l'altra che val, che 'n ciel non è udita?"

E già il poeta innanzi mi saliva, 136
e dicea: "Vienne omai; vedi ch'è tocco
meridïan dal sole, e a la riva

cuopre la notte già col piè Morrocco." 139

CANTO V

I had already left those shades behind
and followed in the footsteps of my guide
when, there beneath me, pointing at me, one
    shade shouted: "See the second climber climb: 4
the sun seems not to shine on his left side,
and when he walks, he walks like one alive!"
    When I had heard these words, I turned my eyes   7
and saw the shades astonished as they stared
at me—at me, and at the broken light.
    "Why have you let your mind get so entwined,"   10
my master said, "that you have slowed your walk?
Why should you care about what's whispered here?
    Come, follow me, and let these people talk: 13
stand like a sturdy tower that does not shake
its summit though the winds may blast; always
    the man in whom thought thrusts ahead of thought   16
allows the goal he's set to move far off—
the force of one thought saps the other's force."
    Could my reply be other than "I come"?   19
And—somewhat colored by the hue that makes
one sometimes merit grace—I spoke those words.
    Meanwhile, along the slope, crossing our road   22
slightly ahead of us, people approached,
singing the *Miserere* verse by verse.
    When they became aware that I allowed   25
no path for rays of light to cross my body,
they changed their song into a long, hoarse "Oh!";
    and two of them, serving as messengers,   28
hurried to meet us, and those two inquired:
"Please tell us something more of what you are."
    My master answered them: "You can return   31
and carry this report to those who sent you:
in truth, the body of this man is flesh.

Ante-Purgatory. From the First to the Second Spur: the
Late-Repentant who died deaths by violence. The shades amazed
by Dante's body. Virgil's rebuke. The Second Spur and its new
company of shades. Jacopo del Cassero. Buonconte da Montefeltro.
La Pia the Sienese.

Io era già da quell' ombre partito,
e seguitava l'orme del mio duca,
quando di retro a me, drizzando 'l dito,
    una gridò: "Ve' che non par che luca   4
lo raggio da sinistra a quel di sotto,
e come vivo par che si conduca!"
    Li occhi rivolsi al suon di questo motto,   7
e vidile guardar per maraviglia
pur me, pur me, e 'l lume ch'era rotto.
    "Perché l'animo tuo tanto s'impiglia,"   10
disse 'l maestro, "che l'andare allenti?
che ti fa ciò che quivi si pispiglia?
    Vien dietro a me, e lascia dir le genti: 13
sta come torre ferma, che non crolla
già mai la cima per soffiar di venti;
    ché sempre l'omo in cui pensier rampolla   16
sovra pensier, da sé dilunga il segno,
perché la foga l'un de l'altro insolla."
    Che potea io ridir, se non "Io vegno"?   19
Dissilo, alquanto del color consperso
che fa l'uom di perdon talvolta degno.
    E 'ntanto per la costa di traverso   22
venivan genti innanzi a noi un poco,
cantando "Miserere" a verso a verso.
    Quando s'accorser ch'i' non dava loco   25
per lo mio corpo al trapassar d'i raggi,
mutar lor canto in un "oh!" lungo e roco;
    e due di loro, in forma di messaggi,   28
corsero incontr' a noi e dimandarne:
"Di vostra condizion fatene saggi."
    E 'l mio maestro: "Voi potete andarne   31
e ritrarre a color che vi mandaro
che 'l corpo di costui è vera carne.

If, as I think, they stopped to see his shadow,   34
that answer is sufficient: let them welcome
him graciously, and that may profit them."

    Never did I see kindled vapors rend   37
clear skies at nightfall or the setting sun
cleave August clouds with a rapidity

    that matched the time it took those two to speed   40
above; and, there arrived, they with the others
wheeled back, like ranks that run without a rein.

    "These people pressing in on us are many;   43
they come beseeching you," the poet said;
"don't stop, but listen as you move ahead."

    "O soul who make your way to gladness with   46
the limbs you had at birth, do stay your steps
awhile," they clamored as they came, "to see

    if there is any of us whom you knew,   49
that you may carry word of him beyond.
Why do you hurry on? Why don't you stop?

    We all were done to death by violence,   52
and we all sinned until our final hour;
then light from Heaven granted understanding,

    so that, repenting and forgiving, we   55
came forth from life at peace with God, and He
instilled in us the longing to see Him."

    And I: "Although I scrutinize your faces,   58
I recognize no one; but, spirits born
to goodness, if there's anything within

    my power that might please you, then—by that   61
same peace which in the steps of such a guide
I seek from world to world—I shall perform it."

    And one began: "We all have faith in your   64
good offices without your oath, as long
as lack of power does not curb your will.

    Thus I, who speak alone—before the others—   67
beseech you, if you ever see the land
that lies between Romagna and the realm

    of Charles, that you be courteous to me,   70
entreating those in Fano to bestow
fair prayers to purge me of my heavy sins.

    My home was Fano; but the piercing wounds   73
from which there poured the blood where my life lived—
those I received among Antenor's sons,

Se per veder la sua ombra restaro,   34
com' io avviso, assai è lor risposto:
fàccianli onore, ed esser può lor caro."

   Vapori accesi non vid' io sì tosto   37
di prima notte mai fender sereno,
né, sol calando, nuvole d'agosto,

   che color non tornasser suso in meno;   40
e, giunti là, con li altri a noi dier volta,
come schiera che scorre sanza freno.

   "Questa gente che preme a noi è molta,   43
e vegnonti a pregar," disse 'l poeta:
"però pur va, e in andando ascolta."

   "O anima che vai per esser lieta   46
con quelle membra con le quai nascesti,"
venian gridando, "un poco il passo queta.

   Guarda s'alcun di noi unqua vedesti,   49
sì che di lui di là novella porti:
deh, perché vai? deh, perché non t'arresti?

   Noi fummo tutti già per forza morti,   52
e peccatori infino a l'ultima ora;
quivi lume del ciel ne fece accorti,

   sì che, pentendo e perdonando, fora   55
di vita uscimmo a Dio pacificati,
che del disio di sé veder n'accora."

   E io: "Perché ne' vostri visi guati,   58
non riconosco alcun; ma s'a voi piace
cosa ch'io possa, spiriti ben nati,

   voi dite, e io farò per quella pace   61
che, dietro a' piedi di sì fatta guida,
di mondo in mondo cercar mi si face."

   E uno incominciò: "Ciascun si fida   64
del beneficio tuo sanza giurarlo,
pur che 'l voler nonpossa non ricida.

   Ond' io, che solo innanzi a li altri parlo,   67
ti priego, se mai vedi quel paese
che siede tra Romagna e quel di Carlo,

   che tu mi sie di tuoi prieghi cortese   70
in Fano, sì che ben per me s'adori
pur ch'i' possa purgar le gravi offese.

   Quindi fu' io; ma li profondi fóri   73
ond' uscì 'l sangue in sul quale io sedea,
fatti mi fuoro in grembo a li Antenori,

there where I thought that I was most secure; 76
for he of Este, hating me far more
than justice warranted, had that deed done.

But had I fled instead toward Mira when 79
they overtook me at Oriaco, then
I should still be beyond, where men draw breath.

I hurried to the marsh. The mud, the reeds 82
entangled me; I fell. And there I saw
a pool, poured from my veins, form on the ground."

Another shade then said: "Ah, so may that 85
desire which draws you up the lofty mountain
be granted, with kind pity help my longing!

I was from Montefeltro, I'm Buonconte; 88
Giovanna and the rest—they all neglect me;
therefore, among these shades, I go in sadness."

And I to him: "What violence or chance 91
so dragged you from the field of Campaldino
that we know nothing of your burial place?"

"Oh," he replied, "across the Casentino 94
there runs a stream called Archiano—born
in the Apennines above the Hermitage.

There, at the place where that stream's name is lost, 97
I came—my throat was pierced—fleeing on foot
and bloodying the plain; and there it was

that I lost sight and speech; and there, as I 100
had finished uttering the name of Mary,
I fell; and there my flesh alone remained.

I'll speak the truth—do you, among the living, 103
retell it: I was taken by God's angel,
but he from Hell cried: 'You from Heaven—why

do you deny me him? For just one tear 106
you carry off his deathless part; but I
shall treat his other part in other wise.'

You are aware how, in the air, moist vapor 109
will gather and again revert to rain
as soon as it has climbed where cold enfolds.

His evil will, which only seeks out evil, 112
conjoined with intellect; and with the power
his nature grants, he stirred up wind and vapor.

And then, when day was done, he filled the valley 115
from Pratomagno far as the great ridge
with mist; the sky above was saturated.

là dov' io più sicuro esser credea:
quel da Esti il fé far, che m'avea in ira
assai più là che dritto non volea.

    Ma s'io fosse fuggito inver' la Mira,   79
quando fu' sovragiunto ad Orïaco,
ancor sarei di là dove si spira.

    Corsi al palude, e le cannucce e 'l braco   82
m'impigliar sì ch'i' caddi; e lì vid' io
de le mie vene farsi in terra laco."

    Poi disse un altro: "Deh, se quel disio   85
si compia che ti tragge a l'alto monte,
con buona pïetate aiuta il mio!

    Io fui di Montefeltro, io son Bonconte;   88
Giovanna o altri non ha di me cura;
per ch'io vo tra costor con bassa fronte."

    E io a lui: "Qual forza o qual ventura   91
ti travïò sì fuor di Campaldino,
che non si seppe mai tua sepultura?"

    "Oh!" rispuos' elli, "a piè del Casentino   94
traversa un'acqua c'ha nome l'Archiano,
che sovra l'Ermo nasce in Apennino.

    Là 've 'l vocabol suo diventa vano,   97
arriva' io forato ne la gola,
fuggendo a piede e sanguinando il piano.

    Quivi perdei la vista e la parola;   100
nel nome di Maria fini', e quivi
caddi, e rimase la mia carne sola.

    Io dirò vero, e tu 'l ridì tra ' vivi: 103
l'angel di Dio mi prese, e quel d'inferno
gridava: 'O tu del ciel, perché mi privi?

    Tu te ne porti di costui l'etterno   106
per una lagrimetta che 'l mi toglie;
ma io farò de l'altro altro governo!'

    Ben sai come ne l'aere si raccoglie   109
quell' umido vapor che in acqua riede,
tosto che sale dove 'l freddo il coglie.

    Giunse quel mal voler che pur mal chiede   112
con lo 'ntelletto, e mosse il fummo e 'l vento
per la virtù che sua natura diede.

    Indi la valle, come 'l dì fu spento,   115
da Pratomagno al gran giogo coperse
di nebbia; e 'l ciel di sopra fece intento,

The dense air was converted into water;   118
rain fell, and then the gullies had to carry
whatever water earth could not receive;

and when that rain was gathered into torrents,   121
it rushed so swiftly toward the royal river
that nothing could contain its turbulence.

The angry Archiano—at its mouth—   124
had found my frozen body; and it thrust
it in the Arno and set loose the cross

that, on my chest, my arms, in pain, had formed.   127
It rolled me on the banks and river bed,
then covered, girded me with its debris."

"Pray, after your returning to the world,   130
when, after your long journeying, you've rested,"
the third soul, following the second, said,

"may you remember me, who am La Pia;   133
Siena made—Maremma unmade—me:
he who, when we were wed, gave me his pledge

and then, as nuptial ring, his gem, knows that."   136

sì che 'l pregno aere in acqua si converse;   118
la pioggia cadde, e a' fossati venne
di lei ciò che la terra non sofferse;

   e come ai rivi grandi si convenne,   121
ver' lo fiume real tanto veloce
si ruinò, che nulla la ritenne.

   Lo corpo mio gelato in su la foce   124
trovò l'Archian rubesto; e quel sospinse
ne l'Arno, e sciolse al mio petto la croce

   ch'i' fe' di me quando 'l dolor mi vinse;   127
voltòmmi per le ripe e per lo fondo,
poi di sua preda mi coperse e cinse.''

   ''Deh, quando tu sarai tornato al mondo   130
e riposato de la lunga via,''
seguitò 'l terzo spirito al secondo,

   ''ricorditi di me, che son la Pia;   133
Siena mi fé, disfecemi Maremma:
salsi colui che 'nnanellata pria

   disposando m'avea con la sua gemma.''   136

BUONCONTE

VI · 149

CANTO VI

When dicing's done and players separate,
the loser's left alone, disconsolate—
rehearsing what he'd thrown, he sadly learns;
    all of the crowd surrounds the one who won—   4
one goes in front, and one tugs at his back,
and at his side one asks to be remembered;
    he does not halt but listens to them all;   7
and when he gives them something, they desist;
and so he can fend off the pressing throng.
    And I, in that persistent pack, was such: 10
this way and that, I turned my face to them
and, making promises, escaped their clutch.
    There was the Aretine who met his death   13
beneath Ghino di Tacco's bestial hands,
and one who drowned when, in pursuit, he ran.
    There, with his outstretched hands, was Federigo   16
Novello, praying, and the Pisan who
made good Marzucco show his fortitude.
    I saw Count Orso, and I saw the soul   19
cleft from its body out of spite and envy—
not, so it said, because it had been guilty—
    I mean Pier de la Brosse (and may the Lady   22
of Brabant, while she's still in this world, watch
her ways—or end among a sadder flock).
    As soon as I was free from all those shades   25
who always pray for others' prayers for them,
so as to reach their blessed state more quickly,
    I started: "O my light, it seems to me   28
that in one passage you deny expressly
that prayer can bend the rule of Heaven, yet
    these people pray precisely for that end.   31
Is their hope, therefore, only emptiness,
or have I not read clearly what you said?"

Ante-Purgatory. Still the Second Spur. The simile of the gamester. Others who died deaths by violence. The efficacy of prayers for the dead. Virgil and his fellow Mantuan, Sordello. Dante's invective against Italy and Florence.

Quando si parte il gioco de la zara,
colui che perde si riman dolente,
repetendo le volte, e tristo impara;

con l'altro se ne va tutta la gente;   4
qual va dinanzi, e qual di dietro il prende,
e qual dallato li si reca a mente;

el non s'arresta, e questo e quello intende;   7
a cui porge la man, più non fa pressa;
e così da la calca si difende.

Tal era io in quella turba spessa,   10
volgendo a loro, e qua e là, la faccia,
e promettendo mi sciogliea da essa.

Quiv' era l'Aretin che da le braccia   13
fiere di Ghin di Tacco ebbe la morte,
e l'altro ch'annegò correndo in caccia.

Quivi pregava con le mani sporte   16
Federigo Novello, e quel da Pisa
che fé parer lo buon Marzucco forte.

Vidi conte Orso e l'anima divisa   19
dal corpo suo per astio e per inveggia,
com' e' dicea, non per colpa commisa;

Pier da la Broccia dico; e qui proveggia,   22
mentr' è di qua, la donna di Brabante,
sì che però non sia di peggior greggia.

Come libero fui da tutte quante   25
quell' ombre che pregar pur ch'altri prieghi,
sì che s'avacci lor divenir sante,

io cominciai: "El par che tu mi nieghi,   28
o luce mia, espresso in alcun testo
che decreto del cielo orazion pieghi;

e questa gente prega pur di questo: 31
sarebbe dunque loro speme vana,
o non m'è 'l detto tuo ben manifesto?"

And he to me: "My text is plain enough, 34
and yet their hope is not delusive if
one scrutinizes it with sober wit;

the peak of justice is not lowered when 37
the fire of love accomplishes in one
instant the expiation owed by all

who dwell here; for where I asserted this— 40
that prayers could not mend their fault—I spoke
of prayers without a passageway to God.

But in a quandary so deep, do not 43
conclude with me, but wait for word that she,
the light between your mind and truth, will speak—

lest you misunderstand, the *she* I mean 46
is Beatrice; upon this mountain's peak,
there you shall see her smiling joyously."

And I: "Lord, let us move ahead more quickly, 49
for now I am less weary than before;
and—you can see—the slope now casts a shadow."

"As long as it is day, we'll make as much 52
headway as possible," he answered; "but
our climb won't be as rapid as you thought.

You will not reach the peak before you see 55
the sun returning: now he hides behind
the hills—you cannot interrupt his light.

But see—beyond—a soul who is completely 58
apart, and seated, looking toward us; he
will show us where to climb most speedily."

We came to him. O Lombard soul, what pride 61
and what disdain were in your stance! Your eyes
moved with such dignity, such gravity!

He said no thing to us but let us pass, 64
his eyes intent upon us only as
a lion watches when it is at rest.

Yet Virgil made his way to him, appealing 67
to him to show us how we'd best ascend;
and he did not reply to that request,

but asked us what our country was and who 70
we were, at which my gentle guide began
"Mantua"—and that spirit, who had been

so solitary, rose from his position 73
saying: "O Mantuan, I am Sordello,
from your own land!" And each embraced the other.

Ed elli a me: "La mia scrittura è piana;   34
e la speranza di costor non falla,
se ben si guarda con la mente sana;

   ché cima di giudicio non s'avvalla   37
perché foco d'amor compia in un punto
ciò che de' sodisfar chi qui s'astalla;

e là dov' io fermai cotesto punto,   40
non s'ammendava, per pregar, difetto,
perché 'l priego da Dio era disgiunto.

   Veramente a così alto sospetto   43
non ti fermar, se quella nol ti dice
che lume fia tra 'l vero e lo 'ntelletto.

   Non so se 'ntendi: io dico di Beatrice;   46
tu la vedrai di sopra, in su la vetta
di questo monte, ridere e felice."

   E io: "Segnore, andiamo a maggior fretta,   49
ché già non m'affatico come dianzi,
e vedi omai che 'l poggio l'ombra getta."

   "Noi anderem con questo giorno innanzi,"   52
rispuose, "quanto più potremo omai;
ma 'l fatto è d'altra forma che non stanzi.

   Prima che sie là sù, tornar vedrai   55
colui che già si cuopre de la costa,
sì che ' suoi raggi tu romper non fai.

   Ma vedi là un'anima che, posta   58
sola soletta, inverso noi riguarda:
quella ne 'nsegnerà la via più tosta."

   Venimmo a lei: o anima lombarda,   61
come ti stavi altera e disdegnosa
e nel mover de li occhi onesta e tarda!

   Ella non ci dicëa alcuna cosa,   64
ma lasciavane gir, solo sguardando
a guisa di leon quando si posa.

   Pur Virgilio si trasse a lei, pregando   67
che ne mostrasse la miglior salita;
e quella non rispuose al suo dimando,

   ma di nostro paese e de la vita   70
ci 'nchiese; e 'l dolce duca incominciava
"Mantüa . . . ," e l'ombra, tutta in sé romita,

   surse ver' lui del loco ove pria stava,   73
dicendo: "O Mantoano, io son Sordello
de la tua terra!"; e l'un l'altro abbracciava.

Ah, abject Italy, you inn of sorrows,   76
you ship without a helmsman in harsh seas,
no queen of provinces but of bordellos!

That noble soul had such enthusiasm: 79
his city's sweet name was enough for him
to welcome—there—his fellow-citizen.

But those who are alive within you now   82
can't live without their warring—even those
whom one same wall and one same moat enclose

gnaw at each other. Squalid Italy,   85
search round your shores and then look inland—see
if any part of you delight in peace.

What use was there in a Justinian   88
mending your bridle, when the saddle's empty?
Indeed, were there no reins, your shame were less.

Ah you—who if you understood what God   91
ordained, would then attend to things devout
and in the saddle surely would allow

Caesar to sit—see how this beast turns fierce   94
because there are no spurs that would correct it,
since you have laid your hands upon the bit!

O German Albert, you who have abandoned   97
that steed become recalcitrant and savage,
you who should ride astride its saddlebows—

upon your blood may the just judgment of   100
the stars descend with signs so strange and plain
that your successor has to feel its terror!

For both you and your father, in your greed   103
for lands that lay more close at hand, allowed
the garden of the Empire to be gutted.

Come—you who pay no heed—do come and see   106
Montecchi, Cappelletti, sad already,
and, filled with fear, Monaldi, Filippeschi.

Come, cruel one, come see the tribulation   109
of your nobility and heal their hurts;
see how disconsolate is Santafior!

Come, see your Rome who, widowed and alone,   112
weeps bitterly; both day and night, she moans:
"My Caesar, why are you not at my side?"

Come, see how much your people love each other!   115
And if no pity for us moves you, may
shame for your own repute move you to act.

Ahi serva Italia, di dolore ostello,
nave sanza nocchiere in gran tempesta,
non donna di provincie, ma bordello!

Quell' anima gentil fu così presta, 79
sol per lo dolce suon de la sua terra,
di fare al cittadin suo quivi festa;

e ora in te non stanno sanza guerra 82
li vivi tuoi, e l'un l'altro si rode
di quei ch'un muro e una fossa serra.

Cerca, misera, intorno da le prode 85
le tue marine, e poi ti guarda in seno,
s'alcuna parte in te di pace gode.

Che val perché ti racconciasse il freno 88
Iustinïano, se la sella è vòta?
Sanz' esso fora la vergogna meno.

Ahi gente che dovresti esser devota, 91
e lasciar seder Cesare in la sella,
se bene intendi ciò che Dio ti nota,

guarda come esta fiera è fatta fella 94
per non esser corretta da li sproni,
poi che ponesti mano a la predella.

O Alberto tedesco ch'abbandoni 97
costei ch'è fatta indomita e selvaggia,
e dovresti inforcar li suoi arcioni,

giusto giudicio da le stelle caggia 100
sovra 'l tuo sangue, e sia novo e aperto,
tal che 'l tuo successor temenza n'aggia!

ch'avete tu e 'l tuo padre sofferto, 103
per cupidigia di costà distretti,
che 'l giardin de lo 'mperio sia diserto.

Vieni a veder Montecchi e Cappelletti, 106
Monaldi e Filippeschi, uom sanza cura:
color già tristi, e questi con sospetti!

Vien, crudel, vieni, e vedi la pressura 109
d'i tuoi gentili, e cura lor magagne;
e vedrai Santafior com' è oscura!

Vieni a veder la tua Roma che piagne 112
vedova e sola, e dì e notte chiama:
"Cesare mio, perché non m'accompagne?"

Vieni a veder la gente quanto s'ama! 115
e se nulla di noi pietà ti move,
a vergognar ti vien de la tua fama.

And if I am allowed, o highest Jove,   118
to ask: You who on earth were crucified
for us—have You turned elsewhere Your just eyes?

Or are You, in Your judgment's depth, devising   121
a good that we cannot foresee, completely
dissevered from our way of understanding?

For all the towns of Italy are full   124
of tyrants, and each townsman who becomes
a partisan is soon a new Marcellus.

My Florence, you indeed may be content   127
that this digression would leave you exempt:
your people's strivings spare you this lament.

Others have justice in their hearts, and thought   130
is slow to let it fly off from their bow;
but your folk keep it ready—on their lips.

Others refuse the weight of public service;   133
whereas your people—eagerly—respond,
even unasked, and shout: "I'll take it on."

You might be happy now, for you have cause!   136
You with your riches, peace, judiciousness!
If I speak truly, facts won't prove me wrong.

Compared to you, Athens and Lacedaemon,   139
though civil cities, with their ancient laws,
had merely sketched the life of righteousness;

for you devise provisions so ingenious—   142
whatever threads October sees you spin,
when mid-November comes, will be unspun.

How often, in the time you can remember,   145
have you changed laws and coinage, offices
and customs, and revised your citizens!

And if your memory has some clarity,   148
then you will see yourself like that sick woman
who finds no rest upon her feather-bed,

but, turning, tossing, tries to ease her pain.   151

E se licito m'è, o sommo Giove 118
che fosti in terra per noi crucifisso,
son li giusti occhi tuoi rivolti altrove?

O è preparazion che ne l'abisso 121
del tuo consiglio fai per alcun bene
in tutto de l'accorger nostro scisso?

Ché le città d'Italia tutte piene 124
son di tiranni, e un Marcel diventa
ogne villan che parteggiando viene.

Fiorenza mia, ben puoi esser contenta 127
di questa digression che non ti tocca,
mercé del popol tuo che si argomenta.

Molti han giustizia in cuore, e tardi scocca 130
per non venir sanza consiglio a l'arco;
ma il popol tuo l'ha in sommo de la bocca.

Molti rifiutan lo comune incarco; 133
ma il popol tuo solicito risponde
sanza chiamare, e grida: "I' mi sobbarco!"

Or ti fa lieta, ché tu hai ben onde: 136
tu ricca, tu con pace e tu con senno!
S'io dico 'l ver, l'effetto nol nasconde.

Atene e Lacedemona, che fenno 139
l'antiche leggi e furon sì civili,
fecero al viver bene un picciol cenno

verso di te, che fai tanto sottili 142
provedimenti, ch'a mezzo novembre
non giugne quel che tu d'ottobre fili.

Quante volte, del tempo che rimembre, 145
legge, moneta, officio e costume
hai tu mutato, e rinovate membre!

E se ben ti ricordi e vedi lume, 148
vedrai te somigliante a quella inferma
che non può trovar posa in su le piume,

ma con dar volta suo dolore scherma. 151

CANTO VII

When glad and gracious welcomings had been
repeated three and four times, then Sordello
drew himself back and asked: "But who are you?"

"Before the spirits worthy of ascent   4
to God had been directed to this mountain,
my bones were buried by Octavian.

I am Virgil, and I am deprived of Heaven   7
for no fault other than my lack of faith."
This was the answer given by my guide.

Even like one who, suddenly, has seen   10
something before him and then, marveling,
does and does not believe, saying, "It is . . .

is not," so did Sordello seem, and then   13
he bent his brow, returned to Virgil humbly,
and clasped him where the lesser presence clasps.

He said: "O glory of the Latins, you   16
through whom our tongue revealed its power, you,
eternal honor of my native city,

what merit or what grace shows you to me?   19
If I deserve to hear your word, then answer:
tell me if you're from Hell and from what cloister."

"Through every circle of the sorry kingdom,"   22
he answered him, "I journeyed here; a power
from Heaven moved me, and with that, I come.

Not for the having—but not having—done,   25
I lost the sight that you desire, the Sun—
that high Sun I was late in recognizing.

There is a place below that only shadows—   28
not torments—have assigned to sadness; there,
lament is not an outcry, but a sigh.

There I am with the infant innocents,   31
those whom the teeth of death had seized before
they were set free from human sinfulness;

Ante-Purgatory. From the Second Spur to the Valley of the Rulers—they too, through negligence, among the Late-Repentant. Rudolph I of Hapsburg; Ottokar II of Bohemia; Philip III of France; Henry I of Navarre; Peter III of Aragon; Charles I of Anjou; Peter, youngest son of Peter III of Aragon; Henry II of England—all thirteenth-century rulers.

Poscia che l'accoglienze oneste e liete
furo iterate tre e quattro volte,
Sordel si trasse, e disse: "Voi, chi siete?"

"Anzi che a questo monte fosser volte   4
l'anime degne di salire a Dio,
fur l'ossa mie per Ottavian sepolte.

Io son Virgilio; e per null' altro rio   7
lo ciel perdei che per non aver fé."
Così rispuose allora il duca mio.

Qual è colui che cosa innanzi sé   10
sùbita vede ond' e' si maraviglia,
che crede e non, dicendo "Ella è . . . non è . . . ,"

tal parve quelli; e poi chinò le ciglia,   13
e umilmente ritornò ver' lui,
e abbracciòl là 've 'l minor s'appiglia.

"O gloria di Latin," disse, "per cui   16
mostrò ciò che potea la lingua nostra,
o pregio etterno del loco ond' io fui,

qual merito o qual grazia mi ti mostra?   19
S'io son d'udir le tue parole degno,
dimmi se vien d'inferno, e di qual chiostra."

"Per tutt' i cerchi del dolente regno,"   22
rispuose lui, "son io di qua venuto;
virtù del ciel mi mosse, e con lei vegno.

Non per far, ma per non fare ho perduto   25
a veder l'alto Sol che tu disiri
e che fu tardi per me conosciuto.

Luogo è là giù non tristo di martìri,   28
ma di tenebre solo, ove i lamenti
non suonan come guai, ma son sospiri.

Quivi sto io coi pargoli innocenti   31
dai denti morse de la morte avante
che fosser da l'umana colpa essenti;

there I am with those souls who were not clothed   34
in the three holy virtues—but who knew
and followed after all the other virtues.

But if you know and you are able to,   37
would you point out the path that leads more quickly
to the true entry point of Purgatory?"

He answered: "No fixed place has been assigned   40
to us; I'm free to range about and climb;
as far as I may go, I'll be your guide.

But see now how the day declines; by night   43
we cannot climb; and therefore it is best
to find some pleasant place where we can rest.

Here to the right are spirits set apart;   46
if you allow me, I shall lead you to them;
and not without delight, you'll come to know them."

"How is that?" he was asked. "Is it that he   49
who tried to climb by night would be impeded
by others, or by his own lack of power?"

And good Sordello, as his finger traced   52
along the ground, said: "Once the sun has set,
then—look—even this line cannot be crossed.

And not that anything except the dark   55
of night prevents your climbing up; it is
the night itself that implicates your will.

Once darkness falls, one can indeed retreat   58
below and wander aimlessly about
the slopes, while the horizon has enclosed

the day." At which my lord, as if in wonder,   61
said: "Lead us then to there where, as you say,
we may derive delight from this night's stay."

We had not gone far off, when I perceived   64
that, just as valleys hollow mountains here
in our world, so that mountain there was hollowed.

That shade said: "It is there that we shall go—   67
to where the slope forms, of itself, a lap;
at that place we'll await the new day's coming."

There was a slanting path, now steep, now flat;   70
it led us to a point beside the valley,
just where its bordering edge had dropped by half.

Gold and fine silver, cochineal, white lead,   73
and Indian lychnite, highly polished, bright,
fresh emerald at the moment it is dampened,

quivi sto io con quei che le tre sante   34
virtù non si vestiro, e sanza vizio
conobber l'altre e seguir tutte quante.

Ma se tu sai e puoi, alcuno indizio   37
dà noi per che venir possiam più tosto
là dove purgatorio ha dritto inizio."

Rispuose: "Loco certo non c'è posto;   40
licito m'è andar suso e intorno;
per quanto ir posso, a guida mi t'accosto.

Ma vedi già come dichina il giorno,   43
e andar sù di notte non si puote;
però è buon pensar di bel soggiorno.

Anime sono a destra qua remote;   46
se mi consenti, io ti merrò ad esse,
e non sanza diletto ti fier note."

"Com' è ciò?" fu risposto. "Chi volesse   49
salir di notte, fora elli impedito
d'altrui, o non sarria ché non potesse?"

E 'l buon Sordello in terra fregò 'l dito,   52
dicendo: "Vedi? sola questa riga
non varcheresti dopo 'l sol partito:

non però ch'altra cosa desse briga,   55
che la notturna tenebra, ad ir suso;
quella col nonpoder la voglia intriga.

Ben si poria con lei tornare in giuso   58
e passeggiar la costa intorno errando,
mentre che l'orizzonte il dì tien chiuso."

Allora il mio segnor, quasi ammirando,   61
"Menane," disse, "dunque là 've dici
ch'aver si può diletto dimorando."

Poco allungati c'eravam di lici,   64
quand' io m'accorsi che 'l monte era scemo,
a guisa che i vallon li sceman quici.

"Colà," disse quell' ombra, "n'anderemo   67
dove la costa face di sé grembo;
e là il novo giorno attenderemo."

Tra erto e piano era un sentiero schembo,   70
che ne condusse in fianco de la lacca,
là dove più ch'a mezzo muore il lembo.

Oro e argento fine, cocco e biacca,   73
indaco, legno lucido e sereno,
fresco smeraldo in l'ora che si fiacca,

if placed within that valley, all would be   76
defeated by the grass and flowers' colors,
just as the lesser gives way to the greater.

    And nature there not only was a painter,   79
but from the sweetness of a thousand odors,
she had derived an unknown, mingled scent.

    Upon the green grass and the flowers, I   82
saw seated spirits singing "*Salve, Regina*";
they were not visible from the outside.

    "Before the meager sun seeks out its nest,"   85
began the Mantuan who led us here,
"do not ask me to guide you down among them.

    From this bank, you'll be better able to   88
make out the acts and features of them all
than if you were to join them in the hollow.

    He who is seated highest, with the look   91
of one too lax in what he undertook—
whose mouth, although the rest sing, does not move—

    was Emperor Rudolph, one who could have healed 94
the wounds that were the death of Italy,
so that another, later, must restore her.

    His neighbor, whose appearance comforts him,   97
governed the land in which are born the waters
the Moldau carries to the Elbe and

    the Elbe to the sea: named Ottokar—   100
in swaddling-bands he was more valiant than
his son, the bearded Wenceslaus, who feeds

    on wantonness and ease. That small-nosed man,   103
who seems so close in counsel with his kindly
friend, died in flight, deflowering the lily:

    see how he beats his breast there! And you see 106
the other shade, who, as he sighs, would rest
his cheek upon his palm as on a bed.

    Father and father-in-law of the pest   109
of France, they know his life—its filth, its vice;
out of that knowledge grows the grief that has

    pierced them. That other, who seems so robust   112
and sings in time with him who has a nose
so manly, wore the cord of every virtue;

    and if the young man seated there behind him   115
had only followed him as king, then valor
might have been poured from vessel unto vessel;

da l'erba e da li fior, dentr' a quel seno
posti, ciascun saria di color vinto,
come dal suo maggiore è vinto il meno.

Non avea pur natura ivi dipinto,   79
ma di soavità di mille odori
vi facea uno incognito e indistinto.

"Salve, Regina" in sul verde e 'n su' fiori   82
quindi seder cantando anime vidi,
che per la valle non parean di fuori.

"Prima che 'l poco sole omai s'annidi,"   85
cominciò 'l Mantoan che ci avea vòlti,
"tra color non vogliate ch'io vi guidi.

Di questo balzo meglio li atti e' volti   88
conoscerete voi di tutti quanti,
che ne la lama giù tra essi accolti.

Colui che più siede alto e fa sembianti   91
d'aver negletto ciò che far dovea,
e che non move bocca a li altrui canti,

Rodolfo imperador fu, che potea   94
sanar le piaghe c'hanno Italia morta,
sì che tardi per altri si ricrea.

L'altro che ne la vista lui conforta,   97
resse la terra dove l'acqua nasce
che Molta in Albia, e Albia in mar ne porta:

Ottacchero ebbe nome, e ne le fasce   100
fu meglio assai che Vincislao suo figlio
barbuto, cui lussuria e ozio pasce.

E quel nasetto che stretto a consiglio   103
par con colui c'ha sì benigno aspetto,
morì fuggendo e disfiorando il giglio:

guardate là come si batte il petto!   106
L'altro vedete c'ha fatto a la guancia
de la sua palma, sospirando, letto.

Padre e suocero son del mal di Francia: 109
sanno la vita sua viziata e lorda,
e quindi viene il duol che sì li lancia.

Quel che par sì membruto e che s'accorda,   112
cantando, con colui dal maschio naso,
d'ogne valor portò cinta la corda;

e se re dopo lui fosse rimaso   115
lo giovanetto che retro a lui siede,
ben andava il valor di vaso in vaso,

one cannot say this of his other heirs; 118
his kingdoms now belong to James and Frederick—
but they do not possess his best bequest.

How seldom human worth ascends from branch 121
to branch, and this is willed by Him who grants
that gift, that one may pray to Him for it!

My words suggest the large-nosed one no less 124
than they refer to Peter, singing with him,
whose heir brings Puglia and Provence distress:

the plant is lesser than its seed, just as 127
the man whom Beatrice and Margaret wed
is lesser than the husband Constance has.

You see the king who led the simple life 130
seated alone: Henry of England—he
has better fortune with his progeny.

He who is seated lowest on the ground, 133
and looking up, is William the Marquis—
for him, both Alexandria and its war

make Monferrato and Canavese mourn." 136

che non si puote dir de l'altre rede;   118
Iacomo e Federigo hanno i reami;
del retaggio miglior nessun possiede.

Rade volte risurge per li rami   121
l'umana probitate; e questo vole
quei che la dà, perché da lui si chiami.

Anche al nasuto vanno mie parole   124
non men ch'a l'altro, Pier, che con lui canta,
onde Puglia e Proenza già si dole.

Tant' è del seme suo minor la pianta,   127
quanto, più che Beatrice e Margherita,
Costanza di marito ancor si vanta.

Vedete il re de la semplice vita   130
seder là solo, Arrigo d'Inghilterra:
questi ha ne' rami suoi migliore uscita.

Quel che più basso tra costor s'atterra,   133
guardando in suso, è Guiglielmo marchese,
per cui e Alessandria e la sua guerra
  fa pianger Monferrato e Canavese."   136

VIII · 30

VIII · 100

CANTO VIII

It was the hour that turns seafarers' longings
homeward—the hour that makes their hearts grow tender
upon the day they bid sweet friends farewell;

the hour that pierces the new traveler   4
with love when he has heard, far off, the bell
that seems to mourn the dying of the day;

when I began to let my hearing fade   7
and watched one of those souls who, having risen,
had signaled with his hand for our attention.

He joined his palms and, lifting them, he fixed   10
all his attention on the east, as if
to say to God: "I care for nothing else."

"*Te lucis ante*" issued from his lips   13
with such devotion and with notes so sweet
that I was moved to move beyond my mind.

And then the other spirits followed him—   16
devoutly, gently—through all of that hymn,
their eyes intent on the supernal spheres.

Here, reader, let your eyes look sharp at truth,   19
for now the veil has grown so very thin—
it is not difficult to pass within.

I saw that company of noble spirits,   22
silent and looking upward, pale and humble,
as if in expectation; and I saw,

emerging and descending from above,   25
two angels bearing flaming swords, of which
the blades were broken off, without their tips.

Their garments, just as green as newborn leaves,   28
were agitated, fanned by their green wings,
and trailed behind them; and one angel came

and stood somewhat above us, while the other   31
descended on the opposite embankment,
flanking that company of souls between them.

Ante-Purgatory. The Valley of the Rulers. Sunset. The two angels. Dante's friend, Nino Visconti. The three stars. The serpent put to flight by the angels. Colloquy with Currado Malaspina.

Era già l'ora che volge il disio
ai navicanti e 'ntenerisce il core
lo dì c'han detto ai dolci amici addio;

e che lo novo peregrin d'amore   4
punge, se ode squilla di lontano
che paia il giorno pianger che si more;

quand' io incominciai a render vano   7
l'udire e a mirare una de l'alme
surta, che l'ascoltar chiedea con mano.

Ella giunse e levò ambo le palme,   10
ficcando li occhi verso l'orïente,
come dicesse a Dio: "D'altro non calme."

"Te lucis ante" sì devotamente   13
le uscìo di bocca e con sì dolci note,
che fece me a me uscir di mente;

e l'altre poi dolcemente e devote   16
seguitar lei per tutto l'inno intero,
avendo li occhi a le superne rote.

Aguzza qui, lettor, ben li occhi al vero,   19
ché 'l velo è ora ben tanto sottile,
certo che 'l trapassar dentro è leggero.

Io vidi quello essercito gentile   22
tacito poscia riguardare in sùe,
quasi aspettando, palido e umìle;

e vidi uscir de l'alto e scender giùe   25
due angeli con due spade affocate,
tronche e private de le punte sue.

Verdi come fogliette pur mo nate   28
erano in veste, che da verdi penne
percosse traean dietro e ventilate.

L'un poco sovra noi a star si venne,   31
e l'altro scese in l'opposita sponda,
sì che la gente in mezzo si contenne.

My eyes made out their blond heads clearly, but   34
my sight was dazzled by their faces—just
like any sense bewildered by excess.

"Both come from Mary's bosom," said Sordello,   37
"to serve as the custodians of the valley
against the serpent that will soon appear."

At this, not knowing where its path might be,   40
frozen with fear, I turned around, pressing
close to the trusty shoulders. And Sordello

continued: "Let us now descend among   43
the great shades in the valley; we shall speak
with them; and seeing you, they will be pleased."

I think that I had taken but three steps   46
to go below, when I saw one who watched
attentively, trying to recognize me.

The hour had now arrived when air grows dark,   49
but not so dark that it deprived my eyes
and his of what—before—they were denied.

He moved toward me, and I advanced toward him.   52
Noble Judge Nino—what delight was mine
when I saw you were not among the damned!

There was no gracious greeting we neglected   55
before he asked me: "When did you arrive,
across long seas, beneath this mountainside?"

I told him, "Oh, by way of the sad regions,   58
I came this morning; I am still within
the first life—although, by this journeying,

I earn the other." When they heard my answer,   61
Sordello and Judge Nino, just behind him,
drew back like people suddenly astonished.

One turned to Virgil, and the other turned   64
and called to one who sat there: "Up, Currado!
Come see what God, out of His grace, has willed!"

Then, when he turned to me: "By that especial   67
gratitude you owe to Him who hides
his primal aim so that no human mind

may find the ford to it, when you return   70
across the wide waves, ask my own Giovanna—
there where the pleas of innocents are answered—

to pray for me. I do not think her mother   73
still loves me: she gave up her white veils—surely,
poor woman, she will wish them back again.

Ben discernëa in lor la testa bionda;   34
ma ne la faccia l'occhio si smarria,
come virtù ch'a troppo si confonda.

   "Ambo vegnon del grembo di Maria,"   37
disse Sordello, "a guardia de la valle,
per lo serpente che verrà vie via."

   Ond' io, che non sapeva per qual calle,   40
mi volsi intorno, e stretto m'accostai,
tutto gelato, a le fidate spalle.

   E Sordello anco: "Or avvalliamo omai   43
tra le grandi ombre, e parleremo ad esse;
grazïoso fia lor vedervi assai."

   Solo tre passi credo ch'i' scendesse,   46
e fui di sotto, e vidi un che mirava
pur me, come conoscer mi volesse.

   Temp' era già che l'aere s'annerava,   49
ma non sì che tra li occhi suoi e ' miei
non dichiarisse ciò che pria serrava.

   Ver' me si fece, e io ver' lui mi fei: 52
giudice Nin gentil, quanto mi piacque
quando ti vidi non esser tra ' rei!

   Nullo bel salutar tra noi si tacque;   55
poi dimandò: "Quant' è che tu venisti
a piè del monte per le lontane acque?"

   "Oh!" diss' io lui, "per entro i luoghi tristi   58
venni stamane, e sono in prima vita,
ancor che l'altra, sì andando, acquisti."

   E come fu la mia risposta udita,   61
Sordello ed elli in dietro si raccolse
come gente di sùbito smarrita.

   L'uno a Virgilio e l'altro a un si volse   64
che sedea lì, gridando: "Sù, Currado!
vieni a veder che Dio per grazia volse."

   Poi, vòlto a me: "Per quel singular grado   67
che tu dei a colui che sì nasconde
lo suo primo perché, che non li è guado,

   quando sarai di là da le larghe onde,   70
dì a Giovanna mia che per me chiami
là dove a li 'nnocenti si risponde.

   Non credo che la sua madre più m'ami,   73
poscia che trasmutò le bianche bende,
le quai convien che, misera!, ancor brami.

Through her, one understands so easily   76
how brief, in woman, is love's fire—when not
rekindled frequently by eye or touch.

The serpent that assigns the Milanese   79
their camping place will not provide for her
a tomb as fair as would Gallura's rooster."

So Nino spoke; his bearing bore the seal   82
of that unswerving zeal which, though it flames
within the heart, maintains a sense of measure.

My avid eyes were steadfast, staring at   85
that portion of the sky where stars are slower,
even as spokes when they approach the axle.

And my guide: "Son, what are you staring at?"   88
And I replied: "I'm watching those three torches
with which this southern pole is all aflame."

Then he to me: "The four bright stars you saw   91
this morning now are low, beyond the pole,
and where those four stars were, these three now are."

Even as Virgil spoke, Sordello drew   94
my guide to him: "See there—our adversary!"
he said; and then he pointed with his finger.

At the unguarded edge of that small valley,   97
there was a serpent—similar, perhaps,
to that which offered Eve the bitter food.

Through grass and flowers the evil streak advanced;   100
from time to time it turned its head and licked
its back, like any beast that preens and sleeks.

I did not see—and therefore cannot say—   103
just how the hawks of heaven made their move,
but I indeed saw both of them in motion.

Hearing the green wings cleave the air, the serpent   106
fled, and the angels wheeled around as each
of them flew upward, back to his high station.

The shade who, when the judge had called, had drawn   109
closer to him, through all of that attack,
had not removed his eyes from me one moment.

"So may the lantern that leads you on high   112
discover in your will the wax one needs—
enough for reaching the enameled peak,"

that shade began, "if you have heard true tidings   115
of Val di Magra or the lands nearby,
tell them to me—for there I once was mighty.

Per lei assai di lieve si comprende 76
quanto in femmina foco d'amor dura,
se l'occhio o 'l tatto spesso non l'accende.

Non le farà sì bella sepultura 79
la vipera che Melanesi accampa,
com' avria fatto il gallo di Gallura."

Così dicea, segnato de la stampa, 82
nel suo aspetto, di quel dritto zelo
che misuratamente in core avvampa.

Li occhi miei ghiotti andavan pur al cielo, 85
pur là dove le stelle son più tarde,
sì come rota più presso a lo stelo.

E 'l duca mio: "Figliuol, che là sù guarde?" 88
E io a lui: "A quelle tre facelle
di che 'l polo di qua tutto quanto arde."

Ond' elli a me: "Le quattro chiare stelle 91
che vedevi staman, son di là basse,
e queste son salite ov' eran quelle."

Com' ei parlava, e Sordello a sé il trasse 94
dicendo: "Vedi là 'l nostro avversaro";
e drizzò il dito perché 'n là guardasse.

Da quella parte onde non ha riparo 97
la picciola vallea, era una biscia,
forse qual diede ad Eva il cibo amaro.

Tra l'erba e ' fior venìa la mala striscia, 100
volgendo ad ora ad or la testa, e 'l dosso
leccando come bestia che si liscia.

Io non vidi, e però dicer non posso, 103
come mosser li astor celestïali;
ma vidi bene e l'uno e l'altro mosso.

Sentendo fender l'aere a le verdi ali, 106
fuggì 'l serpente, e li angeli dier volta,
suso a le poste rivolando iguali.

L'ombra che s'era al giudice raccolta 109
quando chiamò, per tutto quello assalto
punto non fu da me guardare sciolta.

"Se la lucerna che ti mena in alto 112
truovi nel tuo arbitrio tanta cera
quant' è mestiere infino al sommo smalto,"

cominciò ella, "se novella vera 115
di Val di Magra o di parte vicina
sai, dillo a me, che già grande là era.

Currado Malaspina was my name;   118
I'm not the old Currado, but I am
descended from him: to my own I bore
  the love that here is purified." I answered: 121
"I never visited your lands; but can
there be a place in all of Europe where
  they are not celebrated? Such renown   124
honors your house, acclaims your lords and lands—
even if one has yet to journey there.
  And so may I complete my climb, I swear   127
to you: your honored house still claims the prize—
the glory of the purse and of the sword.
  Custom and nature privilege it so   130
that, though the evil head contorts the world,
your kin alone walk straight and shun the path
  of wickedness." And he: "Be sure of that.   133
The sun will not have rested seven times
within the bed that's covered and held fast
  by all the Ram's four feet before this gracious 136
opinion's squarely nailed into your mind
with stouter nails than others' talk provides—
  if the divine decree has not been stayed."   139

Fui chiamato Currado Malaspina;
non son l'antico, ma di lui disceṣi;
a' miei portai l'amor che qui raffina."
    "Oh!" diss' io lui, "per li vostri paesi   121
già mai non fui; ma dove si dimora
per tutta Europa ch'ei non sien palesi?
    La fama che la vostra casa onora,   124
grida i segnori e grida la contrada,
sì che ne sa chi non vi fu ancora;
    e io vi giuro, s'io di sopra vada,   127
che vostra gente onrata non si sfregia
del pregio de la borsa e de la spada.
    Uso e natura sì la privilegia,   130
che, perché il capo reo il mondo torca,
sola va dritta e 'l mal cammin dispregia."
    Ed elli: "Or va; che 'l sol non si ricorca   133
sette volte nel letto che 'l Montone
con tutti e quattro i piè cuopre e inforca,
    che cotesta cortese oppinïone   136
ti fia chiavata in mezzo de la testa
con maggior chiovi che d'altrui sermone,
    se corso di giudicio non s'arresta."   139

CANTO IX

Now she who shares the bed of old Tithonus,
abandoning the arms of her sweet lover,
grew white along the eastern balcony;

the heavens facing her were glittering   4
with gems set in the semblance of the chill
animal that assails men with its tail;

while night within the valley where we were   7
had moved across two of the steps it climbs,
and now the third step made night's wings incline;

when I, who bore something of Adam with me,   10
feeling the need for sleep, lay down upon
the grass where now all five of us were seated.

At that hour close to morning when the swallow   13
begins her melancholy songs, perhaps
in memory of her ancient sufferings,

when, free to wander farther from the flesh   16
and less held fast by cares, our intellect's
envisionings become almost divine—

in dream I seemed to see an eagle poised   19
with golden pinions, in the sky: its wings
were open; it was ready to swoop down.

And I seemed to be there where Ganymede   22
deserted his own family when he
was snatched up for the high consistory.

Within myself I thought: "This eagle may   25
be used to hunting only here; its claws
refuse to carry upward any prey

found elsewhere." Then it seemed to me that, wheeling   28
slightly and terrible as lightning, it
swooped, snatching me up to the fire's orbit.

And there it seemed that he and I were burning;   31
and this imagined conflagration scorched
me so—I was compelled to break my sleep.

Ante-Purgatory. The Valley of the Rulers. Aurora in the northern hemisphere and night in Purgatory. The sleep of Dante. His dream of the Eagle. His waking at morning. The guardian angel. The gate of Purgatory. The seven P's. Entry.

La concubina di Titone antico
già s'imbiancava al balco d'orïente,
fuor de le braccia del suo dolce amico;

di gemme la sua fronte era lucente, 4
poste in figura del freddo animale
che con la coda percuote la gente;

e la notte, de' passi con che sale, 7
fatti avea due nel loco ov' eravamo,
e 'l terzo già chinava in giuso l'ale;

quand' io, che meco avea di quel d'Adamo, 10
vinto dal sonno, in su l'erba inchinai
là 've già tutti e cinque sedavamo.

Ne l'ora che comincia i tristi lai 13
la rondinella presso a la mattina,
forse a memoria de' suo' primi guai,

e che la mente nostra, peregrina 16
più da la carne e men da' pensier presa,
a le sue visïon quasi è divina,

in sogno mi parea veder sospesa 19
un'aguglia nel ciel con penne d'oro,
con l'ali aperte e a calare intesa;

ed esser mi parea là dove fuoro 22
abbandonati i suoi da Ganimede,
quando fu ratto al sommo consistoro.

Fra me pensava: "Forse questa fiede 25
pur qui per uso, e forse d'altro loco
disdegna di portarne suso in piede."

Poi mi parea che, poi rotata un poco, 28
terribil come folgor discendesse,
e me rapisse suso infino al foco.

Ivi parea che ella e io ardesse; 31
e sì lo 'ncendio imaginato cosse,
che convenne che 'l sonno si rompesse.

Just like the waking of Achilles when   34
he started up, casting his eyes about him,
not knowing where he was (after his mother

had stolen him, asleep, away from Chiron   37
and in her arms had carried him to Skyros,
the isle the Greeks would—later—make him leave);

such was my starting up, as soon as sleep   40
had left my eyes, and I went pale, as will
a man who, terrified, turns cold as ice.

The only one beside me was my comfort;   43
by now the sun was more than two hours high;
it was the sea to which I turned my eyes.

My lord said: "Have no fear; be confident,   46
for we are well along our way; do not
restrain, but give free rein to, all your strength.

You have already come to Purgatory: 49
see there the rampart wall enclosing it;
see, where that wall is breached, the point of entry.

Before, at dawn that ushers in the day,   52
when soul was sleeping in your body, on
the flowers that adorn the ground below,

a lady came; she said: 'I am Lucia;   55
let me take hold of him who is asleep,
that I may help to speed him on his way.'

Sordello and the other noble spirits   58
stayed there; and she took you, and once the day
was bright, she climbed—I following behind.

And here she set you down, but first her lovely   61
eyes showed that open entryway to me;
then she and sleep together took their leave."

Just like a man in doubt who then grows sure,   64
exchanging fear for confidence, once truth
has been revealed to him, so was I changed;

and when my guide had seen that I was free   67
from hesitation, then he moved, with me
behind him, up the rocks and toward the heights.

Reader, you can see clearly how I lift   70
my matter; do not wonder, therefore, if
I have to call on more art to sustain it.

Now we were drawing closer; we had reached   73
the part from which—where first I'd seen a breach,
precisely like a gap that cleaves a wall—

Non altrimenti Achille si riscosse,   34
li occhi svegliati rivolgendo in giro
e non sappiendo là dove si fosse,

    quando la madre da Chirón a Schiro   37
trafuggò lui dormendo in le sue braccia,
là onde poi li Greci il dipartiro;

    che mi scoss' io, sì come da la faccia   40
mi fuggì 'l sonno, e diventa' ismorto,
come fa l'uom che, spaventato, agghiaccia.

    Dallato m'era solo il mio conforto,   43
e 'l sole er' alto già più che due ore,
e 'l viso m'era a la marina torto.

    "Non aver tema," disse il mio segnore;   46
"fatti sicur, ché noi semo a buon punto;
non stringer, ma rallarga ogne vigore.

    Tu se' omai al purgatorio giunto: 49
vedi là il balzo che 'l chiude dintorno;
vedi l'entrata là 've par digiunto.

    Dianzi, ne l'alba che procede al giorno,   52
quando l'anima tua dentro dormia,
sovra li fiori ond' è là giù addorno

    venne una donna, e disse: 'I' son Lucia;   55
lasciatemi pigliar costui che dorme;
sì l'agevolerò per la sua via.'

    Sordel rimase e l'altre genti forme;   58
ella ti tolse, e come 'l dì fu chiaro,
sen venne suso; e io per le sue orme.

    Qui ti posò, ma pria mi dimostraro   61
li occhi suoi belli quella intrata aperta;
poi ella e 'l sonno ad una se n'andaro."

    A guisa d'uom che 'n dubbio si raccerta   64
e che muta in conforto sua paura,
poi che la verità li è discoperta,

    mi cambia' io; e come sanza cura   67
vide me 'l duca mio, su per lo balzo
si mosse, e io di rietro inver' l'altura.

    Lettor, tu vedi ben com' io innalzo   70
la mia matera, e però con più arte
non ti maravigliar s'io la rincalzo.

    Noi ci appressammo, ed eravamo in parte   73
che là dove pareami prima rotto,
pur come un fesso che muro diparte,

I now made out a gate and, there below it,　　　　76
three steps—their colors different—leading to it,
and a custodian who had not yet spoken.

　　As I looked more and more directly at him,　　79
I saw him seated on the upper step—
his face so radiant, I could not bear it;

　　and in his hand he held a naked sword,　　　82
which so reflected rays toward us that I,
time and again, tried to sustain that sight

　　in vain. "Speak out from there; what are you seeking?"　85
so he began to speak. "Where is your escort?
Take care, lest you be harmed by climbing here."

　　My master answered him: "But just before,　　88
a lady came from Heaven and, familiar
with these things, told us: 'That's the gate; go there.'"

　　"And may she speed you on your path of goodness!"　91
the gracious guardian of the gate began
again. "Come forward, therefore, to our stairs."

　　There we approached, and the first step was white　94
marble, so polished and so clear that I
was mirrored there as I appear in life.

　　The second step, made out of crumbling rock,　97
rough-textured, scorched, with cracks that ran across
its length and width, was darker than deep purple.

　　The third, resting above more massively,　　100
appeared to me to be of porphyry,
as flaming red as blood that spurts from veins.

　　And on this upper step, God's angel—seated　103
upon the threshold, which appeared to me
to be of adamant—kept his feet planted.

　　My guide, with much good will, had me ascend　106
by way of these three steps, enjoining me:
"Do ask him humbly to unbolt the gate."

　　I threw myself devoutly at his holy　　　109
feet, asking him to open out of mercy;
but first I beat three times upon my breast.

　　Upon my forehead, he traced seven P's　　112
with his sword's point and said: "When you have entered
within, take care to wash away these wounds."

　　Ashes, or dry earth that has just been quarried,　115
would share one color with his robe, and from
beneath that robe he drew two keys; the one

vidi una porta, e tre gradi di sotto   76
per gire ad essa, di color diversi,
e un portier ch'ancor non facea motto.

  E come l'occhio più e più v'apersi,   79
vidil seder sovra 'l grado sovrano,
tal ne la faccia ch'io non lo soffersi;

  e una spada nuda avëa in mano,   82
che reflettëa i raggi sì ver' noi,
ch'io dirizzava spesso il viso in vano.

  "Dite costinci: che volete voi?"   85
cominciò elli a dire, "ov' è la scorta?
Guardate che 'l venir sù non vi nòi."

  "Donna del ciel, di queste cose accorta,"   88
rispuose 'l mio maestro a lui, "pur dianzi
ne disse: 'Andate là: quivi è la porta.'"

  "Ed ella i passi vostri in bene avanzi,"   91
ricominciò il cortese portinaio:
"Venite dunque a' nostri gradi innanzi."

  Là ne venimmo; e lo scaglion primaio   94
bianco marmo era sì pulito e terso,
ch'io mi specchiai in esso qual io paio.

  Era il secondo tinto più che perso,   97
d'una petrina ruvida e arsiccia,
crepata per lo lungo e per traverso.

  Lo terzo, che di sopra s'ammassiccia,   100
porfido mi parea, sì fiammeggiante
come sangue che fuor di vena spiccia.

  Sovra questo tenëa ambo le piante   103
l' angel di Dio sedendo in su la soglia
che mi sembiava pietra di diamante.

  Per li tre gradi sù di buona voglia   106
mi trasse il duca mio, dicendo: "Chiedi
umilemente che 'l serrame scioglia."

  Divoto mi gittai a' santi piedi;   109
misericordia chiesi e ch'el m'aprisse,
ma tre volte nel petto pria mi diedi.

  Sette P ne la fronte mi descrisse   112
col punton de la spada, e "Fa che lavi,
quando se' dentro, queste piaghe" disse.

  Cenere, o terra che secca si cavi,   115
d'un color fora col suo vestimento;
e di sotto da quel trasse due chiavi.

was made of gold, the other was of silver;   118
first with the white, then with the yellow key,
he plied the gate so as to satisfy me.

"Whenever one of these keys fails, not turning   121
appropriately in the lock," he said
to us, "this gate of entry does not open.

One is more precious, but the other needs   124
much art and skill before it will unlock—
that is the key that must undo the knot.

These I received from Peter; and he taught me   127
rather to err in opening than in keeping
this portal shut—whenever souls pray humbly."

Then he pushed back the panels of the holy   130
gate, saying: "Enter; but I warn you—he
who would look back, returns—again—outside."

And when the panels of that sacred portal,   133
which are of massive and resounding metal,
turned in their hinges, then even Tarpeia

(when good Metellus was removed from it,   136
for which that rock was left impoverished)
did not roar so nor show itself so stubborn.

Hearing that gate resound, I turned, attentive;   139
I seemed to hear, inside, in words that mingled
with gentle music, *Te Deum laudamus.*"

And what I heard gave me the very same   142
impression one is used to getting when
one hears a song accompanied by organ,

and now the words are clear and now are lost.   145

L'una era d'oro e l'altra era d'argento; 118
pria con la bianca e poscia con la gialla
fece a la porta sì, ch'i' fu' contento.

   "Quandunque l'una d'este chiavi falla, 121
che non si volga dritta per la toppa,"
diss' elli a noi, "non s'apre questa calla.

   Più cara è l'una; ma l'altra vuol troppa 124
d'arte e d'ingegno avanti che diserri,
perch' ella è quella che 'l nodo digroppa.

   Da Pier le tegno; e dissemi ch'i' erri 127
anzi ad aprir ch'a tenerla serrata,
pur che la gente a' piedi mi s'atterri."

   Poi pinse l'uscio a la porta sacrata, 130
dicendo: "Intrate; ma facciovi accorti
che di fuor torna chi 'n dietro si guata."

   E quando fuor ne' cardini distorti 133
li spigoli di quella regge sacra,
che di metallo son sonanti e forti,

   non rugghiò sì né si mostrò sì acra 136
Tarpëa, come tolto le fu il buono
Metello, per che poi rimase macra.

   Io mi rivolsi attento al primo tuono, 139
e "Te Deum laudamus" mi parea
udire in voce mista al dolce suono.

   Tale imagine a punto mi rendea 142
ciò ch'io udiva, qual prender si suole
quando a cantar con organi si stea;

   ch'or sì or no s'intendon le parole. 145

IX · 19

IX · 112

CANTO X

When I had crossed the threshold of the gate
that—since the soul's aberrant love would make
the crooked way seem straight—is seldom used,

I heard the gate resound and, hearing, knew   4
that it had shut; and if I'd turned toward it,
how could my fault have found a fit excuse?

Our upward pathway ran between cracked rocks;   7
they seemed to sway in one, then the other part,
just like a wave that flees, then doubles back.

"Here we shall need some ingenuity,"   10
my guide warned me, "as both of us draw near
this side or that side where the rock wall veers."

This made our steps so slow and hesitant   13
that the declining moon had reached its bed
to sink back into rest before we had

made our way through that needle's eye; but when   16
we were released from it, in open space
above, a place at which the slope retreats,

I was exhausted; with the two of us   19
uncertain of our way, we halted on
a plateau lonelier than desert paths.

The distance from its edge, which rims the void,   22
in to the base of the steep slope, which climbs
and climbs, would measure three times one man's body;

and for as far as my sight took its flight,   25
now to the left, now to the right-hand side,
that terrace seemed to me equally wide.

There we had yet to let our feet advance   28
when I discovered that the bordering bank—
less sheer than banks of other terraces—

was of white marble and adorned with carvings   31
so accurate—not only Polycletus
but even Nature, there, would feel defeated.

The First Terrace: the Prideful. The hard ascent. The sculptured wall with three examples of humility: the Virgin Mary, David, and Trajan. The Prideful punished by bearing the weight of heavy stones.

CANTO X 85

Poi fummo dentro al soglio de la porta
che 'l mal amor de l'anime disusa,
perché fa parer dritta la via torta,

  sonando la senti' esser richiusa;   4
e s'io avesse li occhi vòlti ad essa,
qual fora stata al fallo degna scusa?

  Noi salavam per una pietra fessa,   7
che si moveva e d'una e d'altra parte,
sì come l'onda che fugge e s'appressa.

  "Qui si conviene usare un poco d'arte,"   10
cominciò 'l duca mio, "in accostarsi
or quinci, or quindi al lato che si parte."

  E questo fece i nostri passi scarsi,   13
tanto che pria lo scemo de la luna
rigiunse al letto suo per ricorcarsi,

  che noi fossimo fuor di quella cruna;   16
ma quando fummo liberi e aperti
sù dove il monte in dietro si rauna,

  ïo stancato e amendue incerti   19
di nostra via, restammo in su un piano
solingo più che strade per diserti.

  Da la sua sponda, ove confina il vano,   22
al piè de l'alta ripa che pur sale,
misurrebbe in tre volte un corpo umano;

  e quanto l'occhio mio potea trar d'ale,   25
or dal sinistro e or dal destro fianco,
questa cornice mi parea cotale.

  Là sù non eran mossi i piè nostri anco,   28
quand' io conobbi quella ripa intorno
che dritto di salita aveva manco,

  esser di marmo candido e addorno   31
d'intagli sì, che non pur Policleto,
ma la natura lì avrebbe scorno.

The angel who reached earth with the decree   34
of that peace which, for many years, had been
invoked with tears, the peace that opened Heaven

after long interdict, appeared before us,   37
his gracious action carved with such precision—
he did not seem to be a silent image.

One would have sworn that he was saying, "Ave";   40
for in that scene there was the effigy
of one who turned the key that had unlocked

the highest love; and in her stance there were   43
impressed these words, "*Ecce ancilla Dei,*"
precisely like a figure stamped in wax.

"Your mind must not attend to just one part,"   46
the gentle master said—he had me on
the side of him where people have their heart.

At this, I turned my face and saw beyond   49
the form of Mary—on the side where stood
the one who guided me—another story

engraved upon the rock; therefore I moved   52
past Virgil and drew close to it, so that
the scene before my eyes was more distinct.

There, carved in that same marble, were the cart   55
and oxen as they drew the sacred ark,
which makes men now fear tasks not in their charge.

People were shown in front; and all that group,   58
divided into seven choirs, made
two of my senses speak—one sense said, "No,"

the other said, "Yes, they do sing"; just so,   61
about the incense smoke shown there, my nose
and eyes contended, too, with *yes* and *no.*

And there the humble psalmist went before   64
the sacred vessel, dancing, lifting up
his robe—he was both less and more than king.

Facing that scene, and shown as at the window   67
of a great palace, Michal watched as would
a woman full of scorn and suffering.

To look more closely at another carving—   70
beyond Michal, it beckoned, gleaming, white—
I made my way still farther to the right.

And there the noble action of a Roman   73
prince was presented—he whose worth had urged
on Gregory to his great victory—

L'angel che venne in terra col decreto   34
de la molt' anni lagrimata pace,
ch'aperse il ciel del suo lungo divieto,

   dinanzi a noi pareva sì verace   37
quivi intagliato in un atto soave,
che non sembiava imagine che tace.

   Giurato si saria ch'el dicesse "*Ave!*";   40
perché iv' era imaginata quella
ch'ad aprir l'alto amor volse la chiave;

   e avea in atto impressa esta favella   43
"*Ecce ancilla Deï!*," propriamente
come figura in cera si suggella.

   "Non tener pur ad un loco la mente,"   46
disse 'l dolce maestro, che m'avea
da quella parte onde 'l cuore ha la gente.

   Per ch'i' mi mossi col viso, e vedea   49
di retro da Maria, da quella costa
onde m'era colui che mi movea,

   un'altra storia ne la roccia imposta;   52
per ch'io varcai Virgilio, e fe'mi presso,
acciò che fosse a li occhi miei disposta.

   Era intagliato lì nel marmo stesso   55
lo carro e ' buoi, traendo l'arca santa,
per che si teme officio non commesso.

   Dinanzi parea gente; e tutta quanta,   58
partita in sette cori, a' due mie' sensi
faceva dir l'un "No," l'altro "Sì, canta."

   Similemente al fummo de li 'ncensi   61
che v'era imaginato, li occhi e 'l naso
e al sì e al no discordi fensi.

   Lì precedeva al benedetto vaso,   64
trescando alzato, l'umile salmista,
e più e men che re era in quel caso.

   Di contra, effigïata ad una vista   67
d'un gran palazzo, Micòl ammirava
sì come donna dispettosa e trista.

   I' mossi i piè del loco dov' io stava,   70
per avvisar da presso un'altra istoria,
che di dietro a Micòl mi biancheggiava.

   Quiv' era storïata l'alta gloria   73
del roman principato, il cui valore
mosse Gregorio a la sua gran vittoria;

I mean the Emperor Trajan; and a poor   76
widow was near his bridle, and she stood
even as one in tears and sadness would.

Around him, horsemen seemed to press and crowd;   79
above their heads, on golden banners, eagles
were represented, moving in the wind.

Among that crowd, the miserable woman   82
seemed to be saying: "Lord, avenge me for
the slaying of my son—my heart is broken."

And he was answering: "Wait now until   85
I have returned." And she, as one in whom
grief presses urgently: "And, lord, if you

do not return?" And he: "The one who'll be   88
in my place will perform it for you." She:
"What good can others' goodness do for you

if you neglect your own?" He: "Be consoled;   91
my duty shall be done before I go:
so justice asks, so mercy makes me stay."

This was the speech made visible by One   94
within whose sight no thing is new—but we,
who lack its likeness here, find novelty.

While I took much delight in witnessing   97
these effigies of true humility—
dear, too, to see because He was their Maker—

the poet murmured: "See the multitude   100
advancing, though with slow steps, on this side:
they will direct us to the higher stairs."

My eyes, which had been satisfied in seeking   103
new sights—a thing for which they long—did not
delay in turning toward him. But I would

not have you, reader, be deflected from   106
your good resolve by hearing from me now
how God would have us pay the debt we owe.

Don't dwell upon the form of punishment: 109
consider what comes after that; at worst
it cannot last beyond the final Judgment.

"Master," I said, "what I see moving toward us   112
does not appear to me like people, but
I can't tell what is there—my sight's bewildered."

And he to me: "Whatever makes them suffer   115
their heavy torment bends them to the ground;
at first I was unsure of what they were.

i' dico di Traiano imperadore;   76
e una vedovella li era al freno,
di lagrime atteggiata e di dolore.

    Intorno a lui parea calcato e pieno   79
di cavalieri, e l'aguglie ne l'oro
sovr' essi in vista al vento si movieno.

    La miserella intra tutti costoro   82
pareva dir: "Segnor, fammi vendetta
di mio figliuol ch'è morto, ond' io m'accoro";

    ed elli a lei rispondere: "Or aspetta   85
tanto ch'i' torni"; e quella: "Segnor mio,"
come persona in cui dolor s'affretta,

    "se tu non torni?"; ed ei: "Chi fia dov' io,   88
la ti farà"; ed ella: "L'altrui bene
a te che fia, se 'l tuo metti in oblio?";

    ond' elli: "Or ti conforta; ch'ei convene   91
ch'i' solva il mio dovere anzi ch'i' mova:
giustizia vuole e pietà mi ritene."

    Colui che mai non vide cosa nova   94
produsse esto visibile parlare,
novello a noi perché qui non si trova.

    Mentr' io mi dilettava di guardare   97
l'imagini di tante umilitadi,
e per lo fabbro loro a veder care,

    "Ecco di qua, ma fanno i passi radi,"   100
mormorava il poeta, "molte genti:
questi ne 'nvïeranno a li alti gradi."

    Li occhi miei, ch'a mirare eran contenti   103
per veder novitadi ond' e' son vaghi,
volgendosi ver' lui non furon lenti.

    Non vo' però, lettor, che tu ti smaghi   106
di buon proponimento per udire
come Dio vuol che 'l debito si paghi.

    Non attender la forma del martìre: 109
pensa la succession; pensa ch'al peggio
oltre la gran sentenza non può ire.

    Io cominciai: "Maestro, quel ch'io veggio   112
muovere a noi, non mi sembian persone,
e non so che, sì nel veder vaneggio."

    Ed elli a me: "La grave condizione   115
di lor tormento a terra li rannicchia,
sì che ' miei occhi pria n'ebber tencione.

But look intently there, and let your eyes   118
unravel what's beneath those stones: you can
already see what penalty strikes each."

O Christians, arrogant, exhausted, wretched,   121
whose intellects are sick and cannot see,
who place your confidence in backward steps,

do you not know that we are worms and born   124
to form the angelic butterfly that soars,
without defenses, to confront His judgment?

Why does your mind presume to flight when you   127
are still like the imperfect grub, the worm
before it has attained its final form?

Just as one sees at times—as corbel for   130
support of ceiling or of roof—a figure
with knees drawn up into its chest (and this

oppressiveness, unreal, gives rise to real   133
distress in him who watches it): such was
the state of those I saw when I looked hard.

They were indeed bent down—some less, some more— 136
according to the weights their backs now bore;
and even he whose aspect showed most patience,

in tears, appeared to say: "I can no more."   139

Ma guarda fiso là, e disviticchia 118
col viso quel che vien sotto a quei sassi:
già scorger puoi come ciascun si picchia."

O superbi cristian, miseri lassi, 121
che, de la vista de la mente infermi,
fidanza avete ne' retrosi passi,

non v'accorgete voi che noi siam vermi 124
nati a formar l'angelica farfalla,
che vola a la giustizia sanza schermi?

Di che l'animo vostro in alto galla, 127
poi siete quasi antomata in difetto,
sì come vermo in cui formazion falla?

Come per sostentar solaio o tetto, 130
per mensola talvolta una figura
si vede giugner le ginocchia al petto,

la qual fa del non ver vera rancura 133
nascere 'n chi la vede; così fatti
vid' io color, quando puosi ben cura.

Vero è che più e meno eran contratti 136
secondo ch'avien più e meno a dosso;
e qual più pazïenza avea ne li atti,

piangendo parea dicer: "Più non posso." 139

CANTO XI

"Our Father, You who dwell within the heavens—
but are not circumscribed by them—out of
Your greater love for Your first works above,

    praised be Your name and Your omnipotence,   4
by every creature, just as it is seemly
to offer thanks to Your sweet effluence.

    Your kingdom's peace come unto us, for if   7
it does not come, then though we summon all
our force, we cannot reach it of our selves.

    Just as Your angels, as they sing Hosanna,   10
offer their wills to You as sacrifice,
so may men offer up their wills to You.

    Give unto us this day the daily manna   13
without which he who labors most to move
ahead through this harsh wilderness falls back.

    Even as we forgive all who have done   16
us injury, may You, benevolent,
forgive, and do not judge us by our worth.

    Try not our strength, so easily subdued,   19
against the ancient foe, but set it free
from him who goads it to perversity.

    This last request we now address to You,   22
dear Lord, not for ourselves—who have no need—
but for the ones whom we have left behind."

    Beseeching, thus, good penitence for us   25
and for themselves, those shades moved on beneath
their weights, like those we sometimes bear in dreams—

    each in his own degree of suffering   28
but all, exhausted, circling the first terrace,
purging themselves of this world's scoriae.

    If there they pray on our behalf, what can   31
be said and done here on this earth for them
by those whose wills are rooted in true worth?

Still on the First Terrace: the Prideful, who now pray a
paraphrase of the Lord's Prayer. Omberto Aldobrandeschi.
Oderisi of Gubbio: his discourse on earthly fame; his presentation
of Provenzan Salvani.

"O Padre nostro, che ne' cieli stai,
non circunscritto, ma per più amore
ch'ai primi effetti di là sù tu hai,

laudato sia 'l tuo nome e 'l tuo valore   4
da ogne creatura, com' è degno
di render grazie al tuo dolce vapore.

Vegna ver' noi la pace del tuo regno,   7
ché noi ad essa non potem da noi,
s'ella non vien, con tutto nostro ingegno.

Come del suo voler li angeli tuoi   10
fan sacrificio a te, cantando *osanna*,
così facciano li uomini de' suoi.

Dà oggi a noi la cotidiana manna,   13
sanza la qual per questo aspro diserto
a retro va chi più di gir s'affanna.

E come noi lo mal ch'avem sofferto   16
perdoniamo a ciascuno, e tu perdona
benigno, e non guardar lo nostro merto.

Nostra virtù che di legger s'adona,   19
non spermentar con l'antico avversaro,
ma libera da lui che sì la sprona.

Quest' ultima preghiera, segnor caro,   22
già non si fa per noi, ché non bisogna,
ma per color che dietro a noi restaro."

Così a sé e noi buona ramogna   25
quell' ombre orando, andavan sotto 'l pondo,
simile a quel che talvolta si sogna,

disparmente angosciate tutte a tondo   28
e lasse su per la prima cornice,
purgando la caligine del mondo.

Se di là sempre ben per noi si dice,   31
di qua che dire e far per lor si puote
da quei c'hanno al voler buona radice?

Indeed we should help them to wash away   34
the stains they carried from this world, so that,
made pure and light, they reach the starry wheels.

    "Ah, so may justice and compassion soon   37
unburden you, so that your wings may move
as you desire them to, and uplift you,

    show us on which hand lies the shortest path   40
to reach the stairs; if there is more than one
passage, then show us that which is less steep;

    for he who comes with me, because he wears   43
the weight of Adam's flesh as dress, despite
his ready will, is slow in his ascent."

    These words, which had been spoken by my guide,   46
were answered by still other words we heard;
for though it was not clear who had replied,

    an answer came: "Come with us to the right   49
along the wall of rock, and you will find
a pass where even one alive can climb.

    And were I not impeded by the stone   52
that, since it has subdued my haughty neck,
compels my eyes to look below, then I

    should look at this man who is still alive   55
and nameless, to see if I recognize
him—and to move his pity for my burden.

    I was Italian, son of a great Tuscan: 58
my father was Guiglielmo Aldobrandesco;
I do not know if you have heard his name.

    The ancient blood and splendid deeds of my   61
forefathers made me so presumptuous
that, without thinking on our common mother,

    I scorned all men past measure, and that scorn   64
brought me my death—the Sienese know how,
as does each child in Campagnatico.

    I am Omberto; and my arrogance   67
has not harmed me alone, for it has drawn
all of my kin into calamity.

    Until God has been satisfied, I bear   70
this burden here among the dead because
I did not bear this load among the living."

    My face was lowered as I listened; and   73
one of those souls—not he who'd spoken—twisted
himself beneath the weight that burdened them;

Ben si de' loro atar lavar le note 34
che portar quinci, sì che, mondi e lievi,
possano uscire a le stellate ruote.

"Deh, se giustizia e pietà vi disgrievi 37
tosto, sì che possiate muover l'ala,
che secondo il disio vostro vi lievi,

mostrate da qual mano inver' la scala 40
si va più corto; e se c'è più d'un varco,
quel ne 'nsegnate che men erto cala;

ché questi che vien meco, per lo 'ncarco 43
de la carne d'Adamo onde si veste,
al montar sù, contra sua voglia, è parco."

Le lor parole, che rendero a queste 46
che dette avea colui cu' io seguiva,
non fur da cui venisser manifeste;

ma fu detto: "A man destra per la riva 49
con noi venite, e troverete il passo
possibile a salir persona viva.

E s'io non fossi impedito dal sasso 52
che la cervice mia superba doma,
onde portar convienmi il viso basso,

cotesti, ch'ancor vive e non si noma, 55
guardere' io, per veder s'i' 'l conosco,
e per farlo pietoso a questa soma.

Io fui latino e nato d'un gran Tosco: 58
Guiglielmo Aldobrandesco fu mio padre;
non so se 'l nome suo già mai fu vosco.

L'antico sangue e l'opere leggiadre 61
d'i miei maggior mi fer sì arrogante,
che, non pensando a la comune madre,

ogn' uomo ebbi in despetto tanto avante, 64
ch'io ne mori', come i Sanesi sanno,
e sallo in Campagnatico ogne fante.

Io sono Omberto; e non pur a me danno 67
superbia fa, ché tutti miei consorti
ha ella tratti seco nel malanno.

E qui convien ch'io questo peso porti 70
per lei, tanto che a Dio si sodisfaccia,
poi ch'io nol fe' tra ' vivi, qui tra ' morti."

Ascoltando chinai in giù la faccia; 73
e un di lor, non questi che parlava,
si torse sotto il peso che li 'mpaccia,

he saw and knew me and called out to me,   76
fixing his eyes on me laboriously
as I, completely hunched, walked on with them.

    "Oh," I cried out, "are you not Oderisi,   79
glory of Gubbio, glory of that art
they call illumination now in Paris?"

    "Brother," he said, "the pages painted by   82
the brush of Franco Bolognese smile
more brightly: all the glory now is his;

    mine, but a part. In truth I would have been   85
less gracious when I lived—so great was that
desire for eminence which drove my heart.

    For such pride, here one pays the penalty;   88
and I'd not be here yet, had it not been
that, while I still could sin, I turned to Him.

    O empty glory of the powers of humans!   91
How briefly green endures upon the peak—
unless an age of dullness follows it.

    In painting Cimabue thought he held   94
the field, and now it's Giotto they acclaim—
the former only keeps a shadowed fame.

    So did one Guido, from the other, wrest   97
the glory of our tongue—and he perhaps
is born who will chase both out of the nest.

    Worldly renown is nothing other than   100
a breath of wind that blows now here, now there,
and changes name when it has changed its course.

    Before a thousand years have passed—a span   103
that, for eternity, is less space than
an eyeblink for the slowest sphere in heaven—

    would you find greater glory if you left   106
your flesh when it was old than if your death
had come before your infant words were spent?

    All Tuscany acclaimed his name—the man   109
who moves so slowly on the path before me,
and now they scarcely whisper of him even

    in Siena, where he lorded it when they   112
destroyed the raging mob of Florence—then
as arrogant as now it's prostitute.

    Your glory wears the color of the grass   115
that comes and goes; the sun that makes it wither
first drew it from the ground, still green and tender."

e videmi e conobbemi e chiamava,   76
tenendo li occhi con fatica fisi
a me che tutto chin con loro andava.

    "Oh!" diss' io lui, "non se' tu Oderisi,   79
l'onor d'Agobbio e l'onor di quell' arte
ch'alluminar chiamata è in Parisi?"

    "Frate," diss' elli, "più ridon le carte   82
che pennelleggia Franco Bolognese;
l'onore è tutto or suo, e mio in parte.

    Ben non sare' io stato sì cortese   85
mentre ch'io vissi, per lo gran disio
de l'eccellenza ove mio core intese.

    Di tal superbia qui si paga il fio;   88
e ancor non sarei qui, se non fosse
che, possendo peccar, mi volsi a Dio.

    Oh vana gloria de l'umane posse!   91
com' poco verde in su la cima dura,
se non è giunta da l'etati grosse!

    Credette Cimabue ne la pittura   94
tener lo campo, e ora ha Giotto il grido,
sì che la fama di colui è scura.

    Così ha tolto l'uno a l'altro Guido   97
la gloria de la lingua; e forse è nato
chi l'uno e l'altro caccerà del nido.

    Non è il mondan romore altro ch'un fiato   100
di vento, ch'or vien quinci e or vien quindi,
e muta nome perché muta lato.

    Che voce avrai tu più, se vecchia scindi   103
da te la carne, che se fossi morto
anzi che tu lasciassi il 'pappo' e 'l 'dindi,'

    pria che passin mill' anni? ch'è più corto   106
spazio a l'etterno, ch'un muover di ciglia
al cerchio che più tardi in cielo è torto.

    Colui che del cammin sì poco piglia   109
dinanzi a me, Toscana sonò tutta;
e ora a pena in Siena sen pispiglia,

    ond' era sire quando fu distrutta   112
la rabbia fiorentina, che superba
fu a quel tempo sì com' ora è putta

    La vostra nominanza è color d'erba,   115
che viene e va, e quei la discolora
per cui ella esce de la terra acerba."

And I to him: "Your truthful speech has filled   118
my soul with sound humility, abating
my overswollen pride; but who is he
    of whom you spoke now?" "Provenzan Salvani,"   121
he answered, "here because—presumptuously—
he thought his grip could master all Siena.

    So he has gone, and so he goes, with no   124
rest since his death; this is the penalty
exacted from those who—there—overreached."

    And I: "But if a spirit who awaits   127
the edge of life before repenting must—
unless good prayers help him—stay below

    and not ascend here for as long a time   130
as he had spent alive, do tell me how
Salvani's entry here has been allowed."

    "When he was living in his greatest glory"   133
said he, "then of his own free will he set
aside all shame and took his place upon

    the Campo of Siena; there, to free   136
his friend from suffering in Charles's prison,
humbling himself, he trembled in each vein.

    I say no more; I know I speak obscurely;   139
but soon enough you'll find your neighbor's acts
are such that what I say can be explained.

    This deed delivered him from those confines."   142

E io a lui: "Tuo vero dir m'incora   118
bona umiltà, e gran tumor m'appiani;
ma chi è quei di cui tu parlavi ora?"

"Quelli è," rispuose, "Provenzan Salvani;   121
ed è qui perché fu presuntüoso
a recar Siena tutta a le sue mani.

Ito è così e va, sanza riposo,   124
poi che morì; cotal moneta rende
a sodisfar chi è di là troppo oso."

E io: "Se quello spirito ch'attende,   127
pria che si penta, l'orlo de la vita,
qua giù dimora e qua sù non ascende,

se buona orazïon lui non aita,   130
prima che passi tempo quanto visse,
come fu la venuta lui largita?"

"Quando vivea più glorïoso," disse,   133
"liberamente nel Campo di Siena,
ogne vergogna diposta, s'affisse;

e lì, per trar l'amico suo di pena,   136
ch'e' sostenea ne la prigion di Carlo,
si condusse a tremar per ogne vena.

Più non dirò, e scuro so che parlo;   139
ma poco tempo andrà, che ' tuoi vicini
faranno sì che tu potrai chiosarlo.

Quest' opera li tolse quei confini."   142

OMBERTO

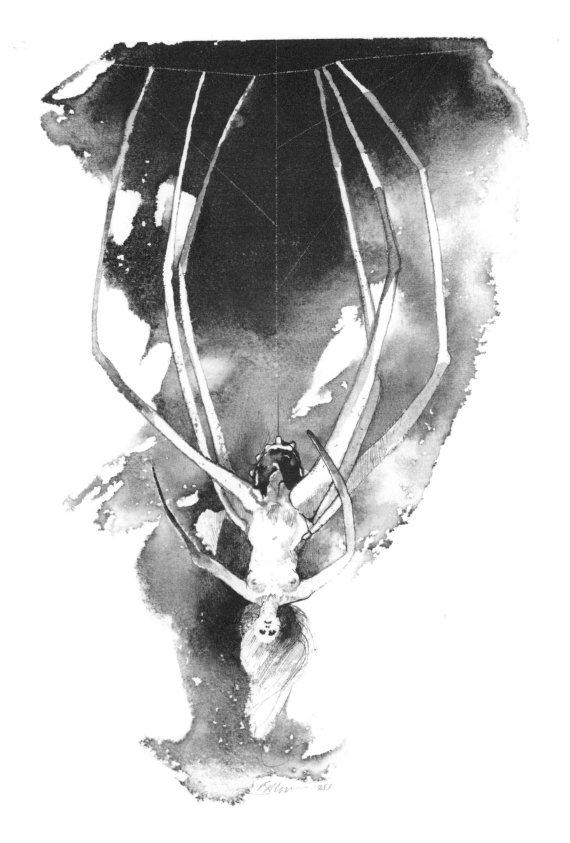

ARACHNE

CANTO XII

As oxen, yoked, proceed abreast, so I
moved with that burdened soul as long as my
kind pedagogue allowed me to; but when

he said: "Leave him behind, and go ahead;   4
for here it's fitting that with wings and oars
each urge his boat along with all his force,"

I drew my body up again, erect—   7
the stance most suitable to man—and yet
the thoughts I thought were still submissive, bent.

Now I was on my way, and willingly   10
I followed in my teacher's steps, and we
together showed what speed we could command.

He said to me: "Look downward, for the way   13
will offer you some solace if you pay
attention to the pavement at your feet."

As, on the lids of pavement tombs, there are   16
stone effigies of what the buried were
before, so that the dead may be remembered;

and there, when memory—which pierces only   19
the pious—has renewed their mourning, men
are often led to shed their tears again;

so did I see, but carved more skillfully,   22
with greater sense of likeness, effigies
on all the path protruding from the mountain.

I saw, to one side of the path, one who   25
had been created nobler than all other
beings, falling lightning-like from Heaven.

I saw, upon the other side, Briareus   28
transfixed by the celestial shaft: he lay,
ponderous, on the ground, in fatal cold.

I saw Thymbraeus, I saw Mars and Pallas,   31
still armed, as they surrounded Jove, their father,
gazing upon the Giants' scattered limbs.

Still on the First Terrace: the Prideful. The sculptured pavement with thirteen examples of punished pride: Satan, Briareus, the Giants, Nimrod, Niobe, Saul, Arachne, Rehoboam, Eriphyle, Sennacherib, Cyrus, Holofernes, Troy. The angel of humility. Ascent to the Second Terrace. The First Beatitude. One P erased.

CANTO XII 103

Di pari, come buoi che vanno a giogo,
m'andava io con quell' anima carca,
fin che 'l sofferse il dolce pedagogo.

Ma quando disse: "Lascia lui e varca;   4
ché qui è buono con l'ali e coi remi,
quantunque può, ciascun pinger sua barca";

dritto sì come andar vuolsi rife'mi   7
con la persona, avvegna che i pensieri
mi rimanessero e chinati e scemi.

Io m'era mosso, e seguia volontieri   10
del mio maestro i passi, e amendue
già mostravam com' eravam leggeri;

ed el mi disse: "Volgi li occhi in giùe: 13
buon ti sarà, per tranquillar la via,
veder lo letto de le piante tue."

Come, perché di lor memoria sia,   16
sovra i sepolti le tombe terragne
portan segnato quel ch'elli eran pria,

onde lì molte volte si ripiagne   19
per la puntura de la rimembranza,
che solo a' pii dà de le calcagne;

sì vid' io lì, ma di miglior sembianza   22
secondo l'artificio, figurato
quanto per via di fuor del monte avanza.

Vedëa colui che fu nobil creato   25
più ch'altra creatura, giù dal cielo
folgoreggiando scender, da l'un lato.

Vedea Brïareo fitto dal telo   28
celestïal giacer, da l'altra parte,
grave a la terra per lo mortal gelo.

Vedea Timbreo, vedea Pallade e Marte,   31
armati ancora, intorno al padre loro,
mirar le membra d'i Giganti sparte.

I saw bewildered Nimrod at the foot   34
of his great labor; watching him were those
of Shinar who had shared his arrogance.

O Niobe, what tears afflicted me   37
when, on that path, I saw your effigy
among your slaughtered children, seven and seven!

O Saul, you were portrayed there as one who   40
had died on his own sword, upon Gilboa,
which never after knew the rain, the dew!

O mad Arachne, I saw you already   43
half spider, wretched on the ragged remnants
of work that you had wrought to your own hurt!

O Rehoboam, you whose effigy   46
seems not to menace there, and yet you flee
by chariot, terrified, though none pursues!

It also showed—that pavement of hard stone—   49
how much Alcmaeon made his mother pay:
the cost of the ill-omened ornament.

It showed the children of Sennacherib   52
as they assailed their father in the temple,
then left him, dead, behind them as they fled.

It showed the slaughter and the devastation   55
wrought by Tomyris when she taunted Cyrus:
"You thirsted after blood; with blood I fill you."

It showed the rout of the Assyrians,   58
sent reeling after Holofernes' death,
and also showed his body—what was left.

I saw Troy turned to caverns and to ashes;   61
o Ilium, your effigy in stone—
it showed you there so squalid, so cast down!

What master of the brush or of the stylus   64
had there portrayed such masses, such outlines
as would astonish all discerning minds?

The dead seemed dead and the alive, alive: 67
I saw, head bent, treading those effigies,
as well as those who'd seen those scenes directly.

Now, sons of Eve, persist in arrogance,   70
in haughty stance, do not let your eyes bend,
lest you be forced to see your evil path!

We now had circled round more of the mountain   73
and much more of the sun's course had been crossed
than I, my mind absorbed, had gauged, when he

Vedea Nembròt a piè del gran lavoro 34
quasi smarrito, e riguardar le genti
che 'n Sennaàr con lui superbi fuoro.

O Nïobè, con che occhi dolenti 37
vedea io te segnata in su la strada,
tra sette e sette tuoi figliuoli spenti!

O Saùl, come in su la propria spada 40
quivi parevi morto in Gelboè,
che poi non sentì pioggia né rugiada!

O folle Aragne, sì vedea io te 43
già mezza ragna, trista in su li stracci
de l'opera che mal per te si fé.

O Roboàm, già non par che minacci 46
quivi 'l tuo segno; ma pien di spavento
nel porta un carro, canza ch'altri il cacci.

Mostrava ancor lo duro pavimento 49
come Almeon a sua madre fé caro
parer lo sventurato addornamento.

Mostrava come i figli si gittaro 52
sovra Sennacherìb dentro dal tempio,
e come, morto lui, quivi il lasciaro.

Mostrava la ruina e 'l crudo scempio 55
che fé Tamiri, quando disse a Ciro:
"Sangue sitisti, e io di sangue t'empio."

Mostrava come in rotta si fuggiro 58
li Assiri, poi che fu morto Oloferne,
e anche le reliquie del martiro.

Vedeva Troia in cenere e in caverne; 61
o Ilïón, come te basso e vile
mostrava il segno che lì si discerne!

Qual di pennel fu maestro o di stile 64
che ritraesse l'ombre e ' tratti ch'ivi
mirar farieno uno ingegno sottile?

Morti li morti e i vivi parean vivi: 67
non vide mei di me chi vide il vero,
quant' io calcai, fin che chinato givi.

Or superbite, e via col viso altero, 70
figliuoli d'Eva, e non chinate il volto
sì che veggiate il vostro mal sentero!

Più era già per noi del monte vòlto 73
e del cammin del sole assai più speso
che non stimava l'animo non sciolto,

who always looked ahead insistently, 76
as he advanced, began: "Lift up your eyes;
it's time to set these images aside.

See there an angel hurrying to meet us, 79
and also see the sixth of the handmaidens
returning from her service to the day.

Adorn your face and acts with reverence, 82
that he be pleased to send us higher. Remember—
today will never know another dawn."

I was so used to his insistent warnings 85
against the loss of time; concerning that,
his words to me could hardly be obscure.

That handsome creature came toward us; his clothes 88
were white, and in his aspect he seemed like
the trembling star that rises in the morning.

He opened wide his arms, then spread his wings; 91
he said: "Approach: the steps are close at hand;
from this point on one can climb easily.

This invitation's answered by so few: 94
o humankind, born for the upward flight,
why are you driven back by wind so slight?"

He led us to a cleft within the rock, 97
and then he struck my forehead with his wing;
that done, he promised me safe journeying.

As on the right, when one ascends the hill 100
where—over Rubaconte's bridge—there stands
the church that dominates the well-ruled city,

the daring slope of the ascent is broken 103
by steps that were constructed in an age
when record books and measures could be trusted,

so was the slope that plummets there so steeply 106
down from the other ring made easier;
but on this side and that, high rock encroaches.

While we began to move in that direction, 109
"Beati pauperes spiritu" was sung
so sweetly—it can not be told in words.

How different were these entryways from those 112
of Hell! For here it is with song one enters;
down there, it is with savage lamentations.

Now we ascended by the sacred stairs, 115
but I seemed to be much more light than I
had been, before, along the level terrace.

quando colui che sempre innanzi atteso
andava, cominciò: "Drizza la testa;
non è più tempo di gir sì sospeso.

Vedi colà un angel che s'appresta   79
per venir verso noi; vedi che torna
dal servigio del dì l'ancella sesta.

Di reverenza il viso e li atti addorna,   82
sì che i diletti lo 'nvïarci in suso;
pensa che questo dì mai non raggiorna!"

Io era ben del suo ammonir uso   85
pur di non perder tempo, sì che 'n quella
materia non potea parlarmi chiuso.

A noi venìa la creatura bella,   88
biancovestito e ne la faccia quale
par tremolando mattutina stella.

Le braccia aperse, e indi aperse l'ale;   91
disse: "Venite: qui son presso i gradi,
e agevolemente omai si sale.

A questo invito vegnon molto radi: 94
o gente umana, per volar sù nata,
perché a poco vento così cadi?"

Menocci ove la roccia era tagliata;   97
quivi mi batté l'ali per la fronte;
poi mi promise sicura l'andata.

Come a man destra, per salire al monte   100
dove siede la chiesa che soggioga
la ben guidata sopra Rubaconte,

si rompe del montar l'ardita foga   103
per le scalee che si fero ad etade
ch'era sicuro il quaderno e la doga;

così s'allenta la ripa che cade   106
quivi ben ratta da l'altro girone;
ma quinci e quindi l'alta pietra rade.

Noi volgendo ivi le nostre persone,   109
"Beati pauperes spiritu!" voci
cantaron sì, che nol diria sermone.

Ahi quanto son diverse quelle foci   112
da l'infernali! ché quivi per canti
s'entra, e là giù per lamenti feroci.

Già montavam su per li scaglion santi,   115
ed esser mi parea troppo più lieve
che per lo pian non mi parea davanti.

At this I asked: "Master, tell me, what heavy   118
weight has been lifted from me, so that I,
in going, notice almost no fatigue?"

He answered: "When the *P*'s that still remain   121
upon your brow—now almost all are faint—
have been completely, like this *P*, erased,

your feet will be so mastered by good will   124
that they not only will not feel travail
but will delight when they are urged uphill."

Then I behaved like those who make their way   127
with something on their head of which they're not
aware, till others' signs make them suspicious,

at which, the hand helps them to ascertain;   130
it seeks and finds and touches and provides
the services that sight cannot supply;

so, with my right hand's outspread fingers, I   133
found just six of the letters once inscribed
by him who holds the keys, upon my forehead;

and as he watched me do this, my guide smiled.   136

Ond' io: "Maestro, dì, qual cosa greve   118
levata s'è da me, che nulla quasi
per me fatica, andando, si riceve?"

    Rispuose: "Quando i P che son rimasi   121
ancor nel volto tuo presso che stinti,
saranno, com' è l'un, del tutto rasi,

    fier li tuoi piè dal buon voler sì vinti,   124
che non pur non fatica sentiranno,
ma fia diletto loro esser sù pinti."

    Allor fec' io come color che vanno   127
con cosa in capo non da lor saputa,
se non che ' cenni altrui sospecciar fanno;

    per che la mano ad accertar s'aiuta,   130
e cerca e truova e quello officio adempie
che non si può fornir per la veduta;

    e con le dita de la destra scempie   133
trovai pur sei le lettere che 'ncise
quel da le chiavi a me sovra le tempie:

    a che guardando, il mio duca sorrise.   136

CANTO XIII

We now had reached the summit of the stairs
where once again the mountain whose ascent
delivers man from sin has been indented.

There, just as in the case of the first terrace,   4
a second terrace runs around the slope,
except that it describes a sharper arc.

No effigy is there and no outline: 7
the bank is visible, the naked path—
only the livid color of raw rock.

"If we wait here in order to inquire   10
of those who pass," the poet said, "I fear
our choice of path may be delayed too long."

And then he fixed his eyes upon the sun;   13
letting his right side serve to guide his movement,
he wheeled his left around and changed direction.

"O gentle light, through trust in which I enter   16
on this new path, may you conduct us here,"
he said, "for men need guidance in this place.

You warm the world and you illumine it;   19
unless a higher Power urge us elsewhere,
your rays must always be the guides that lead."

We had already journeyed there as far   22
as we should reckon here to be a mile,
and done it in brief time—our will was eager—

when we heard spirits as they flew toward us,   25
though they could not be seen—spirits pronouncing
courteous invitations to love's table.

The first voice that flew by called out aloud: 28
"*Vinum non habent,*" and behind us that
same voice reiterated its example.

And as that voice drew farther off, before   31
it faded finally, another cried:
"I am Orestes." It, too, did not stop.

The Second Terrace: the Envious. Virgil's apostrophe to the sun.
Voices calling out three incitements to fraternal love: the examples
of the Virgin Mary and Orestes, and a dictum of Jesus. The
Litany of the Saints. The Envious punished by having their
eyelids sewn up with iron wires. Sapia of Siena.

Noi eravamo al sommo de la scala,
dove secondamente si risega
lo monte che salendo altrui dismala.

Ivi così una cornice lega   4
dintorno il poggio, come la primaia;
se non che l'arco suo più tosto piega.

Ombra non li è né segno che si paia: 7
parsi la ripa e parsi la via schietta
col livido color de la petraia.

"Se qui per dimandar gente s'aspetta,"   10
ragionava il poeta, "io temo forse
che troppo avrà d'indugio nostra eletta."

Poi fisamente al sole li occhi porse;   13
fece del destro lato a muover centro,
e la sinistra parte di sé torse.

"O dolce lume a cui fidanza i' entro   16
per lo novo cammin, tu ne conduci,"
dicea, "come condur si vuol quinc' entro.

Tu scaldi il mondo, tu sovr' esso luci;   19
s'altra ragione in contrario non ponta,
esser dien sempre li tuoi raggi duci."

Quanto di qua per un migliaio si conta,   22
tanto di là eravam noi già iti,
con poco tempo, per la voglia pronta;

e verso noi volar furon sentiti,   25
non però visti, spiriti parlando
a la mensa d'amor cortesi inviti.

La prima voce che passò volando   28
"Vinum non habent" altamente disse,
e dietro a noi l'andò reïterando.

E prima che del tutto non si udisse   31
per allungarsi, un'altra "I' sono Oreste"
passò gridando, e anco non s'affisse.

"What voices are these, father?" were my words; 34
and as I asked him this, I heard a third
voice say: "Love those by whom you have been hurt."

And my good master said: "The sin of envy 37
is scourged within this circle; thus, the cords
that form the scourging lash are plied by love.

The sounds of punished envy, envy curbed, 40
are different; if I judge right, you'll hear
those sounds before we reach the pass of pardon.

But let your eyes be fixed attentively 43
and, through the air, you will see people seated
before us, all of them on the stone terrace."

I opened—wider than before—my eyes; 46
I looked ahead of me, and I saw shades
with cloaks that shared their color with the rocks.

And once we'd moved a little farther on, 49
I heard the cry of, "Mary, pray for us,"
and then heard, "Michael," "Peter," and "All saints."

I think no man now walks upon the earth 52
who is so hard that he would not have been
pierced by compassion for what I saw next;

for when I had drawn close enough to see 55
clearly the way they paid their penalty,
the force of grief pressed tears out of my eyes.

Those souls–it seemed–were cloaked in coarse haircloth; 58
another's shoulder served each shade as prop,
and all of them were bolstered by the rocks:

so do the blind who have to beg appear 61
on pardon days to plead for what they need,
each bending his head back and toward the other,

that all who watch feel—quickly—pity's touch 64
not only through the words that would entreat
but through the sight, which can—no less—beseech.

And just as, to the blind, no sun appears, 67
so to the shades—of whom I now speak—here,
the light of heaven would not give itself;

for iron wire pierces and sews up 70
the lids of all those shades, as untamed hawks
are handled, lest, too restless, they fly off.

It seemed to me a gross discourtesy 73
for me, going, to see and not be seen;
therefore, I turned to my wise counselor.

"Oh!" diss' io, "padre, che voci son queste?"   34
E com' io domandai, ecco la terza
dicendo: "Amate da cui male aveste."

E 'l buon maestro: "Questo cinghio sferza   37
la colpa de la invidia, e però sono
tratte d'amor le corde de la ferza.

Lo fren vuol esser del contrario suono;   40
credo che l'udirai, per mio avviso,
prima che giunghi al passo del perdono.

Ma ficca li occhi per l'aere ben fiso,   43
e vedrai gente innanzi a noi sedersi,
e ciascun è lungo la grotta assiso."

Allora più che prima li occhi apersi;   46
guarda'mi innanzi, e vidi ombre con manti
al color de la pietra non diversi.

E poi che fummo un poco più avanti,   49
udia gridar: "Maria, òra per noi":
gridar "Michele" e "Pietro" e "Tutti santi."

Non credo che per terra vada ancoi   52
omo sì duro, che non fosse punto
per compassion di quel ch'i' vidi poi;

ché, quando fui sì presso di lor giunto,   55
che li atti loro a me venivan certi,
per li occhi fui di grave dolor munto.

Di vil ciliccio mi parean coperti,   58
e l'un sofferia l'altro con la spalla,
e tutti da la ripa eran sofferti.

Così li ciechi a cui la roba falla,   61
stanno a' perdoni a chieder lor bisogna,
e l'uno il capo sopra l'altro avvalla,

perché 'n altrui pietà tosto si pogna,   64
non pur per lo sonar de le parole,
ma per la vista che non meno agogna.

E come a li orbi non approda il sole,   67
così a l'ombre quivi, ond' io parlo ora,
luce del ciel di sé largir non vole;

ché a tutti un fil di ferro i cigli fóra   70
e cusce sì, come a sparvier selvaggio
si fa però che queto non dimora.

A me pareva, andando, fare oltraggio,   73
veggendo altrui, non essendo veduto:
per ch'io mi volsi al mio consiglio saggio.

He knew quite well what I, though mute, had meant;   76
and thus he did not wait for my request,
but said: "Speak, and be brief and to the point."

Virgil was to my right, along the outside,   79
nearer the terrace-edge—no parapet
was there to keep a man from falling off;

and to my other side were the devout   82
shades; through their eyes, sewn so atrociously,
those spirits forced the tears that bathed their cheeks.

I turned to them; and "You who can be certain,"   85
I then began, "of seeing that high light
which is the only object of your longing,

may, in your conscience, all impurity   88
soon be dissolved by grace, so that the stream
of memory flow through it limpidly;

tell me, for I shall welcome such dear words,   91
if any soul among you is Italian;
if I know that, then I—perhaps—can help him."

"My brother, each of us is citizen   94
of one true city: what you meant to say
was 'one who lived in Italy as pilgrim.'"

My hearing placed the point from which this answer   97
had come somewhat ahead of me; therefore,
I made myself heard farther on; moving,

I saw one shade among the rest who looked   100
expectant; and if any should ask how—
its chin was lifted as a blind man's is.

"Spirit," I said, "who have subdued yourself   103
that you may climb, if it is you who answered,
then let me know you by your place or name."

"I was a Sienese," she answered, "and   106
with others here I mend my wicked life,
weeping to Him that He grant us Himself.

I was not sapient, though I was called Sapia;   109
and I rejoiced far more at others' hurts
than at my own good fortune. And lest you

should think I have deceived you, hear and judge   112
if I was not, as I have told you, mad
when my years' arc had reached its downward part.

My fellow citizens were close to Colle,   115
where they'd joined battle with their enemies,
and I prayed God for that which He had willed.

Ben sapev' ei che volea dir lo muto;
e però non attese mia dimanda,
ma disse: "Parla, e sie breve e arguto."

Virgilio mi venìa da quella banda   79
de la cornice onde cader si puote,
perché da nulla sponda s'inghirlanda;

da l'altra parte m'eran le divote   82
ombre, che per l'orribile costura
premevan sì, che bagnavan le gote.

Volsimi a loro e: "O gente sicura,"   85
incominciai, "di veder l'alto lume
che 'l disio vostro solo ha in sua cura,

se tosto grazia resolva le schiume   88
di vostra coscïenza sì che chiaro
per essa scenda de la mente il fiume,

ditemi, ché mi fia grazioso e caro,   91
s'anima è qui tra voi che sia latina;
e forse lei sarà buon s'i' l'apparo."

"O frate mio, ciascuna è cittadina   94
d'una vera città; ma tu vuo' dire
che vivesse in Italia peregrina."

Questo mi parve per risposta udire   97
più innanzi alquanto che là dov' io stava,
ond' io mi feci ancor più là sentire.

Tra l'altre vidi un'ombra ch'aspettava   100
in vista; e se volesse alcun dir "Come?"
lo mento a guisa d'orbo in sù levava.

"Spirto," diss' io, "che per salir ti dome,   103
se tu se' quelli che mi rispondesti,
fammiti conto o per luogo o per nome."

"Io fui sanese," rispuose, "e con questi   106
altri rimendo qui la vita ria,
lagrimando a colui che sé ne presti.

Savia non fui, avvegna che Sapìa   109
fossi chiamata, e fui de li altrui danni
più lieta assai che di ventura mia.

E perché tu non creda ch'io t'inganni,   112
odi s'i' fui, com' io ti dico, folle,
già discendendo l'arco d'i miei anni.

Eran li cittadin miei presso a Colle   115
in campo giunti co' loro avversari,
e io pregava Iddio di quel ch'e' volle.

There they were routed, beaten; they were reeling   118
along the bitter paths of flight; and seeing
that chase, I felt incomparable joy,

so that I lifted up my daring face   121
and cried to God: 'Now I fear you no more!'—
as did the blackbird after brief fair weather.

I looked for peace with God at my life's end;   124
the penalty I owe for sin would not
be lessened now by penitence had not

one who was sorrowing for me because   127
of charity in him—Pier Pettinaio—
remembered me in his devout petitions.

But who are you, who question our condition   130
as you move on, whose eyes—if I judge right—
have not been sewn, who uses breath to speak?"

"My eyes," I said, "will be denied me here,   133
but only briefly; the offense of envy
was not committed often by their gaze.

I fear much more the punishment below;   136
my soul is anxious, in suspense; already
I feel the heavy weights of the first terrace."

And she: "Who, then, led you up here among us,   139
if you believe you will return below?"
And I: "He who is with me and is silent.

I am alive; and therefore, chosen spirit,   142
if you would have me move my mortal steps
on your behalf, beyond, ask me for that."

"Oh, this," she answered, "is so strange a thing   145
to hear: the sign is clear—you have God's love.
Thus, help me sometimes with your prayers. I ask

of you, by that which you desire most,   148
if you should ever tread the Tuscan earth,
to see my name restored among my kin.

You will see them among those vain ones who   151
have put their trust in Talamone (their loss
in hope will be more than Diana cost);

but there the admirals will lose the most."   154

Rotti fuor quivi e vòlti ne li amari
passi di fuga; e veggendo la caccia,
letizia presi a tutte altre dispari,

    tanto ch'io volsi in sù l'ardita faccia,   121
gridando a Dio: 'Omai più non ti temo!'
come fé 'l merlo per poca bonaccia.

    Pace volli con Dio in su lo stremo   124
de la mia vita; e ancor non sarebbe
lo mio dover per penitenza scemo,

    se ciò non fosse, ch'a memoria m'ebbe   127
Pier Pettinaio in sue sante orazioni,
a cui di me per caritate increbbe.

    Ma tu chi se', che nostre condizioni   130
vai dimandando, e porti li occhi sciolti,
sì com' io credo, e spirando ragioni?"

    "Li occhi," diss' io, "mi fieno ancor qui tolti,   133
ma picciol tempo, ché poca è l'offesa
fatta per esser con invidia vòlti.

    Troppa è più la paura ond' è sospesa   136
l'anima mia del tormento di sotto,
che già lo 'ncarco di là giù mi pesa."

    Ed ella a me: "Chi t'ha dunque condotto   139
qua sù tra noi, se giù ritornar credi?"
E io: "Costui ch'è meco e non fa motto.

    E vivo sono; e però mi richiedi,   142
spirito eletto, se tu vuo' ch'i' mova
di là per te ancor li mortai piedi."

    "Oh, questa è a udir sì cosa nuova,"   145
rispuose, "che gran segno è che Dio t'ami;
però col priego tuo talor mi giova.

    E cheggioti, per quel che tu più brami,   148
se mai calchi la terra di Toscana,
che a' miei propinqui tu ben mi rinfami.

    Tu li vedrai tra quella gente vana   151
che spera in Talamone, e perderagli
più di speranza ch'a trovar la Diana;

    ma più vi perderanno li ammiragli."   154

XIII · 70

AGLAUROS

CANTO XIV

"Who is this man who, although death has yet
to grant him flight, can circle round our mountain
and can, at will, open and shut his eyes?"

"I don't know who he is, but I do know   4
he's not alone; you're closer; question him
and greet him gently, so that he replies."

So were two spirits, leaning toward each other,   7
discussing me, along my right-hand side;
then they bent back their heads to speak to me,

and one began: "O soul who—still enclosed   10
within the body—make your way toward Heaven,
may you, through love, console us; tell us who

you are, from where you come; the grace that you've 13
received—a thing that's never come to pass
before—has caused us much astonishment."

And I: "Through central Tuscany there spreads   16
a little stream first born in Falterona;
one hundred miles can't fill the course it needs.

I bring this body from that river's banks;   19
to tell you who I am would be to speak
in vain—my name has not yet gained much fame."

"If, with my understanding, I have seized   22
your meaning properly," replied to me
the one who'd spoken first, "you mean the Arno."

The other said to him: "Why did he hide   25
that river's name, even as one would do
in hiding something horrible from view?"

The shade to whom this question was addressed   28
repaid with this: "I do not know; but it
is right for such a valley's name to perish,

for from its source (at which the rugged chain—   31
from which Pelorus was cut off—surpasses
most other places with its mass of mountains)

*Still the Second Terrace: the Envious. Two spirits, Guido del
Duca and Rinieri da Calboli. Guido's denunciation of the cities in
the valley of the Arno, of Rinieri's grandson, Fulcieri da Calboli,
and of Romagna. Voices calling out examples of punished envy:
Cain and Aglauros.*

"Chi è costui che 'l nostro monte cerchia
prima che morte li abbia dato il volo,
e apre li occhi a sua voglia e coverchia?"

"Non so chi sia, ma so ch'e' non è solo;   4
domandal tu che più li t'avvicini,
e dolcemente, sì che parli, acco'lo."

Così due spirti, l'uno a l'altro chini,   7
ragionavan di me ivi a man dritta;
poi fer li visi, per dirmi, supini;

e disse l'uno: "O anima che fitta   10
nel corpo ancora inver' lo ciel ten vai,
per carità ne consola e ne ditta

onde vieni e chi se'; ché tu ne fai   13
tanto maravigliar de la tua grazia,
quanto vuol cosa che non fu più mai."

E io: "Per mezza Toscana si spazia   16
un fiumicel che nasce in Falterona,
e cento miglia di corso nol sazia.

Di sovr' esso rech' io questa persona: 19
dirvi ch'i' sia, saria parlare indarno,
ché 'l nome mio ancor molto non suona."

"Se ben lo 'ntendimento tuo accarno   22
con lo 'ntelletto," allora mi rispuose
quei che diceva pria, "tu parli d'Arno."

E l'altro disse lui: "Perché nascose   25
questi il vocabol di quella riviera,
pur com' om fa de l'orribili cose?"

E l'ombra che di ciò domandata era,   28
si sdebitò così: "Non so; ma degno
ben è che 'l nome di tal valle pèra;

ché dal principio suo, ov' è sì pregno   31
l'alpestro monte ond' è tronco Peloro,
che 'n pochi luoghi passa oltra quel segno,

until its end point (where it offers back   34
those waters that evaporating skies
drew from the sea, that streams may be supplied),
    virtue is seen as serpent, and all flee   37
from it as if it were an enemy,
either because the site is ill-starred or
    their evil custom goads them so; therefore,   40
the nature of that squalid valley's people
has changed, as if they were in Circe's pasture.
    That river starts its miserable course   43
among foul hogs, more fit for acorns than
for food devised to serve the needs of man.
    Then, as that stream descends, it comes on curs   46
that, though their force is feeble, snap and snarl;
scornful of them, it swerves its snout away.
    And, downward, it flows on; and when that ditch,   49
ill-fated and accursed, grows wider, it
finds, more and more, the dogs becoming wolves.
    Descending then through many dark ravines,   52
it comes on foxes so full of deceit—
there is no trap that they cannot defeat.
    Nor will I keep from speech because my comrade   55
hears me (and it will serve you, too, to keep
in mind what prophecy reveals to me).
    I see your grandson: he's become a hunter   58
of wolves along the banks of the fierce river,
and he strikes every one of them with terror.
    He sells their flesh while they are still alive;   61
then, like an ancient beast, he turns to slaughter,
depriving many of life, himself of honor.
    Bloody, he comes out from the wood he's plundered,   64
leaving it such that in a thousand years
it will not be the forest that it was."
    Just as the face of one who has heard word   67
of pain and injury becomes perturbed,
no matter from what side that menace stirs,
    so did I see that other soul, who'd turned   70
to listen, growing anxious and dejected
when he had taken in his comrade's words.
    The speech of one, the aspect of the other   73
had made me need to know their names, and I
both queried and beseeched at the same time,

infin là 've si rende per ristoro 34
di quel che 'l ciel de la marina asciuga,
ond' hanno i fiumi ciò che va con loro,

vertù così per nimica si fuga 37
da tutti come biscia, o per sventura
del luogo, o per mal uso che li fruga:

ond' hanno sì mutata lor natura 40
li abitator de la misera valle,
che par che Circe li avesse in pastura.

Tra brutti porci, più degni di galle 43
che d'altro cibo fatto in uman uso,
dirizza prima il suo povero calle.

Botoli trova poi, venendo giuso, 46
ringhiosi più che non chiede lor possa,
e da lor disdegnosa torce il muso.

Vassi caggendo; e quant' ella più 'ngrossa, 49
tanto più trova di can farsi lupi
la maladetta e sventurata fossa

Discesa poi per più pelaghi cupi, 52
trova le volpi sì piene di froda,
che non temono ingegno che le occùpi.

Né lascerò di dir perch' altri m'oda; 55
e buon sarà costui, s'ancor s'ammenta
di ciò che vero spirto mi disnoda

Io veggio tuo nepote che diventa 58
cacciator di quei lupi in su la riva
del fiero fiume, e tutti li sgomenta.

Vende la carne loro essendo viva; 61
poscia li ancide come antica belva;
molti di vita e sé di pregio priva.

Sanguinoso esce de la trista selva; 64
lasciala tal, che di qui a mille anni
ne lo stato primaio non si rinselva."

Com' a l'annunzio di dogliosi danni 67
si turba il viso di colui ch'ascolta,
da qual che parte il periglio l'assanni,

così vid' io l'altr' anima, che volta 70
stava a udir, turbarsi e farsi trista,
poi ch'ebbe la parola a sé raccolta.

Lo dir de l'una e de l'altra la vista 73
mi fer voglioso di saper lor nomi,
e dimanda ne fei con prieghi mista;

at which the spirit who had spoken first   76
to me began again: "You'd have me do
for you that which, to me, you have refused.

But since God would, in you, have His grace glow   79
so brightly, I shall not be miserly;
know, therefore, that I was Guido del Duca.

My blood was so afire with envy that,   82
when I had seen a man becoming happy,
the lividness in me was plain to see.

From what I've sown, this is the straw I reap: 85
o humankind, why do you set your hearts
there where our sharing cannot have a part?

This is Rinieri, this is he—the glory,   88
the honor of the house of Calboli;
but no one has inherited his worth.

It's not his kin alone, between the Po   91
and mountains, and the Reno and the coast,
who've lost the truth's grave good and lost the good

of gentle living, too; those lands are full   94
of poisoned stumps; by now, however much
one were to cultivate, it is too late.

Where is good Lizio? Arrigo Manardi?   97
Pier Traversaro? Guido di Carpigna?
O Romagnoles returned to bastardy!

When will a Fabbro flourish in Bologna?   100
When, in Faenza, a Bernadin di Fosco,
the noble offshoot of a humble plant?

Don't wonder, Tuscan, if I weep when I   103
remember Ugolino d'Azzo, one
who lived among us, and Guido da Prata,

the house of Traversara, of Anastagi   106
(both houses without heirs), and Federigo
Tignoso and his gracious company,

the ladies and the knights, labors and leisure   109
to which we once were urged by courtesy
and love, where hearts now host perversity.

O Bretinoro, why do you not flee—   112
when you've already lost your family
and many men who've fled iniquity?

Bagnacaval does well: it breeds no more—   115
and Castrocuro ill, and Conio worse,
for it insists on breeding counts so cursed.

per che lo spirto che di pria parlòmi
ricominciò: "Tu vuo' ch'io mi deduca
nel fare a te ciò che tu far non vuo'mi.

Ma da che Dio in te vuol che traluca   79
tanto sua grazia, non ti sarò scarso;
però sappi ch'io fui Guido del Duca.

Fu il sangue mio d'invidia sì rïarso,   82
che se veduto avesse uom farsi lieto,
visto m'avresti di livore sparso.

Di mia semente cotal paglia mieto;   85
o gente umana, perché poni 'l core
là 'v' è mestier di consorte divieto?

Questi è Rinier; questi è 'l pregio e l'onore   88
de la casa da Calboli, ove nullo
fatto s'è reda poi del suo valore.

E non pur lo suo sangue è fatto brullo,   91
tra 'l Po e 'l monte e la marina e 'l Reno,
del ben richesto al vero e al trastullo;

ché dentro a questi termini è ripieno   94
di venenosi sterpi, sì che tardi
per coltivare omai verrebber meno.

Ov' è 'l buon Lizio e Arrigo Mainardi?   97
Pier Traversaro e Guido di Carpigna?
Oh Romagnuoli tornati in bastardi!

Quando in Bologna un Fabbro si ralligna?   100
quando in Faenza un Bernardin di Fosco,
verga gentil di picciola gramigna?

Non ti maravigliar s'io piango, Tosco,   103
quando rimembro, con Guido da Prata,
Ugolin d'Azzo che vivette nosco,

Federigo Tignoso e sua brigata,   106
la casa Traversara e li Anastagi
(e l'una gente e l'altra è diretata),

le donne e ' cavalier, li affanni e li agi   109
che ne 'nvogliava amore e cortesia
là dove i cuor son fatti sì malvagi.

O Bretinoro, ché non fuggi via,   112
poi che gita se n'è la tua famiglia
e molta gente per non esser ria?

Ben fa Bagnacaval, che non rifiglia;   115
e mal fa Castrocaro, e peggio Conio,
che di figliar tai conti più s'impiglia.

Once freed of their own demon, the Pagani 118
will do quite well, but not so well that any
will testify that they are pure and worthy.

Your name, o Ugolin de' Fantolini, 121
is safe, since one no longer waits for heirs
to blacken it with their degeneracy.

But, Tuscan, go your way; I am more pleased 124
to weep now than to speak: for that which we
have spoken presses heavily on me!"

We knew those gentle souls had heard us move 127
away; therefore, their silence made us feel
more confident about the path we took.

When we, who'd gone ahead, were left alone, 130
a voice that seemed like lightning as it splits
the air encountered us, a voice that said:

"Whoever captures me will slaughter me"; 133
and then it fled like thunder when it fades
after the cloud is suddenly ripped through.

As soon as that first voice had granted us 136
a truce, another voice cried out with such
uproar—like thunder quick to follow thunder:

"I am Aglauros, who was turned to stone"; 139
and then, to draw more near the poet, I
moved to my right instead of moving forward.

By now the air on every side was quiet; 142
and he told me: "That is the sturdy bit
that should hold every man within his limits.

But you would take the bait, so that the hook 145
of the old adversary draws you to him;
and thus, you've little use for curb or warning.

Heaven would call—and it encircles—you; 148
it lets you see its never-ending beauties;
and yet your eyes would only see the ground;

thus, He who sees all things would strike you down." 151

Ben faranno i Pagan, da che 'l demonio   118
lor sen girà; ma non però che puro
già mai rimagna d'essi testimonio.

O Ugolin de' Fantolin, sicuro   121
è 'l nome tuo, da che più non s'aspetta
chi far lo possa, tralignando, scuro.

Ma va via, Tosco omai; ch'or mi diletta   124
troppo di pianger più che di parlare,
sì m'ha nostra ragion la mente stretta."

Noi sapavam che quell' anime care   127
ci sentivano andar; però, tacendo,
facëan noi del cammin confidare.

Poi fummo fatti soli procedendo,   130
folgore parve quando l'aere fende,
voce che giunse di contra dicendo:

"Anciderammi qualunque m'apprende";   133
e fuggì come tuon che si dilegua,
se sùbito la nuvola scoscende.

Come da lei l'udir nostro ebbe triegua,   136
ed ecco l'altra con sì gran fracasso,
che somigliò tonar che tosto segua:

"Io sono Aglauro che divenni sasso";   139
e allor, per ristrignermi al poeta,
in destro feci, e non innanzi, il passo.

Già era l'aura d'ogne parte queta;   142
ed el mi disse: "Quel fu 'l duro camo
che dovria l'uom tener dentro a sua meta.

Ma voi prendete l'esca, sì che l'amo   145
de l'antico avversaro a sé vi tira;
e però poco val freno o richiamo.

Chiamavi 'l cielo e 'ntorno vi si gira,   148
mostrandovi le sue bellezze etterne,
e l'occhio vostro pur a terra mira;

onde vi batte chi tutto discerne."   151

CANTO XV

As many as the hours in which the sphere
that's always playing like a child appears
from daybreak to the end of the third hour,
    so many were the hours of light still left   4
before the course of day had reached sunset;
vespers was there; and where we are, midnight.
    When sunlight struck directly at our faces,   7
for we had circled so much of the mountain
that now we headed straight into the west,
    then I could feel my vision overcome   10
by radiance greater than I'd sensed before,
and unaccounted things left me amazed;
    at which, that they might serve me as a shade,   13
I lifted up my hands above my brow,
to limit some of that excessive splendor.
    As when a ray of light, from water or   16
a mirror, leaps in the opposed direction
and rises at an angle equal to
    its angle of descent, and to each side   19
the distance from the vertical is equal,
as science and experiment have shown;
    so did it seem to me that I had been   22
struck there by light reflected, facing me,
at which my eyes turned elsewhere rapidly.
    "Kind father, what is that against which I   25
have tried in vain," I said, "to screen my eyes?
It seems to move toward us." And he replied:
    "Don't wonder if you are still dazzled by   28
the family of Heaven: a messenger
has come, and he invites us to ascend.
    Soon, in the sight of such things, there will be   31
no difficulty for you, but delight—
as much as nature fashioned you to feel."

From the Second to the Third Terrace: the Wrathful. CANTO XV 129
Mid-afternoon. The Fifth Beatitude. Virgil on the sharing of
heavenly goods. The Third Terrace, where Dante sees, in ecstatic
vision, examples of gentleness: the Virgin Mary, Pisistratus, St.
Stephen. Virgil on Dante's vision. Black smoke.

Quanto tra l'ultimar de l'ora terza
e 'l principio del dì par de la spera
che sempre a guisa di fanciullo scherza,

   tanto pareva già inver' la sera   4
essere al sol del suo corso rimaso;
vespero là, e qui mezza notte era.

   E i raggi ne ferien per mezzo 'l naso,   7
perché per noi girato era sì 'l monte,
che già dritti andavamo inver' l'occaso,

   quand' io senti' a me gravar la fronte   10
a lo splendore assai più che di prima,
e stupor m'eran le cose non conte;

   ond' io levai le mani inver' la cima   13
de le mie ciglia, e fecimi 'l solecchio,
che del soverchio visibile lima.

   Come quando da l'acqua o da lo specchio   16
salta lo raggio a l'opposita parte,
salendo su per lo modo parecchio

   a quel che scende, e tanto si diparte   19
dal cader de la pietra in igual tratta,
sì come mostra esperïenza e arte;

   così mi parve da luce rifratta   22
quivi dinanzi a me esser percosso;
per che a fuggir la mia vista fu ratta.

   "Che è quel, dolce padre, a che non posso   25
schermar lo viso tanto che mi vaglia,"
diss' io, "e pare inver' noi esser mosso?"

   "Non ti maravigliar s'ancor t'abbaglia   28
la famiglia del cielo," a me rispuose:
"messo è che viene ad invitar ch'om saglia.

   Tosto sarà ch'a veder queste cose   31
non ti fia grave, ma fieti diletto
quanto natura a sentir ti dispuose."

No sooner had we reached the blessed angel   34
than with glad voice he told us: "Enter here;
these are less steep than were the other stairs."

We climbed, already past that point; behind us,   37
we heard *"Beati misericordes"* sung
and then "Rejoice, you who have overcome."

I and my master journeyed on alone,   40
we two together, upward; as we walked,
I thought I'd gather profit from his words;

and even as I turned toward him, I asked: 43
"What did the spirit of Romagna mean
when he said, 'Sharing cannot have a part'?"

And his reply: "He knows the harm that lies   46
in his worst vice; if he chastises it,
to ease its expiation—do not wonder.

For when your longings center on things such   49
that sharing them apportions less to each,
then envy stirs the bellows of your sighs.

But if the love within the Highest Sphere   52
should turn your longings heavenward, the fear
inhabiting your breast would disappear;

for there, the more there are who would say 'ours,' 55
so much the greater is the good possessed
by each—so much more love burns in that cloister."

"I am more hungry now for satisfaction"   58
I said, "than if I'd held my tongue before;
I host a deeper doubt within my mind.

How can a good that's shared by more possessors   61
enable each to be more rich in it
than if that good had been possessed by few?"

And he to me: "But if you still persist   64
in letting your mind fix on earthly things,
then even from true light you gather darkness.

That Good, ineffable and infinite,   67
which is above, directs Itself toward love
as light directs itself to polished bodies.

Where ardor is, that Good gives of Itself;   70
and where more love is, there that Good confers
a greater measure of eternal worth.

And when there are more souls above who love,   73
there's more to love well there, and they love more,
and, mirror-like, each soul reflects the other.

Poi giunti fummo a l'angel benedetto,   34
con lieta voce disse: "Intrate quinci
ad un scaleo vie men che li altri eretto."

Noi montavam, già partiti di linci,   37
e "*Beati misericordes!*" fue
cantato retro, e "Godi tu che vinci!"

Lo mio maestro e io soli amendue   40
suso andavamo; e io pensai, andando,
prode acquistar ne le parole sue;

e dirizza'mi a lui sì dimandando: 43
"Che volse dir lo spirto di Romagna,
e 'divieto' e 'consorte' menzionando?"

Per ch'elli a me: "Di sua maggior magagna   46
conosce il danno; e però non s'ammiri
se ne riprende perché men si piagna.

Perché s'appuntano i vostri disiri   49
dove per compagnia parte si scema,
invidia move il mantaco a' sospiri.

Ma se l'amor de la spera supprema   52
torcesse in suso il disiderio vostro,
non vi sarebbe al petto quella tema;

ché, per quanti si dice più lì 'nostro,'   55
tanto possiede più di ben ciascuno,
e più di caritate arde in quel chiostro."

"Io son d'esser contento più digiuno,"   58
diss' io, "che se mi fosse pria taciuto,
e più di dubbio ne la mente aduno.

Com' esser puote ch'un ben, distributo   61
in più posseditor, faccia più ricchi
di sé che se da pochi è posseduto?"

Ed elli a me: "Però che tu rificchi   64
la mente pur a le cose terrene,
di vera luce tenebre dispicchi.

Quello infinito e ineffabil bene   67
che là sù è, così corre ad amore
com' a lucido corpo raggio vene.

Tanto si dà quanto trova d'ardore;   70
sì che, quantunque carità si stende,
cresce sovr' essa l'etterno valore.

E quanta gente più là sù s'intende,   73
più v'è da bene amare, e più vi s'ama,
e come specchio l'uno a l'altro rende.

And if my speech has not appeased your hunger,   76
you will see Beatrice—she will fulfill
this and all other longings that you feel.

Now only strive, so that the other five   79
wounds may be canceled quickly, as the two
already are—the wounds contrition heals."

But wanting then to say, "You have appeased me,"   82
I saw that I had reached another circle,
and my desiring eyes made me keep still.

There I seemed, suddenly, to be caught up   85
in an ecstatic vision and to see
some people in a temple; and a woman

just at the threshold, in the gentle manner   88
that mothers use, was saying: "O my son,
why have you done this to us? You can see

how we have sought you—sorrowing, your father   91
and I." And at this point, as she fell still,
what had appeared at first now disappeared.

Then there appeared to me another woman: 94
upon her cheeks—the tears that grief distills
when it is born of much scorn for another.

She said: "If you are ruler of that city   97
to name which even goddesses once vied—
where every science had its source of light—

revenge yourself on the presumptuous   100
arms that embraced our daughter, o Pisistratus."
And her lord seemed to me benign and mild,

his aspect temperate, as he replied: 103
"What shall we do to one who'd injure us
if one who loves us earns our condemnation?"

Next I saw people whom the fire of wrath   106
had kindled, as they stoned a youth and kept
on shouting loudly to each other: "Kill!"

"Kill!" "Kill!" I saw him now, weighed down by death,   109
sink to the ground, although his eyes were bent
always on Heaven—they were Heaven's gates—

praying to his high Lord, despite the torture,   112
to pardon those who were his persecutors;
his look was such that it unlocked compassion.

And when my soul returned outside itself   115
and met the things outside it that are real,
I then could recognize my not false errors.

E se la mia ragion non ti disfama,
vedrai Beatrice, ed ella pienamente
ti torrà questa e ciascun' altra brama.

   Procaccia pur che tosto sieno spente,   79
come son già le due, le cinque piaghe,
che si richiudon per esser dolente."

   Com' io voleva dicer "Tu m'appaghe,"   82
vidimi giunto in su l'altro girone,
sì che tacer mi fer le luci vaghe.

   Ivi mi parve in una visïone   85
estatica di sùbito esser tratto,
e vedere in un tempio più persone;

   e una donna, in su l'entrar, con atto   88
dolce di madre dicer: "Figliuol mio,
perché hai tu così verso noi fatto?

   Ecco, dolenti, lo tuo padre e io   91
ti cercavamo." E come qui si tacque,
ciò che pareva prima, dispario.

   Indi m'apparve un'altra con quell' acque   94
giù per le gote che 'l dolor distilla
quando di gran dispetto in altrui nacque,

   e dir: "Se tu se' sire de la villa   97
del cui nome ne' dèi fu tanta lite,
e onde ogne scïenza disfavilla,

   vendica te di quelle braccia ardite   100
ch'abbracciar nostra figlia, o Pisistràto."
E 'l segnor mi parea, benigno e mite,

   risponder lei con viso temperato: 103
"Che farem noi a chi mal ne disira,
se quei che ci ama è per noi condannato?"

   Poi vidi genti accese in foco d'ira   106
con pietre un giovinetto ancider, forte
gridando a sé pur: "Martira, martira!"

   E lui vedea chinarsi, per la morte   109
che l'aggravava già, inver' la terra,
ma de li occhi facea sempre al ciel porte,

   orando a l'alto Sire, in tanta guerra,   112
che perdonasse a' suoi persecutori,
con quello aspetto che pietà diserra.

   Quando l'anima mia tornò di fori   115
a le cose che son fuor di lei vere,
io riconobbi i miei non falsi errori.

My guide, on seeing me behave as if   118
I were a man who's freed himself from sleep,
said: "What is wrong with you? You can't walk straight;

for more than half a league now you have moved   121
with clouded eyes and lurching legs, as if
you were a man whom wine or sleep has gripped!"

"Oh, my kind father, if you hear me out,   124
I'll tell you what appeared to me," I said,
"when I had lost the right use of my legs."

And he: "Although you had a hundred masks   127
upon your face, that still would not conceal
from me the thoughts you thought, however slight.

What you have seen was shown lest you refuse   130
to open up your heart unto the waters
of peace that pour from the eternal fountain.

I did not ask 'What's wrong with you?' as one   133
who only sees with earthly eyes, which—once
the body, stripped of soul, lies dead—can't see;

I asked so that your feet might find more force: 136
so must one urge the indolent, too slow
to use their waking time when it returns."

We made our way until the end of vespers,   139
peering, as far ahead as sight could stretch,
at rays of light that, although late, were bright.

But, gradually, smoke as black as night   142
began to overtake us; and there was
no place where we could have avoided it.

This smoke deprived us of pure air and sight.   145

Lo duca mio, che mi potea vedere
far sì com' om che dal sonno si slega,
disse: "Che hai che non ti puoi tenere,

    ma se' venuto più che mezza lega   121
velando li occhi e con le gambe avvolte,
a guisa di cui vino o sonno piega?"

    "O dolce padre mio, se tu m'ascolte,   124
io ti dirò," diss' io, "ciò che m'apparve
quando le gambe mi furon sì tolte."

    Ed ei: "Se tu avessi cento larve   127
sovra la faccia, non mi sarian chiuse
le tue cogitazion, quantunque parve.

    Ciò che vedesti fu perché non scuse   130
d'aprir lo core a l'acque de la pace
che da l'etterno fonte son diffuse.

    Non dimandai 'Che hai?' per quel che face   133
chi guarda pur con l'occhio che non vede,
quando disanimato il corpo giace;

    ma dimandai per darti forza al piede: 136
così frugar conviensi i pigri, lenti
ad usar lor vigilia quando riede."

    Noi andavam per lo vespero, attenti   139
oltre quanto potean li occhi allungarsi
contra i raggi serotini e lucenti.

    Ed ecco a poco a poco un fummo farsi   142
verso di noi come la notte oscuro;
né da quello era loco da cansarsi.

    Questo ne tolse li occhi e l'aere puro.   145

XV·107

XVI · 6

CANTO XVI

Darkness of Hell and of a night deprived
of every planet, under meager skies,
as overcast by clouds as sky can be,

had never served to veil my eyes so thickly   4
nor covered them with such rough-textured stuff
as smoke that wrapped us there in Purgatory;

my eyes could not endure remaining open,   7
so that my faithful, knowledgeable escort
drew closer as he offered me his shoulder.

Just as a blind man moves behind his guide,   10
that he not stray or strike against some thing
that may do damage to—or even kill—him,

so I moved through the bitter, filthy air,   13
while listening to my guide, who kept repeating:
"Take care that you are not cut off from me."

But I heard voices, and each seemed to pray   16
unto the Lamb of God, who takes away
our sins, for peace and mercy. "Agnus Dei"

was sung repeatedly as their exordium,   19
words sung in such a way—in unison—
that fullest concord seemed to be among them.

"Master, are those whom I hear, spirits?" I   22
asked him. "You have grasped rightly," he replied,
"and as they go they loose the knot of anger."

"Then who are you whose body pierces through   25
our smoke, who speak of us exactly like
a man who uses months to measure time?"

A voice said this. On hearing it, my master   28
turned round to me: "Reply to him, then ask
if this way leads us to the upward path."

And I: "O creature who—that you return   31
fair unto Him who made you—cleanse yourself,
you shall hear wonders if you follow me."

Still the Third Terrace: the Wrathful. Their sin punished by dark smoke. Marco Lombardo's discourse on free will, on the causes of corruption, and on three worthy old men, living examples of ancient virtue.

CANTO XVI 139

Buio d'inferno e di notte privata
d'ogne pianeto, sotto pover cielo,
quant' esser può di nuvol tenebrata,

  non fece al viso mio sì grosso velo   4
come quel fummo ch'ivi ci coperse,
né a sentir di così aspro pelo,

  che l'occhio stare aperto non sofferse;   7
onde la scorta mia saputa e fida
mi s'accostò e l'omero m'offerse.

  Sì come cieco va dietro a sua guida   10
per non smarrirsi e per non dar di cozzo
in cosa che 'l molesti, o forse ancida,

  m'andava io per l'aere amaro e sozzo,   13
ascoltando il mio duca che diceva
pur: "Guarda che da me tu non sia mozzo."

  Io sentia voci, e ciascuna pareva   16
pregar per pace e per misericordia
l'Agnel di Dio che le peccata leva.

  Pur *"Agnus Dei"* eran le loro essordia;   19
una parola in tutte era e un modo,
sì che parea tra esse ogne concordia.

  "Quei sono spirti, maestro, ch'i' odo?"   22
diss' io. Ed elli a me: "Tu vero apprendi,
e d'iracundia van solvendo il nodo."

  "Or tu chi se' che 'l nostro fummo fendi,   25
e di noi parli pur come se tue
partissi ancor lo tempo per calendi?"

  Così per una voce detto fue;   28
onde 'l maestro mio disse: "Rispondi,
e domanda se quinci si va sùe."

  E io: "O creatura che ti mondi   31
per tornar bella a colui che ti fece,
maraviglia udirai, se mi secondi."

"I'll follow you as far as I'm allowed,"   34
he answered, "and if smoke won't let us see,
hearing will serve instead to keep us linked."

    Then I began: "With those same swaddling-bands   37
that death unwinds I take my upward path:
I have come here by way of Hell's exactions;

    since God's so gathered me into His grace   40
that He would have me, in a manner most
unusual for moderns, see His court,

    do not conceal from me who you once were,   43
before your death, and tell me if I go
straight to the pass; your words will be our escort."

    "I was a Lombard and I was called Marco;   46
I knew the world's ways, and I loved those goods
for which the bows of all men now grow slack.

    The way you've taken leads directly upward."   49
So he replied, and then he added: "I
pray you to pray for me when you're above."

    And I to him: "I pledge my faith to you   52
to do what you have asked; and yet a doubt
will burst in me if it finds no way out.

    Before, my doubt was simple; but your statement   55
has doubled it and made me sure that I
am right to couple your words with another's.

    The world indeed has been stripped utterly   58
of every virtue; as you said to me,
it cloaks—and is cloaked by—perversity.

    Some place the cause in heaven, some, below;   61
but I beseech you to define the cause,
that, seeing it, I may show it to others."

    A sigh, from which his sorrow formed an "Oh,"   64
was his beginning; then he answered: "Brother,
the world is blind, and you come from the world.

    You living ones continue to assign   67
to heaven every cause, as if it were
the necessary source of every motion.

    If this were so, then your free will would be   70
destroyed, and there would be no equity
in joy for doing good, in grief for evil.

    The heavens set your appetites in motion—   73
not all your appetites, but even if
that were the case, you have received both light

"Io ti seguiterò quanto mi lece,"   34
rispuose; "e se veder fummo non lascia,
l'udir ci terrà giunti in quella vece."

Allora incominciai: "Con quella fascia   37
che la morte dissolve men vo suso,
e venni qui per l'infernale ambascia.

E se Dio m'ha in sua grazia rinchiuso,   40
tanto che vuol ch'i' veggia la sua corte
per modo tutto fuor del moderno uso,

non mi celar chi fosti anzi la morte,   43
ma dilmi, e dimmi s'i' vo bene al varco;
e tue parole fier le nostre scorte."

"Lombardo fui, e fu' chiamato Marco;   46
del mondo seppi, e quel valore amai
al quale ha or ciascun disteso l'arco.

Per montar sù dirittamente vai."   49
Così rispuose, e soggiunse: "I' ti prego
che per me prieghi quando sù sarai."

E io a lui: "Per fede mi ti lego   52
di far ciò che mi chiedi; ma io scoppio
dentro ad un dubbio, s'io non me ne spiego.

Prima era scempio, e ora è fatto doppio   55
ne la sentenza tua, che mi fa certo
qui, e altrove, quello ov' io l'accoppio.

Lo mondo è ben così tutto diserto   58
d'ogne virtute, come tu mi sone,
e di malizia gravido e coverto;

ma priego che m'addite la cagione,   61
sì ch'i' la veggia e ch'i' la mostri altrui;
ché nel cielo uno, e un qua giù la pone."

Alto sospir, che duolo strinse in "uhi!"   64
mise fuor prima; e poi cominciò: "Frate,
lo mondo è cieco, e tu vien ben da lui.

Voi che vivete ogne cagion recate   67
pur suso al cielo, pur come se tutto
movesse seco di necessitate.

Se così fosse, in voi fora distrutto   70
libero arbitrio, e non fora giustizia
per ben letizia, e per male aver lutto.

Lo cielo i vostri movimenti inizia;   73
non dico tutti, ma, posto ch'i' 'l dica,
lume v'è dato a bene e a malizia,

on good and evil, and free will, which though   76
it struggle in its first wars with the heavens,
then conquers all, if it has been well nurtured.

On greater power and a better nature   79
you, who are free, depend; that Force engenders
the mind in you, outside the heavens' sway.

Thus, if the present world has gone astray,   82
in you is the cause, in you it's to be sought;
and now I'll serve as your true exegete.

Issuing from His hands, the soul—on which   85
He thought with love before creating it—
is like a child who weeps and laughs in sport;

that soul is simple, unaware; but since   88
a joyful Maker gave it motion, it
turns willingly to things that bring delight.

At first it savors trivial goods; these would   91
beguile the soul, and it runs after them,
unless there's guide or rein to rule its love.

Therefore, one needed law to serve as curb;   94
a ruler, too, was needed, one who could
discern at least the tower of the true city.

The laws exist, but who applies them now?   97
No one—the shepherd who precedes his flock
can chew the cud but does not have cleft hooves;

and thus the people, who can see their guide   100
snatch only at that good for which they feel
some greed, would feed on that and seek no further.

Misrule, you see, has caused the world to be   103
malevolent; the cause is clearly not
celestial forces—they do not corrupt.

For Rome, which made the world good, used to have   106
two suns; and they made visible two paths—
the world's path and the pathway that is God's.

Each has eclipsed the other; now the sword   109
has joined the shepherd's crook; the two together
must of necessity result in evil,

because, so joined, one need not fear the other: 112
and if you doubt me, watch the fruit and flower,
for every plant is known by what it seeds.

Within the territory watered by   115
the Adige and Po, one used to find
valor and courtesy—that is, before

e libero voler; che, se fatica 76
ne le prime battaglie col ciel dura,
poi vince tutto, se ben si notrica.

A maggior forza e a miglior natura 79
liberi soggiacete; e quella cria
la mente in voi, che 'l ciel non ha in sua cura.

Però, se 'l mondo presente disvia, 82
in voi è la cagione, in voi si cheggia;
e io te ne sarò or vera spia.

Esce di mano a lui che la vagheggia 85
prima che sia, a guisa di fanciulla
che piangendo e ridendo pargoleggia,

l'anima semplicetta che sa nulla, 88
salvo che, mossa da lieto fattore,
volontier torna a ciò che la trastulla.

Di picciol bene in pria sente sapore; 91
quivi s'inganna, e dietro ad esso corre,
se guida o fren non torce suo amore.

Onde convenne legge per fren porre; 94
convenne rege aver, che discernesse
de la vera cittade almen la torre.

Le leggi son, ma chi pon mano ad esse? 97
Nullo, però che 'l pastor che procede,
rugumar può, ma non ha l'unghie fesse;

per che la gente, che sua guida vede 100
pur a quel ben fedire ond' ella è ghiotta,
di quel si pasce, e più oltre non chiede.

Ben puoi veder che la mala condotta 103
è la cagion che 'l mondo ha fatto reo,
e non natura che 'n voi sia corrotta.

Soleva Roma, che 'l buon mondo feo, 106
due soli aver, che l'una e l'altra strada
facean vedere, e del mondo e di Deo.

L'un l'altro ha spento; ed è giunta la spada 109
col pasturale, e l'un con l'altro insieme
per viva forza mal convien che vada;

però che, giunti, l'un l'altro non teme: 112
se non mi credi, pon mente a la spiga,
ch'ogn' erba si conosce per lo seme.

In sul paese ch'Adice e Po riga, 115
solea valore e cortesia trovarsi,
prima che Federigo avesse briga;

Frederick was met by strife; now anyone   118
ashamed of talking with the righteous or
of meeting them can journey there, secure.

True, three old men are there, in whom old times   121
reprove the new; and they find God is slow
in summoning them to a better life:

Currado da Palazzo, good Gherardo,   124
and Guido da Castel, whom it is better
to call, as do the French, the candid Lombard.

You can conclude: the Church of Rome confounds   127
two powers in itself; into the filth,
it falls and fouls itself and its new burden."

"Good Marco," I replied, "you reason well;   130
and now I understand why Levi's sons
were not allowed to share in legacies.

But what Gherardo is this whom you mention   133
as an example of the vanished people
whose presence would reproach this savage age?"

"Either your speech deceives me or would tempt me," 136
he answered then, "for you, whose speech is Tuscan,
seem to know nothing of the good Gherardo.

There is no other name by which I know him,   139
unless I speak of him as Gaia's father.
God be with you; I come with you no farther.

You see the rays that penetrate the smoke   142
already whitening; I must take leave—
the angel has arrived—before he sees me."

So he turned back and would not hear me more.   145

or può sicuramente indi passarsi   118
per qualunque lasciasse, per vergogna,
di ragionar coi buoni o d'appressarsi.

    Ben v'èn tre vecchi ancora in cui rampogna   121
l'antica età la nova, e par lor tardo
che Dio a miglior vita li ripogna:

    Currado da Palazzo e 'l buon Gherardo   124
e Guido da Castel, che mei si noma,
francescamente, il semplice Lombardo.

    Dì oggimai che la Chiesa di Roma,   127
per confondere in sé due reggimenti,
cade nel fango, e sé brutta e la soma."

    "O Marco mio," diss' io, "bene argomenti;   130
e or discerno perché dal retaggio
li figli di Levì furono essenti.

    Ma qual Gherardo è quel che tu per saggio   133
di' ch'è rimaso de la gente spenta,
in rimprovèro del secol selvaggio?"

    "O tuo parlar m'inganna, o el mi tenta,"   136
rispuose a me; "ché, parlandomi tosco,
par che del buon Gherardo nulla senta.

    Per altro sopranome io nol conosco,   139
s'io nol togliessi da sua figlia Gaia.
Dio sia con voi, ché più non vegno vosco.

    Vedi l'albor che per lo fummo raia   142
già biancheggiare, e me convien partirmi
(l'angelo è ivi) prima ch'io li paia."

    Così tornò, e più non volle udirmi.   145

CANTO XVII

Remember, reader, if you've ever been
caught in the mountains by a mist through which
you only saw as moles see through their skin,

    how, when the thick, damp vapors once begin   4
to thin, the sun's sphere passes feebly through them,
then your imagination will be quick

    to reach the point where it can see how I   7
first came to see the sun again—when it
was almost at the point at which it sets.

    So, my steps matched my master's trusty steps;   10
out of that cloud I came, reaching the rays
that, on the shores below, by now were spent.

    O fantasy, you that at times would snatch   13
us so from outward things—we notice nothing
although a thousand trumpets sound around us—

    who moves you when the senses do not spur you?   16
A light that finds its form in Heaven moves you—
directly or led downward by God's will.

    Within my fantasy I saw impressed   19
the savagery of one who then, transformed,
became the bird that most delights in song;

    at this, my mind withdrew to the within,   22
to what imagining might bring; no thing
that came from the without could enter in.

    Then into my deep fantasy there rained   25
one who was crucified; and as he died,
he showed his savagery and his disdain.

    Around him were great Ahasuerus and   28
Esther his wife, and the just Mordecai,
whose saying and whose doing were so upright.

    And when this image shattered of itself,   31
just like a bubble that has lost the water
beneath which it was formed, there then rose up

From the Third to the Fourth Terrace. Examples of wrath:
Procne, Haman, Amata. The angel of gentleness. The Seventh
Beatitude. Ascent to the Fourth Terrace. Virgil on love and on
Purgatory's seven terraces punishing the seven sins: pride,
envy, and wrath—resulting from perverted love; sloth—from
defective love; avarice, gluttony, and lust—from excessive love
of earthly goods.

Ricorditi, lettor, se mai ne l'alpe
ti colse nebbia per la qual vedessi
non altrimenti che per pelle talpe,

come, quando i vapori umidi e spessi   4
a diradar cominciansi, la spera
del sol debilemente entra per essi;

e fia la tua imagine leggera   7
in giugnere a veder com' io rividi
lo sole in pria, che già nel corcar era.

Sì, pareggiando i miei co' passi fidi   10
del mio maestro, usci' fuor di tal nube
ai raggi morti già ne' bassi lidi.

O imaginativa che ne rube   13
talvolta sì di fuor, ch'om non s'accorge
perché dintorno suonin mille tube,

chi move te, se 'l senso non ti porge?   16
Moveti lume che nel ciel s'informa,
per sé o per voler che giù lo scorge.

De l'empiezza di lei che mutò forma   19
ne l'uccel ch'a cantar più si diletta,
ne l'imagine mia apparve l'orma;

e qui fu la mia mente sì ristretta   22
dentro da sé, che di fuor non venìa
cosa che fosse allor da lei ricetta.

Poi piovve dentro a l'alta fantasia   25
un crucifisso, dispettoso e fero
ne la sua vista, e cotal si moria;

intorno ad esso era il grande Assüero,   28
Estèr sua sposa e 'l giusto Mardoceo,
che fu al dire e al far così intero.

E come questa imagine rompeo   31
sé per sé stessa, a guisa d'una bulla
cui manca l'acqua sotto qual si feo,

in my envisioning a girl who wept 34
most bitterly and said: "O queen, why did
you, in your wrath, desire to be no more?

So as to keep Lavinia, you killed 37
yourself; now you have lost me! I am she,
mother, who mourns your fall before another's."

Even as sleep is shattered when new light 40
strikes suddenly against closed eyes and, once
it's shattered, gleams before it dies completely,

so my imagination fell away 43
as soon as light—more powerful than light
we are accustomed to—beat on my eyes

I looked about to see where I might be; 46
but when a voice said: "Here one can ascend,"
then I abandoned every other intent.

That voice made my will keen to see the one 49
who'd spoken—with the eagerness that cannot
be still until it faces what it wants.

But even as the sun, become too strong, 52
defeats our vision, veiling its own form,
so there my power of sight was overcome.

"This spirit is divine; and though unasked, 55
he would conduct us to the upward path;
he hides himself with that same light he sheds.

He does with us as men do with themselves; 58
for he who sees a need but waits to be
asked is already set on cruel refusal.

Now let our steps accept his invitation, 61
and let us try to climb before dark falls—
then, until day returns, we'll have to halt."

So said my guide; and toward a stairway, he 64
and I, together, turned; and just as soon
as I was at the first step, I sensed something

much like the motion of a wing, and wind 67
that beat against my face, and words: "*Beati
pacifici*, those free of evil anger!"

Above us now the final rays before 70
the fall of night were raised to such a height
that we could see the stars on every side.

"O why, my strength, do you so melt away?" 73
I said within myself, because I felt
the force within my legs compelled to halt.

surse in mia visïone una fanciulla   34
piangendo forte, e dicea: "O regina,
perché per ira hai voluto esser nulla?

  Ancisa t'hai per non perder Lavina;   37
or m'hai perduta! Io son essa che lutto,
madre, a la tua pria ch'a l'altrui ruina."

  Come si frange il sonno ove di butto   40
nova luce percuote il viso chiuso,
che fratto guizza pria che muoia tutto;

  così l'imaginar mio cadde giuso   43
tosto che lume il volto mi percosse,
maggior assai che quel ch'è in nostro uso.

  I' mi volgea per veder ov' io fosse,   46
quando una voce disse "Qui si monta,"
che da ogne altro intento mi rimosse;

  e fece la mia voglia tanto pronta   49
di riguardar chi era che parlava,
che mai non posa, se non si raffronta.

  Ma come al sol che nostra vista grava   52
e per soverchio sua figura vela,
così la mia virtù quivi mancava.

  "Questo è divino spirito, che ne la   55
via da ir sù ne drizza sanza prego,
e col suo lume sé medesmo cela.

  Sì fa con noi, come l'uom si fa sego;   58
ché quale aspetta prego e l'uopo vede,
malignamente già si mette al nego.

  Or accordiamo a tanto invito il piede;   61
procacciam di salir pria che s'abbui,
ché poi non si poria, se 'l dì non riede."

  Così disse il mio duca, e io con lui   64
volgemmo i nostri passi ad una scala;
e tosto ch'io al primo grado fui,

  senti'mi presso quasi un muover d'ala   67
e ventarmi nel viso e dir: "*Beati
pacifici*, che son sanz' ira mala!"

  Già eran sovra noi tanto levati   70
li ultimi raggi che la notte segue,
che le stelle apparivan da più lati.

  "O virtù mia, perché sì ti dilegue?"   73
fra me stesso dicea, ché mi sentiva
la possa de le gambe posta in triegue.

We'd reached a point at which the upward stairs 76
no longer climbed, and we were halted there
just like a ship when it has touched the shore.

I listened for a while, hoping to hear 79
whatever there might be in this new circle;
then I turned toward my master, asking him:

"Tell me, my gentle father: what offense 82
is purged within the circle we have reached?
Although our feet must stop, your words need not."

And he to me: "Precisely here, the love 85
of good that is too tepidly pursued
is mended; here the lazy oar plies harder.

But so that you may understand more clearly, 88
now turn your mind to me, and you will gather
some useful fruit from our delaying here.

My son, there's no Creator and no creature 91
who ever was without love—natural
or mental; and you know that," he began.

"The natural is always without error, 94
but mental love may choose an evil object
or err through too much or too little vigor.

As long as it's directed toward the First Good 97
and tends toward secondary goods with measure,
it cannot be the cause of evil pleasure;

but when it twists toward evil, or attends 100
to good with more or less care than it should,
those whom He made have worked against their Maker.

From this you see that—of necessity— 103
love is the seed in you of every virtue
and of all acts deserving punishment.

Now, since love never turns aside its eyes 106
from the well-being of its subject, things
are surely free from hatred of themselves;

and since no being can be seen as self- 109
existing and divorced from the First Being,
each creature is cut off from hating Him.

Thus, if I have distinguished properly, 112
ill love must mean to wish one's neighbor ill;
and this love's born in three ways in your clay.

There's he who, through abasement of another, 115
hopes for supremacy; he only longs
to see his neighbor's excellence cast down.

Noi eravam dove più non saliva   76
la scala sù, ed eravamo affissi,
pur come nave ch'a la piaggia arriva.

  E io attesi un poco, s'io udissi   79
alcuna cosa nel novo girone;
poi mi volsi al maestro mio, e dissi:

  "Dolce mio padre, dì, quale offensione   82
si purga qui nel giro dove semo?
Se i piè si stanno, non stea tuo sermone."

  Ed elli a me: "L'amor del bene, scemo   85
del suo dover, quiritta si ristora;
qui si ribatte il mal tardato remo.

  Ma perché più aperto intendi ancora,   88
volgi la mente a me, e prenderai
alcun buon frutto di nostra dimora."

  "Né creator né creatura mai,"   91
cominciò el, "figliuol, fu sanza amore,
o naturale o d'animo; e tu 'l sai.

  Lo naturale è sempre sanza errore,   94
ma l'altro puote errar per malo obietto
o per troppo o per poco di vigore.

  Mentre ch'elli è nel primo ben diretto,   97
e ne' secondi sé stesso misura,
esser non può cagion di mal diletto;

  ma quando al mal si torce, o con più cura   100
o con men che non dee corre nel bene,
contra 'l fattore adovra sua fattura.

  Quinci comprender puoi ch'esser convene   103
amor sementa in voi d'ogne virtute
e d'ogne operazion che merta pene.

  Or, perché mai non può da la salute   106
amor del suo subietto volger viso,
da l'odio proprio son le cose tute;

  e perché intender non si può diviso,   109
e per sé stante, alcuno esser dal primo,
da quello odiare ogne effetto è deciso.

  Resta, se dividendo bene stimo,   112
che 'l mal che s'ama è del prossimo; ed esso
amor nasce in tre modi in vostro limo.

  E chi, per esser suo vicin soppresso,   115
spera eccellenza, e sol per questo brama
ch'el sia di sua grandezza in basso messo;

Then there is one who, when he is outdone,   118
fears his own loss of fame, power, honor, favor;
his sadness loves misfortune for his neighbor.

And there is he who, over injury   121
received, resentful, for revenge grows greedy
and, angrily, seeks out another's harm.

This threefold love is expiated here   124
below; now I would have you understand
the love that seeks the good distortedly.

Each apprehends confusedly a Good   127
in which the mind may rest, and longs for It;
and, thus, all strive to reach that Good; but if

the love that urges you to know It or   130
to reach that Good is lax, this terrace, after
a just repentance, punishes for that.

There is a different good, which does not make   133
men glad; it is not happiness, is not
true essence, fruit and root of every good.

The love that—profligately—yields to that   136
is wept on in three terraces above us;
but I'll not say what three shapes that loves takes—

may you seek those distinctions for yourself."   139

è chi podere, grazia, onore e fama 118
teme di perder perch' altri sormonti,
onde s'attrista sì che 'l contrario ama;

   ed è chi per ingiuria par ch'aonti, 121
sì che si fa de la vendetta ghiotto,
e tal convien che 'l male altrui impronti.

   Questo triforme amor qua giù di sotto 124
si piange: or vo' che tu de l'altro intende,
che corre al ben con ordine corrotto.

   Ciascun confusamente un bene apprende 127
nel qual si queti l'animo, e disira;
per che di giugner lui ciascun contende.

   Se lento amore a lui veder vi tira 130
o a lui quistar, acquesta cornice,
dopo giusto penter, ve ne martira.

   Altro ben è che non fa l'uom felice; 133
non è felicità, non è la buona
essenza, d'ogne ben frutto e radice.

   L'amor ch'ad esso troppo s'abbandona, 136
di sovr' a noi si piange per tre cerchi;
ma come tripartito si ragiona,

   tacciolo, acciò che tu per te ne cerchi." 139

HAMAN

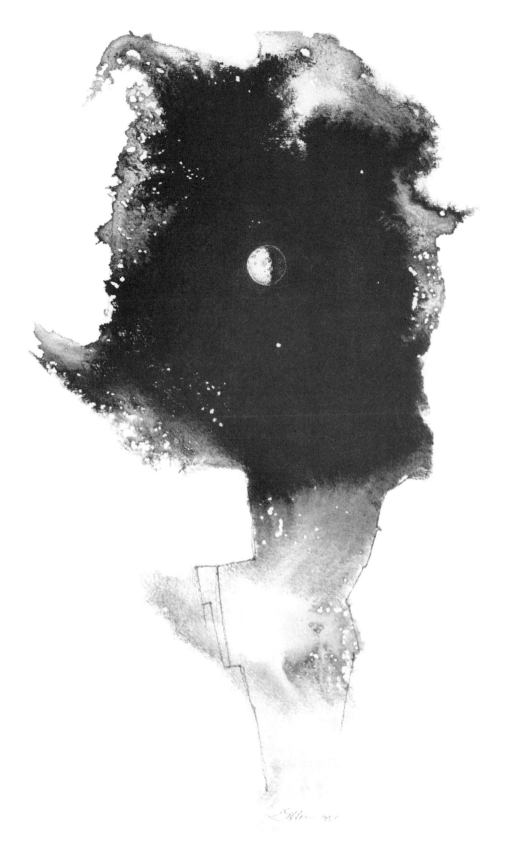

XVIII · 76

CANTO XVIII

The subtle teacher had completed his
discourse to me; attentively he watched
my eyes to see if I seemed satisfied.

And I, still goaded by new thirst, was silent   4
without, although within I said: "Perhaps
I have displeased him with too many questions."

But that true father, who had recognized   7
the timid want I would not tell aloud,
by speaking, gave me courage to speak out.

At which I said: "Master, my sight is so   10
illumined by your light—I recognize
all that your words declare or analyze.

Therefore, I pray you, gentle father dear,   13
to teach me what love is: you have reduced
to love both each good and its opposite."

He said: "Direct your intellect's sharp eyes   16
toward me, and let the error of the blind
who'd serve as guides be evident to you.

The soul, which is created quick to love,   19
responds to everything that pleases, just
as soon as beauty wakens it to act.

Your apprehension draws an image from   22
a real object and expands upon
that object until soul has turned toward it;

and if, so turned, the soul tends steadfastly,   25
then that propensity is love—it's nature
that joins the soul in you, anew, through beauty.

Then, just as flames ascend because the form   28
of fire was fashioned to fly upward, toward
the stuff of its own sphere, where it lasts longest,

so does the soul, when seized, move into longing,   31
a motion of the spirit, never resting
till the beloved thing has made it joyous.

The Fourth Terrace: the Slothful. Virgil on love, free will, and
responsibility. Dante's drowsiness. The Slothful shouting
examples of zeal: the Virgin Mary and Caesar. The punishment
of the Slothful, made to run without respite. The Abbot of San
Zeno. Shouted examples of sloth: the Jews in the desert and the
reluctant Trojans in Sicily. Dante overcome by sleep.

Posto avea fine al suo ragionamento
l'alto dottore, e attento guardava
ne la mia vista s'io parea contento;

e io, cui nova sete ancor frugava,   4
di fuor tacea, e dentro dicea: "Forse
lo troppo dimandar ch'io fo li grava."

Ma quel padre verace, che s'accorse   7
del timido voler che non s'apriva,
parlando, di parlare ardir mi porse.

Ond' io: "Maestro, il mio veder s'avviva   10
sì nel tuo lume, ch'io discerno chiaro
quanto la tua ragion parta o descriva.

Però ti prego, dolce padre caro,   13
che mi dimostri amore, a cui reduci
ogne buono operare e 'l suo contraro."

"Drizza," disse, "ver' me l'agute luci   16
de lo 'ntelletto, e fieti manifesto
l'error de' ciechi che si fanno duci.

L'animo, ch'è creato ad amar presto,   19
ad ogne cosa è mobile che piace,
tosto che dal piacere in atto è desto.

Vostra apprensiva da esser verace   22
tragge intenzione, e dentro a voi la spiega,
sì che l'animo ad essa volger face;

e se, rivolto, inver' di lei si piega,   25
quel piegare è amor, quell'è natura
che per piacer di novo in voi si lega.

Poi, come 'l foco movesi in altura   28
per la sua forma ch'è nata a salire
là dove più in sua matera dura,

così l'animo preso entra in disire,   31
ch'è moto spiritale, e mai non posa
fin che la cosa amata il fa gioire.

Now you can plainly see how deeply hidden   34
truth is from scrutinists who would insist
that every love is, in itself, praiseworthy;
    and they are led to error by the matter   37
of love, because it may seem—always—good;
but not each seal is fine, although the wax is."
    "Your speech and my own wit that followed it,"   40
I answered him, "have shown me what love is;
but that has filled me with still greater doubt;
    for if love's offered to us from without   43
and is the only foot with which soul walks,
soul—going straight or crooked—has no merit."
    And he to me: "What reason can see here,   46
I can impart; past that, for truth of faith,
it's Beatrice alone you must await.
    Every substantial form, at once distinct   49
from matter and conjoined to it, ingathers
the force that is distinctively its own,
    a force unknown to us until it acts—   52
it's never shown except in its effects,
just as green boughs display the life in plants.
    And thus man does not know the source of his   55
intelligence of primal notions and
his tending toward desire's primal objects:
    both are in you just as in bees there is   58
the honey-making urge; such primal will
deserves no praise, and it deserves no blame.
    Now, that all other longings may conform   61
to this first will, there is in you, inborn,
the power that counsels, keeper of the threshold
    of your assent: this is the principle   64
on which your merit may be judged, for it
garners and winnows good and evil longings.
    Those reasoners who reached the roots of things   67
learned of this inborn freedom; the bequest
that, thus, they left unto the world is ethics.
    Even if we allow necessity   70
as source for every love that flames in you,
the power to curb that love is still your own.
    This noble power is what Beatrice   73
means by free will; therefore, remember it,
if she should ever speak of it to you."

Or ti puote apparer quant' è nascosa 34
la veritate a la gente ch'avvera
ciascun amore in sé laudabil cosa;

   però che forse appar la sua matera 37
sempre esser buona, ma non ciascun segno
è buono, ancor che buona sia la cera."

   "Le tue parole e 'l mio seguace ingegno," 40
rispuos' io lui, "m'hanno amor discoverto,
ma ciò m'ha fatto di dubbiar più pregno;

   ché, s'amore è di fuori a noi offerto 43
e l'anima non va con altro piede,
se dritta o torta va, non è suo merto."

   Ed elli a me: "Quanto ragion qui vede, 46
dir ti poss' io; da indi in là t'aspetta
pur a Beatrice, ch'è opra di fede.

   Ogne forma sustanzïal, che setta 49
è da matera ed è con lei unita,
specifica vertute ha in sé colletta,

   la qual sanza operar non è sentita, 52
né si dimostra mai che per effetto,
come per verdi fronde in pianta vita.

   Però, là onde vegna lo 'ntelletto 55
de le prime notizie, omo non sape,
e de' primi appetibili l'affetto,

   che sono in voi sì come studio in ape 58
di far lo mele; e questa prima voglia
merto di lode o di biasmo non cape.

   Or perché a questa ogn' altra si raccoglia, 61
innata v'è la virtù che consiglia,
e de l'assenso de' tener la soglia.

   Quest' è 'l principio là onde si piglia 64
ragion di meritare in voi, secondo
che buoni e rei amori accoglie e viglia.

   Color che ragionando andaro al fondo, 67
s'accorser d'esta innata libertate;
però moralità lasciaro al mondo.

   Onde, poniam che di necessitate 70
surga ogne amor che dentro a voi s'accende,
di ritenerlo è in voi la podestate.

   La nobile virtù Beatrice intende 73
per lo libero arbitrio, e però guarda
che l'abbi a mente, s'a parlar ten prende."

The moon, delayed almost to midnight, made 76
the stars seem scarcer to us; it was shaped
just like a copper basin, gleaming, new;

and countercourse, it crossed those paths the sun 79
ignites when those in Rome can see it set
between the Corsicans and the Sardinians.

That gracious shade for whom Pietola 82
won more renown than any Mantuan town
had freed me from the weight of doubt I bore;

so that I, having harvested his clear 85
and open answers to my questions, stood
like one who, nearing sleep, has random visions.

But readiness for sleep was suddenly 88
taken from me by people who, behind
our backs, already turned in our direction.

Just as—of old—Ismenus and Asopus, 91
at night, along their banks, saw crowds and clamor
whenever Thebans had to summon Bacchus,

such was the arching crowd that curved around 94
that circle, driven on, as I made out,
by righteous will as well as by just love.

Soon all that mighty throng drew near us, for 97
they ran and ran; and two, in front of them,
who wept, were crying: "In her journey, Mary

made haste to reach the mountain, and, in order 100
to conquer Lérida, first Caesar thrust
against Marseilles, and then to Spain he rushed."

Following them, the others cried: "Quick, quick, 103
lest time be lost through insufficient love;
where urge for good is keen, grace finds new green."

"O people in whom eager fervor now 106
may compensate for sloth and negligence
you showed in doing good half-heartedly,

he—who's alive, and surely I don't lie 109
to you—would climb above as soon as he
has seen the sun shed light on us again;

then, tell us where the passage lies at hand." 112
My guide said this. One of the souls replied:
"Come, follow us, and you will find the gap.

We are so fully anxious to advance— 115
we cannot halt; and do forgive us, should
you take our penance for discourtesy.

La luna, quasi a mezza notte tarda,
facea le stelle a noi parer più rade,
fatta com' un secchion che tuttor arda;

   e correa contra 'l ciel per quelle strade   79
che 'l sole infiamma allor che quel da Roma
tra ' Sardi e ' Corsi il vede quando cade.

   E quell' ombra gentil per cui si noma   82
Pietola più che villa mantoana,
del mio carcar diposta avea la soma;

   per ch'io, che la ragione aperta e piana   85
sovra le mie quistioni avea ricolta,
stava com' om che sonnolento vana.

   Ma questa sonnolenza mi fu tolta   88
subitamente da gente che dopo
le nostre spalle a noi era già volta.

   E quale Ismeno già vide e Asopo   91
lungo di sé di notte furia e calca,
pur che i Teban di Bacco avesser uopo,

   cotal per quel giron suo passo falca,   94
per quel ch'io vidi di color, venendo,
cui buon volere e giusto amor cavalca.

   Tosto fur sovr' a noi, perché correndo   97
si movea tutta quella turba magna;
e due dinanzi gridavan piangendo:

   "Maria corse con fretta a la montagna;   100
e Cesare, per soggiogare Ilerda,
punse Marsilia e poi corse in Ispagna."

   "Ratto, ratto, che 'l tempo non si perda   103
per poco amor," gridavan li altri appresso,
"che studio di ben far grazia rinverda."

   "O gente in cui fervore aguto adesso   106
ricompie forse negligenza e indugio
da voi per tepidezza in ben far messo,

   questi che vive, e certo i' non vi bugio,   109
vuole andar sù, pur che 'l sol ne riluca;
però ne dite ond' è presso il pertugio."

   Parole furon queste del mio duca;   112
e un di quelli spirti disse: "Vieni
di retro a noi, e troverai la buca.

   Noi siam di voglia a muoverci sì pieni,   115
che restar non potem; però perdona,
se villania nostra giustizia tieni.

I was St. Zeno's abbot in Verona   118
under the rule of valiant Barbarossa,
of whom Milan still speaks with so much sorrow.

And there is one with one foot in the grave,   121
who soon will weep over that monastery,
lamenting that he once had power there,

because, in place of its true shepherd, he   124
put one who was unsound of body and,
still more, of mind, and born in sin—his son."

I don't know if he said more or was silent—   127
he had already raced so far beyond us;
but I heard this much and was pleased to hear it.

And he who was my help in every need   130
said: "Turn around: see those two coming—they
whose words mock sloth." And I heard those two say

behind all of the rest: "The ones for whom   133
the sea parted were dead before the Jordan
saw those who had inherited its lands;

and those who did not suffer trials until   136
the end together with Anchises' son
gave themselves up to life without renown."

Then, when those shades were so far off from us   139
that seeing them became impossible,
a new thought rose inside of me and, from

that thought, still others—many and diverse—   142
were born: I was so drawn from random thought
to thought that, wandering in mind, I shut

my eyes, transforming thought on thought to dream. 145

Io fui abate in San Zeno a Verona
sotto lo 'mperio del buon Barbarossa,
di cui dolente ancor Milan ragiona.

E tale ha già l'un piè dentro la fossa,   121
che tosto piangerà quel monastero,
e tristo fia d'avere avuta possa;

perché suo figlio, mal del corpo intero,   124
e de la mente peggio, e che mal nacque,
ha posto in loco di suo pastor vero."

Io non so se più disse o s'ei si tacque,   127
tant' era già di là da noi trascorso;
ma questo intesi, e ritener mi piacque.

E quei che m'era ad ogne uopo soccorso   130
disse: "Volgiti qua: vedine due
venir dando a l'accidïa di morso."

Di retro a tutti dicean: "Prima fue   133
morta la gente a cui il mar s'aperse,
che vedesse Iordan le rede sue.

E quella che l'affanno non sofferse   136
fino a la fine col figlio d'Anchise,
sé stessa a vita sanza gloria offerse."

Poi quando fuor da noi tanto divise   139
quell' ombre, che veder più non potiersi,
novo pensiero dentro a me si mise,

del qual più altri nacquero e diversi;   142
e tanto d'uno in altro vaneggiai,
che li occhi per vaghezza ricopersi,

e 'l pensamento in sogno trasmutai.   145

CANTO XIX

In that hour when the heat of day, defeated
by Earth and, sometimes, Saturn, can no longer
warm up the moon-sent cold, when geomancers
   can, in the east, see their *Fortuna major*   4
rising before the dawn along a path
that will be darkened for it only briefly—
   a stammering woman came to me in dream: 7
her eyes askew, and crooked on her feet,
her hands were crippled, her complexion sallow.
   I looked at her; and just as sun revives   10
cold limbs that night made numb, so did my gaze
loosen her tongue and then, in little time,
   set her contorted limbs in perfect order;   13
and, with the coloring that love prefers,
my eyes transformed the wanness of her features.
   And when her speech had been set free, then she   16
began to sing so, that it would have been
most difficult for me to turn aside.
   "I am," she sang, "I am the pleasing siren,   19
who in midsea leads mariners astray—
there is so much delight in hearing me.
   I turned aside Ulysses, although he   22
had longed to journey; who grows used to me
seldom departs—I satisfy him so."
   Her lips were not yet done when, there beside me,   25
a woman showed herself, alert and saintly,
to cast the siren into much confusion.
   "O Virgil, Virgil, tell me: who is this?"   28
she asked most scornfully; and he came forward,
his eyes intent upon that honest one.
   He seized the other, baring her in front,   31
tearing her clothes, and showing me her belly;
the stench that came from there awakened me.

From the Fourth to the Fifth Terrace: the Avaricious and the
Prodigal. Dante's dream of the Siren. Waking to the third
morning. The angel of zeal. The Third Beatitude. Ascent to the
Fifth Terrace. Colloquy with Pope Adrian V. The punishment of
the Avaricious: given to earthly goods, they now, bound hand
and foot lie stretched on the ground, face down.

Ne l'ora che non può 'l calor dïurno
intepidar più 'l freddo de la luna,
vinto da terra, e talor da Saturno

—quando i geomanti lor Maggior Fortuna   4
veggiono in orïente, innanzi a l'alba,
surger per via che poco le sta bruna—

mi venne in sogno una femmina balba,   7
ne li occhi guercia, e sovra i piè distorta,
con le man monche, e di colore scialba.

Io la mirava; e come 'l sol conforta   10
le fredde membra che la notte aggrava,
così lo sguardo mio le facea scorta

la lingua, e poscia tutta la drizzava   13
in poco d'ora, e lo smarrito volto,
com' amor vuol, così le colorava.

Poi ch'ell' avea 'l parlar così disciolto,   16
cominciava a cantar sì, che con pena
da lei avrei mio intento rivolto.

"Io son," cantava, "io son dolce serena,   19
che ' marinari in mezzo mar dismago;
tanto son di piacere a sentir piena!

Io volsi Ulisse del suo cammin vago   22
al canto mio; e qual meco s'ausa,
rado sen parte; sì tutto l'appago!"

Ancor non era sua bocca richiusa,   25
quand' una donna apparve santa e presta
lunghesso me per far colei confusa.

"O Virgilio, Virgilio, chi è questa?"   28
fieramente dicea; ed el venìa
con li occhi fitti pur in quella onesta.

L'altra prendea, e dinanzi l'apria   31
fendendo i drappi, e mostravami 'l ventre;
quel mi svegliò col puzzo che n'uscia.

I moved my eyes, and my good master cried: 34
"At least three times I've called you. Rise and come:
let's find the opening where you may enter."

I rose; the daylight had already filled 37
the circles of the sacred mountain—we
were journeying with new sun at our back.

I followed him, bearing my brow like one 40
whose thoughts have weighed him down, who bends as if
he were the semiarch that forms a bridge,

and then I heard: "Draw near; the pass is here," 43
said in a manner so benign and gentle
as, in our mortal land, one cannot hear.

He who addressed us so had open wings, 46
white as a swan's; and he directed us
upward, between two walls of the hard rock.

And then he moved his plumes and, fanning us, 49
affirmed that those "*Qui lugent*" would be blessed—
their souls would be possessed of consolation.

"What makes you keep your eyes upon the ground?" 52
my guide began to say to me when both
of us had climbed a little, past the angel.

And I: "What makes me move with such misgiving 55
is a new vision: it has so beguiled me
that I cannot relinquish thoughts of it."

"The one you saw," he said, "that ancient witch— 58
for her alone one must atone above;
you saw how man can free himself from her.

Let that suffice, and hurry on your way; 61
fasten your eyes upon the lure that's spun
by the eternal King with His great spheres."

Just like a falcon, who at first looks down, 64
then, answering the falconer's call, bends forward,
craving the food that's ready for him there,

so I became—and so remained until, 67
through the cleft rock that lets one climb above,
I reached the point at which the circle starts.

When I was in the clearing, the fifth level, 70
my eyes discovered people there who wept,
lying upon the ground, all turned face down.

"*Adhaesit pavimento anima mea*" 73
I heard them say with sighs so deep that it
was hard to comprehend the words they spoke.

Io mossi li occhi, e 'l buon maestro: "Almen tre   34
voci t'ho messe!" dicea, "Surgi e vieni;
troviam l'aperta per la qual tu entre."

Sù mi levai, e tutti eran già pieni   37
de l'alto dì i giron del sacro monte,
e andavam col sol novo a le reni.

Seguendo lui, portava la mia fronte   40
come colui che l'ha di pensier carca,
che fa di sé un mezzo arco di ponte;

quand' io udi' "Venite; qui si varca"   43
parlare in modo soave e benigno,
qual non si sente in questa mortal marca.

Con l'ali aperte, che parean di cigno,   46
volseci in sù colui che sì parlonne
tra due pareti del duro macigno.

Mosse le penne poi e ventilonne,   49
"Qui lugent" affermando esser beati,
ch'avran di consolar l'anime donne.

"Che hai che pur inver' la terra guati?"   52
la guida mia incominciò a dirmi,
poco amendue da l'angel sormontati.

E io: "Con tanta sospeccion fa irmi   55
novella visïon ch'a sé mi piega,
sì ch'io non posso dal pensar partirmi."

"Vedesti," disse, "quell'antica strega   58
che sola sovr' a noi omai si piagne;
vedesti come l'uom da lei si slega.

Bastiti, e batti a terra le calcagne;   61
li occhi rivolgi al logoro che gira
lo rege etterno con le rote magne."

Quale 'l falcon, che prima a' piè si mira,   64
indi si volge al grido e si protende
per lo disio del pasto che là il tira,

tal mi fec' io; e tal, quanto si fende   67
la roccia per dar via a chi va suso,
n'andai infin dove 'l cerchiar si prende.

Com' io nel quinto giro fui dischiuso,   70
vidi gente per esso che piangea,
giacendo a terra tutta volta in giuso.

"Adhaesit pavimento anima mea"   73
sentia dir lor con sì alti sospiri,
che la parola a pena s'intendea.

"O God's elect, whose sufferings both hope   76
and justice make less difficult, direct
us to the stairway meant for our ascent."

"If you come here but do not need to be   79
prostrate, and you would find the path most quickly,
then keep your right hand always to the outside."

So did the poet ask, so did reply   82
come from a little way ahead; and I,
hearing that voice reply, learned what was hidden.

I turned my eyes to find my master's eyes;   85
at this, with a glad sign, he ratified
what I had asked for with my eager eyes.

When, free to do as I had wanted to,   88
I moved ahead and bent over that soul
whose words—before—had made me notice him,

saying: "Spirit, within whom weeping ripens   91
that without which there's no return to God,
suspend awhile—for me—your greater care.

Tell me: Who were you? And why are your backs   94
turned up? And there—where I, alive, set out—
would you have me beseech some good for you?"

And he to me: "Why Heaven turns our backs   97
against itself, you are to know; but first
scias quod ego fui successor Petri.

Between Sestri and Chiavari descends   100
a handsome river; and its name is set
upon the upper portion of my crest.

For one month and a little more I learned   103
how the great mantle weighs on him who'd keep it
out of the mire—all other weights seem feathers.

Alas! How tardy my conversion was!   106
But when I had been named the Roman shepherd,
then I discovered the deceit of life.

I saw that there the heart was not at rest,   109
nor could I, in that life, ascend more high;
so that, in me, love for this life was kindled.

Until that point I was a squalid soul,   112
from God divided, wholly avaricious;
now, as you see, I'm punished here for that.

What avarice enacts is here declared   115
in the purgation of converted souls;
the mountain has no punishment more bitter.

"O eletti di Dio, li cui soffriri
e giustizia e speranza fa men duri,
drizzate noi verso li alti saliri."

"Se voi venite dal giacer sicuri,   79
e volete trovar la via più tosto,
le vostre destre sien sempre di fori."

Così pregò 'l poeta, e sì risposto   82
poco dinanzi a noi ne fu; per ch'io
nel parlare avvisai l'altro nascosto,

e volsi li occhi a li occhi al segnor mio: 85
ond' elli m'assentì con lieto cenno
ciò che chiedea la vista del disio.

Poi ch'io potei di me fare a mio senno,   88
trassimi sovra quella creatura
le cui parole pria notar mi fenno,

dicendo: "Spirto in cui pianger matura   91
quel sanza 'l quale a Dio tornar non pòssi.
sosta un poco per me tua maggior cura.

Chi fosti e perché vòlti avete i dossi   94
al sù, mi dì, e se vuo' ch'io t'impetri
cosa di là ond' io vivendo mossi."

Ed elli a me: "Perché i nostri diretri   97
rivolga il cielo a sé, saprai; ma prima
scias quod ego fui successor Petri.

Intra Sïestri e Chiaveri s'adima   100
una fiumana bella, e del suo nome
lo titol del mio sangue fa sua cima.

Un mese e poco più prova' io come   103
pesa il gran manto a chi dal fango il guarda,
che piuma sembran tutte l'altre some.

La mia conversïone, omè!, fu tarda;   106
ma, come fatto fui roman pastore,
così scopersi la vita bugiarda.

Vidi che lì non s'acquetava il core,   109
né più salir potiesi in quella vita;
per che di questa in me s'accese amore.

Fino a quel punto misera e partita   112
da Dio anima fui, del tutto avara;
or, come vedi, qui ne son punita.

Quel ch'avarizia fa, qui si dichiara   115
in purgazion de l'anime converse;
e nulla pena il monte ha più amara.

Just as we did not lift our eyes on high 118
but set our sight on earthly things instead,
so justice here impels our eyes toward earth.

As avarice annulled in us the love 121
of any other good, and thus we lost
our chance for righteous works, so justice here

fetters our hands and feet and holds us captive; 124
and for as long as it may please our just
Lord, here we'll be outstretched and motionless."

I'd kneeled, wishing to speak; but just as I 127
began—and through my voice alone—he sensed
that I had meant to do him reverence.

"What reason makes you bend your body so?" 130
he said. And I to him: "Your dignity
made conscience sting me as I stood erect."

"Brother, straighten your legs, rise up!" he answered. 133
"Don't be mistaken; I, with you and others,
am but a fellow-servant of one Power.

If you have ever understood the holy 136
sound of the Gospel that says '*Neque nubent*,'
then you will see why I have spoken so.

Now go your way: I'd not have you stop longer; 139
your staying here disturbs my lamentations,
the tears that help me ripen what you mentioned.

Beyond, I have a niece whose name's Alagia; 142
she, in herself, is good, as long as our
house, by example, brings her not to evil;

and she alone is left to me beyond." 145

Sì come l'occhio nostro non s'aderse
in alto, fisso a le cose terrene,
così giustizia qui a terra il merse.

Come avarizia spense a ciascun bene 121
lo nostro amore, onde operar perdési,
così giustizia qui stretti ne tene,

ne' piedi e ne le man legati e presi; 124
e quanto fia piacer del giusto Sire,
tanto staremo immobili e distesi."

Io m'era iginocchiato e volea dire; 127
ma com' io cominciai ed el s'accorse,
solo ascoltando, del mio reverire,

"Qual cagion," disse, "in giù così ti torse?" 130
E io a lui: "Pur vostra dignitate
mia coscïenza dritto mi rimorse."

"Drizza le gambe, lèvati sù, frate!" 133
rispuose; "non errar: conservo sono
teco e con li altri ad una podestate.

Se mai quel santo evangelico suono 136
che dice 'Neque nubent' intendesti,
ben puoi veder perch' io così ragiono.

Vattene omai: non vo' che più t'arresti; 139
ché la tua stanza mio pianger disagia,
col qual maturo ciò che tu dicesti.

Nepote ho io di là c'ha nome Alagia, 142
buona da sé, pur che la nostra casa
non faccia lei per essempro malvagia;

e questa sola di là m'è rimasa." 145

XIX · 32

XIX·124

CANTO XX

Against a better will, the will fights weakly;
therefore, against my pleasure, to please him,
I drew my unquenched sponge out of the water.

I moved on, and my guide moved through the un-   4
encumbered space, hugging the rock, as one
walks on a wall, close to the battlements;

for those whose eyes would melt down, drop by drop,   7
the evil that possesses all the world
were too close to the edge, on the far side.

May you be damned, o ancient wolf, whose power   10
can claim more prey than all the other beasts—
your hungering is deep and never-ending!

O heavens, through whose revolutions many   13
think things on earth are changed, when will he come—
the one whose works will drive that wolf away?

Our steps were short and slow as we moved on;   16
I was attentive to the shades; I heard
the sorrow in their tears and lamentations.

Then I, by chance, heard one ahead of us   19
crying in his lament, "Sweet Mary," as
a woman would outcry in labor pains.

And he continued: "In that hostel where   22
you had set down your holy burden, there
one can discover just how poor you were."

Following this I heard: "O good Fabricius,   25
you chose, as your possessions, indigence
with virtue rather than much wealth with vice."

These words had been so pleasing to me—I   28
moved forward, so that I might come to know
the spirit from whom they had seemed to come.

He kept on speaking, telling the largesse   31
of Nicholas—the gifts he gave the maidens
so that they might be honorably wed.

Still the Fifth Terrace, the Avaricious and the Prodigal.
Excoriation of avarice. Examples of poverty and generosity:
the Virgin Mary, Fabricius, St. Nicholas. Hugh Capet's
condemnation of his descendants. Examples of avarice: Pygmalion,
Midas, Achan, Sapphira and her husband Ananias, Heliodorus,
and Polymnestor. The mountain's trembling. The shout of the
souls on Purgatory.

CANTO XX 175

Contra miglior voler voler mal pugna;
onde contra 'l piacer mio, per piacerli,
trassi de l'acqua non sazia la spugna.

Mossimi; e 'l duca mio si mosse per li   4
luoghi spediti pur lungo la roccia,
come si va per muro stretto a' merli;

ché la gente che fonde a goccia a goccia   7
per li occhi il mal che tutto 'l mondo occupa,
da l'altra parte in fuor troppo s'approccia.

Maladetta sie tu, antica lupa,   10
che più che tutte l'altre bestie hai preda
per la tua fame sanza fine cupa!

O ciel, nel cui girar par che si creda   13
le condizion di qua giù trasmutarsi,
quando verrà per cui questa disceda?

Noi andavam con passi lenti e scarsi,   16
e io attento a l'ombre, ch'i' sentia
pietosamente piangere e lagnarsi;

e per ventura udi' "Dolce Maria!"   19
dinanzi a noi chiamar così nel pianto
come fa donna che in parturir sia;

e seguitar: "Povera fosti tanto,   22
quanto veder si può per quello ospizio
dove sponesti il tuo portato santo."

Seguentemente intesi: "O buon Fabrizio,   25
con povertà volesti anzi virtute
che gran ricchezza posseder con vizio."

Queste parole m'eran sì piaciute,   28
ch'io mi trassi oltre per aver contezza
di quello spirto onde parean venute.

Esso parlava ancor de la larghezza   31
che fece Niccolò a le pulcelle,
per condurre ad onor lor giovinezza.

"O soul who speaks of so much righteousness,   34
do tell me who you were," I said, "and why
just you alone renew these seemly praises.

Your speaking to me will not go unthanked   37
when I return to finish the short span
of that life which now hurries toward its end."

And he: "I'll tell you—not because I hope   40
for solace from your world, but for such grace
as shines in you before your death's arrived.

I was the root of the obnoxious plant   43
that overshadows all the Christian lands,
so that fine fruit can rarely rise from them.

But if Douai and Lille and Bruges and Ghent   46
had power, then they'd soon take vengeance on it;
and this I beg of Him who judges all.

The name I bore beyond was Hugh Capet: 49
of me were born the Louises and Philips
by whom France has been ruled most recently.

I was the son of a Parisian butcher.   52
When all the line of ancient kings was done
and only one—a monk in gray—survived,

I found the reins that ruled the kingdom tight   55
within my hands, and I held so much new-
gained power and possessed so many friends

that, to the widowed crown, my own son's head   58
was elevated, and from him began
the consecrated bones of all those kings.

Until the giant dowry of Provence   61
removed all sense of shame within my house,
my line was not worth much, but did no wrong.

There its rapine began with lies and force;   64
and then it seized—that it might make amends—
Ponthieu and Normandy and Gascony.

Charles came to Italy and, for amends,   67
made Conradin a victim, and then thrust
back Thomas into Heaven, for amends.

I see a time—not too far off—in which   70
another Charles advances out of France
to make himself and his descendants famous.

He does not carry weapons when he comes,   73
only the lance that Judas tilted; this
he couches so—he twists the paunch of Florence.

"O anima che tanto ben favelle,   34
dimmi chi fosti," dissi, "e perché sola
tu queste degne lode rinovelle.

Non fia sanza mercé la tua parola,   37
s'io ritorno a compiér lo cammin corto
di quella vita ch'al termine vola."

Ed elli: "Io ti dirò, non per conforto   40
ch'io attenda di là, ma perché tanta
grazia in te luce prima che sie morto.

Io fui radice de la mala pianta   43
che la terra cristiana tutta aduggia,
sì che buon frutto rado se ne schianta.

Ma se Doagio, Lilla, Guanto e Bruggia 46
potesser, tosto ne saria vendetta;
e io la cheggio a lui che tutto giuggia.

Chiamato fui di là Ugo Ciappetta;   49
di me son nati i Filippi e i Luigi
per cui novellamente è Francia retta.

Figliuol fu' io d'un beccaio di Parigi: 52
quando li regi antichi venner meno
tutti, fuor ch'un renduto in panni bigi,

trova'mi stretto ne le mani il freno   55
del governo del regno, e tanta possa
di nuovo acquisto, e sì d'amici pieno,

ch'a la corona vedova promossa   58
la testa di mio figlio fu, dal quale
cominciar di costor le sacrate ossa.

Mentre che la gran dota provenzale   61
al sangue mio non tolse la vergogna,
poco valea, ma pur non facea male.

Lì cominciò con forza e con menzogna 64
la sua rapina; e poscia, per ammenda,
Pontì e Normandia prese e Guascogna.

Carlo venne in Italia e, per ammenda, 67
vittima fé di Curradino; e poi
ripinse al ciel Tommaso, per ammenda.

Tempo vegg' io, non molto dopo ancoi, 70
che tragge un altro Carlo fuor di Francia,
per far conoscer meglio e sé e ' suoi.

Sanz' arme n'esce e solo con la lancia 73
con la qual giostrò Giuda, e quella ponta
sì, ch'a Fiorenza fa scoppiar la pancia.

From this he'll gain not land, just shame and sin,   76
which will be all the heavier for him
as he would reckon lightly such disgrace.

The other, who once left his ship as prisoner—   79
I see him sell his daughter, bargaining
as pirates haggle over female slaves.

O avarice, my house is now your captive: 82
it traffics in the flesh of its own children—
what more is left for you to do to us?

That past and future evil may seem less,   85
I see the fleur-de-lis enter Anagni
and, in his vicar, Christ made prisoner.

I see Him mocked a second time; I see   88
the vinegar and gall renewed—and He
is slain between two thieves who're still alive.

And I see the new Pilate, one so cruel   91
that, still not sated, he, without decree,
carries his greedy sails into the Temple.

O You, my Lord, when will You let me be   94
happy on seeing vengeance that, concealed,
makes sweet Your anger in Your secrecy?

What I have said about the only bride   97
the Holy Ghost has known, the words that made
you turn to me for commentary—these

words serve as answer to our prayers as long   100
as it is day; but when night falls, then we
recite examples that are contrary.

Then we tell over how Pygmalion,   103
out of his greedy lust for gold, became
a thief and traitor and a parricide;

the wretchedness of avaricious Midas,   106
resulting from his ravenous request,
the consequence that always makes men laugh;

and each of us recalls the foolish Acan—   109
how he had robbed the spoils, so that the anger
of Joshua still seems to sting him here.

Then we accuse Sapphira and her husband;   112
we praise the kicks Heliodorus suffered;
and Polymnestor, who killed Polydorus,

resounds, in infamy, round all this mountain;   115
and finally, what we cry here is: 'Crassus,
tell us, because you know: "How does gold taste?"'

Quindi non terra, ma peccato e onta
guadagnerà, per sé tanto più grave.
quanto più lieve simil danno conta.

    L'altro, che già uscì preso di nave,   79
veggio vender sua figlia e patteggiarne
come fanno i corsar de l'altre schiave.

    O avarizia, che puoi tu più farne,   82
poscia c'ha' il mio sangue a te sì tratto,
che non si cura de la propria carne?

    Perché men paia il mal futuro e 'l fatto,   85
veggio in Alagna intrar lo fiordaliso,
e nel vicario suo Cristo esser catto.

    Veggiolo un'altra volta esser deriso;   88
veggio rinovellar l'aceto e 'l fiele,
e tra vivi ladroni esser anciso.

    Veggio il novo Pilato sì crudele,   91
che ciò nol sazia, ma sanza decreto
portar nel Tempio le cupide vele.

    O Segnor mio, quando sarò io lieto   94
a veder la vendetta che, nascosa,
fa dolce l'ira tua nel tuo secreto?

    Ciò ch'io dicea di quell' unica sposa   97
de lo Spirito Santo e che ti fece
verso me volger per alcuna chiosa,

    tanto è risposto a tutte nostre prece   100
quanto 'l dì dura; ma com' el s'annotta,
contrario suon prendemo in quella vece.

    Noi repetiam Pigmalïon allotta,   103
cui traditore e ladro e paricida
fece la voglia sua de l'oro ghiotta;

    e la miseria de l'avaro Mida,   106
che seguì a la sua dimanda gorda,
per la qual semper convien che si rida.

    Del folle Acàn ciascun poi si ricorda,   109
come furò le spoglie, sì che l'ira
di Iosüè qui par ch'ancor lo morda.

    Indi accusiam col marito Saffira;   112
lodiamo i calci ch'ebbe Elïodoro;
e in infamia tutto 'l monte gira

    Polinestòr ch'ancise Polidoro;   115
ultimamente ci si grida: 'Crasso,
dilci, che 'l sai: di che sapore è l'oro?'

At times one speaks aloud, another low,   118
according to the sentiment that goads
us now to be more swift and now more slow:
    thus, I was not alone in speaking of   121
the good we cite by day, but here nearby
no other spirit raised his voice as high."
    We had already taken leave of him   124
and were already struggling to advance
along that road as far as we were able,
    when I could feel the mountain tremble like   127
a falling thing; at which a chill seized me
as cold grips one who goes to meet his death.
    Delos had surely not been buffeted   130
so hard before Latona planted there
the nest in which to bear the sky's two eyes.
    Then such a shout rose up on every side   133
that, drawing near to me, my master said:
"Don't be afraid, as long as I'm your guide."
    "Gloria in excelsis Deo," they all cried—   136
so did I understand from those nearby,
whose shouted words were able to be heard.
    Just like the shepherds who first heard that song,   139
we stood, and did not move, in expectation,
until the trembling stopped, the song was done.
    Then we took up again our holy path,   142
watching the shades who lay along the ground,
who had resumed their customary tears.
    My ignorance has never struggled so,   145
has never made me long so much to know—
if memory does not mislead me now—
    as it seemed then to long within my thoughts;   148
nor did I dare to ask—we were so rushed;
nor, by myself, could I discern the cause.
    So, timid, pensive, I pursued my way.   151

Talor parla l'uno alto e l'altro basso,   118
secondo l'affezion ch'ad ir ci sprona
ora a maggiore e ora a minor passo:
   però al ben che 'l dì ci si ragiona,   121
dianzi non era io sol; ma qui da presso
non alzava la voce altra persona."
   Noi eravam partiti già da esso,   124
e brigavam di soverchiar la strada
tanto quanto al poder n'era permesso,
   quand' io senti', come cosa che cada,   127
tremar lo monte; onde mi prese un gelo
qual prender suol colui ch'a morte vada.
   Certo non si scoteo sì forte Delo,   130
pria che Latona in lei facesse 'l nido
a parturir li due occhi del cielo.
   Poi cominciò da tutte parti un grido   133
tal, che 'l maestro inverso me si feo,
dicendo: "Non dubbiar, mentr' io ti guido."
   "Glorïa in excelsis" tutti *"Deo"*   136
dicean, per quel ch'io da' vicin compresi,
onde intender lo grido si poteo.
   No' istavamo immobili e sospesi   139
come i pastor che prima udir quel canto,
fin che 'l tremar cessò ed el compiési.
   Poi ripigliammo nostro cammin santo,   142
guardando l'ombre che giacean per terra,
tornate già in su l'usato pianto.
   Nulla ignoranza mai con tanta guerra   145
mi fé desideroso di sapere,
se la memoria mia in ciò non erra,
   quanta pareami allor, pensando, avere;   148
né per la fretta dimandare er' oso,
né per me lì potea cosa vedere:
   così m'andava timido e pensoso.   151

CANTO XXI

The natural thirst that never can be quenched
except by water that gives grace—the draught
the simple woman of Samaria sought—

    tormented me; haste spurred me on the path   4
crowded with souls, behind my guide; and I
felt pity, though their pain was justified.

    And here—even as Luke records for us   7
that Christ, new-risen from his burial cave,
appeared to two along his way—a shade

    appeared; and he advanced behind our backs   10
while we were careful not to trample on
the outstretched crowd. We did not notice him

    until he had addressed us with: "God give   13
you, o my brothers, peace!" We turned at once;
then, after offering suitable response,

    Virgil began: "And may that just tribunal   16
which has consigned me to eternal exile
place you in peace within the blessed assembly!"

    "What!" he exclaimed, as we moved forward quickly. 19
"If God's not deemed you worthy of ascent,
who's guided you so far along His stairs?"

    "If you observe the signs the angel traced   22
upon this man," my teacher said, "you'll see
plainly—he's meant to reign with all the righteous;

    but since she who spins night and day had not   25
yet spun the spool that Clotho sets upon
the distaff and adjusts for everyone,

    his soul, the sister of your soul and mine,   28
in its ascent, could not—alone—have climbed
here, for it does not see the way we see.

    Therefore, I was brought forth from Hell's broad jaws 31
to guide him in his going; I shall lead
him just as far as where I teach can reach.

*Still the Fifth Terrace: the Avaricious and the Prodigal. The
appearance of Statius. Virgil's explanation of Dante's and his
presence in Purgatory. Statius' explanation of the earthquake
and the exultation. Statius on himself and on his love for the
Aeneid. Dante's embarrassment, then his introduction of Virgil
to Statius. Statius' reverence for Virgil.*

La sete natural che mai non sazia
se non con l'acqua onde la femminetta
samaritana domandò la grazia,

   mi travagliava, e pungeami la fretta   4
per la 'mpacciata via dietro al mio duca,
e condoleami a la giusta vendetta.

   Ed ecco, sì come ne scrive Luca   7
che Cristo apparve a' due ch'erano in via,
giù surto fuor de la sepulcral buca,

   ci apparve un'ombra, e dietro a noi venìa,   10
dal piè guardando la turba che giace;
né ci addemmo di lei, sì parlò pria,

   dicendo: "O frati miei, Dio vi dea pace."   13
Noi ci volgemmo sùbiti, e Virgilio
rendéli 'l cenno ch'a ciò si conface.

   Poi cominciò: "Nel beato concilio   16
ti ponga in pace la verace corte
che me rilega ne l'etterno essilio."

   "Come!" diss' elli, e parte andavam forte: 19
"se voi siete ombre che Dio sù non degni,
chi v'ha per la sua scala tanto scorte?"

   E 'l dottor mio: "Se tu riguardi a' segni   22
che questi porta e che l'angel profila,
ben vedrai che coi buon convien ch'e' regni.

   Ma perché lei che dì e notte fila   25
non li avea tratta ancora la conocchia
che Cloto impone a ciascuno e compila,

   l'anima sua, ch'è tua e mia serocchia,   28
venendo sù, non potea venir sola,
però ch'al nostro modo non adocchia.

   Ond' io fui tratto fuor de l'ampia gola   31
d'inferno per mostrarli, e mosterrolli
oltre, quanto 'l potrà menar mia scola.

But tell me, if you can, why, just before,   34
the mountain shook and shouted, all of it—
for so it seemed—down to its sea-bathed shore.''

His question threaded so the needle's eye   37
of my desire that just the hope alone
of knowing left my thirst more satisfied.

That other shade began: "The sanctity   40
of these slopes does not suffer anything
that's without order or uncustomary.

This place is free from every perturbation: 43
what heaven from itself and in itself
receives may serve as cause here—no thing else.

Therefore, no rain, no hail, no snow, no dew,   46
no hoarfrost falls here any higher than
the stairs of entry with their three brief steps;

neither thick clouds nor thin appear, nor flash   49
of lightning; Thaumas' daughter, who so often
shifts places in your world, is absent here.

Dry vapor cannot climb up any higher   52
than to the top of the three steps of which
I spoke—where Peter's vicar plants his feet.

Below that point, there may be small or ample   55
tremors; but here above, I know not why,
no wind concealed in earth has ever caused

a tremor; for it only trembles here   58
when some soul feels it's cleansed, so that it rises
or stirs to climb on high; and that shout follows.

The will alone is proof of purity   61
and, fully free, surprises soul into
a change of dwelling place—effectively.

Soul had the will to climb before, but that   64
will was opposed by longing to do penance
(as once, to sin), instilled by divine justice.

And I, who have lain in this suffering   67
five hundred years and more, just now have felt
my free will for a better threshold: thus,

you heard the earthquake and the pious spirits   70
throughout the mountain as they praised the Lord—
and may He send them speedily upward.''

So did he speak to us; and just as joy   73
is greater when we quench a greater thirst,
the joy he brought cannot be told in words.

Ma dimmi, se tu sai, perché tai crolli 34
diè dianzi 'l monte, e perché tutto ad una
parve gridare infino a' suoi piè molli."

Sì mi diè, dimandando, per la cruna 37
del mio disio, che pur con la speranza
si fece la mia sete men digiuna.

Quei cominciò: "Cosa non è che sanza 40
ordine senta la religïone
de la montagna, o che sia fuor d'usanza.

Libero è qui da ogne alterazione: 43
di quel che 'l ciel da sé in sé riceve
esser ci puote, e non d'altro, cagione.

Per che non pioggia, non grando, non neve, 46
non rugiada, non brina più sù cade
che la scaletta di tre gradi breve;

nuvole spesse non paion né rade, 49
né coruscar, né figlia di Taumante,
che di là cangia sovente contrade;

secco vapor non surge più avante 52
ch'al sommo d'i tre gradi ch'io parlai,
dov' ha 'l vicario di Pietro le piante.

Trema forse più giù poco o assai; 55
ma per vento che 'n terra si nasconda,
non so come, qua sù non tremò mai.

Tremaci quando alcuna anima monda 58
sentesi, sì che surga o che si mova
per salir sù; e tal grido seconda.

De la mondizia sol voler fa prova, 61
che, tutto libero a mutar convento,
l'alma sorprende, e di voler le giova.

Prima vuol ben, ma non lascia il talento 64
che divina giustizia, contra voglia,
come fu al peccar, pone al tormento.

E io, che son giaciuto a questa doglia 67
cinquecent' anni e più, pur mo sentii
libera volontà di miglior soglia:

però sentisti il tremoto e li pii 70
spiriti per lo monte render lode
a quel Segnor, che tosto sù li 'nvii."

Così ne disse; e però ch'el si gode 73
tanto del ber quant' è grande la sete,
non saprei dir quant' el mi fece prode.

And my wise guide: "I now can see the net   76
impeding you, how one slips through, and why
it quakes here, and what makes you all rejoice.

And now may it please you to tell me who   79
you were, and in your words may I find why
you've lain here for so many centuries."

"In that age when the worthy Titus, with   82
help from the Highest King, avenged the wounds
from which the blood that Judas sold had flowed,

I had sufficient fame beyond," that spirit   85
replied; "I bore the name that lasts the longest
and honors most—but faith was not yet mine.

So gentle was the spirit of my verse   88
that Rome drew me, son of Toulouse, to her,
and there my brow deserved a crown of myrtle.

On earth my name is still remembered—Statius: 91
I sang of Thebes and then of great Achilles;
I fell along the way of that last labor.

The sparks that warmed me, the seeds of my ardor,   94
were from the holy fire—the same that gave
more than a thousand poets light and flame.

I speak of the *Aeneid*; when I wrote   97
verse, it was mother to me, it was nurse;
my work, without it, would not weigh an ounce.

And to have lived on earth when Virgil lived—   100
for that I would extend by one more year
the time I owe before my exile's end."

These words made Virgil turn to me, and as   103
he turned, his face, through silence, said: "Be still"
(and yet the power of will cannot do all,

for tears and smiles are both so faithful to   106
the feelings that have prompted them that true
feeling escapes the will that would subdue).

But I smiled like a man whose eyes would signal;   109
at this, the shade was silent, and he stared
where sentiment is clearest—at my eyes—

and said: "So may your trying labor end   112
successfully, do tell me why—just now—
your face showed me the flashing of a smile."

Now I am held by one side and the other: 115
one keeps me still, the other conjures me
to speak; but when, therefore, I sigh, my master

E 'l savio duca: "Omai veggio la rete
che qui vi 'mpiglia e come si scalappia,
perché ci trema e di che congaudete.

Ora chi fosti, piacciati ch'io sappia,   79
e perché tanti secoli giaciuto
qui se', ne le parole tue mi cappia."

"Nel tempo che 'l buon Tito, con l'aiuto   82
del sommo rege, vendicò le fóra
ond' uscì 'l sangue per Giuda venduto,

col nome che più dura e più onora   85
era io di là," rispuose quello spirto,
"famoso assai, ma non con fede ancora.

Tanto fu dolce mio vocale spirto,   88
che, tolosano, a sé mi trasse Roma,
dove mertai le tempie ornar di mirto.

Stazio la gente ancor di là mi noma: 91
cantai di Tebe, e poi del grande Achille;
ma caddi in via con la seconda soma.

Al mio ardor fuor seme le faville,   94
che mi scaldar, de la divina fiamma
onde sono allumati più di mille;

de l'Eneïda dico, la qual mamma   97
fummi, e fummi nutrice, poetando:
sanz' essa non fermai peso di dramma.

E per esser vivuto di là quando   100
visse Virgilio, assentirei un sole
più che non deggio al mio uscir di bando."

Volser Virgilio a me queste parole   103
con viso che, tacendo, disse "Taci";
ma non può tutto la virtù che vuole;

ché riso e pianto son tanto seguaci   106
a la passion di che ciascun si spicca,
che men seguon voler ne' più veraci.

Io pur sorrisi come l'uom ch'ammicca;   109
per che l'ombra si tacque, e riguardommi
ne li occhi ove 'l sembiante più si ficca;

e "Se tanto labore in bene assommi,"   112
disse, "perché la tua faccia testeso
un lampeggiar di riso dimostrommi?"

Or son io d'una parte e d'altra preso: 115
l'una mi fa tacer, l'altra scongiura
ch'io dica; ond' io sospiro, e sono inteso

knows why and tells me: "Do not be afraid   118
to speak, but speak and answer what he has
asked you to tell him with such earnestness."

At this, I answered: "Ancient spirit, you   121
perhaps are wondering at the smile I smiled:
but I would have you feel still more surprise.

He who is guide, who leads my eyes on high,   124
is that same Virgil from whom you derived
the power to sing of men and of the gods.

Do not suppose my smile had any source   127
beyond the speech you spoke; be sure—it was
those words you said of him that were the cause."

Now he had bent to kiss my teacher's feet,   130
but Virgil told him: "Brother, there's no need—
you are a shade, a shade is what you see."

And, rising, he: "Now you can understand   133
how much love burns in me for you, when I
forget our insubstantiality,

treating the shades as one treats solid things."   136

dal mio maestro, e "Non aver paura,"   118
mi dice, "di parlar; ma parla e digli
quel ch'e' dimanda con cotanta cura."

    Ond' io: "Forse che tu ti maravigli,   121
antico spirto, del rider ch'io fei;
ma più d'ammirazion vo' che ti pigli.

    Questi che guida in alto li occhi miei,   124
è quel Virgilio dal qual tu togliesti
forte a cantar de li uomini e d'i dèi.

    Se cagion altra al mio rider credesti,   127
lasciala per non vera, ed esser credi
quelle parole che di lui dicesti."

    Già s'inchinava ad abbracciar li piedi   130
al mio dottor, ma el li disse: "Frate,
non far, ché tu se' ombra e ombra vedi."

    Ed ei surgendo: "Or puoi la quantitate   133
comprender de l'amor ch'a te mi scalda,
quand' io dismento nostra vanitate,

    trattando l'ombre come cosa salda."   136

VIRGIL & STATIUS

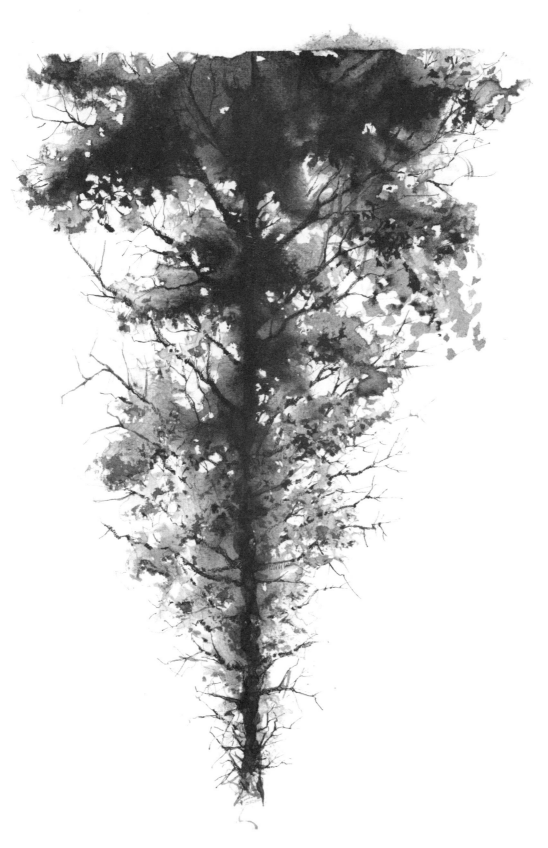

XXII ·131

CANTO XXII

The angel now was left behind us, he
who had directed us to the sixth terrace,
having erased one *P* that scarred my face;

he had declared that those who longed for justice   4
are blessed, and his voice concluded that
message with "*sitiunt*," without the rest.

And while I climbed behind the two swift spirits,   7
not laboring at all, for I was lighter
than I had been along the other stairs,

Virgil began: "Love that is kindled by   10
virtue, will, in another, find reply,
as long as that love's flame appears without;

so, from the time when Juvenal, descending   13
among us, in Hell's Limbo, had made plain
the fondness that you felt for me, my own

benevolence toward you has been much richer   16
than any ever given to a person
one has not seen; thus, now these stairs seem short.

But tell me (and, as friend, forgive me if   19
excessive candor lets my reins relax,
and, as a friend, exchange your words with me):

how was it that you found within your breast   22
a place for avarice, when you possessed
the wisdom you had nurtured with such care?"

These words at first brought something of a smile   25
to Statius; then he answered: "Every word
you speak, to me is a dear sign of love.

Indeed, because true causes are concealed,   28
we often face deceptive reasoning
and things provoke perplexity in us.

Your question makes me sure that you're convinced—   31
perhaps because my circle was the fifth—
that, in the life I once lived, avarice

From the Fifth to the Sixth Terrace: the Gluttonous. The angel
of justice. First part of the Fourth Beatitude. Ascent to the Sixth
Terrace. Statius: his true sin, prodigality; his conversion. Virgil
on the other souls in Limbo. The Sixth Terrace. The strange tree.
Voices citing examples of temperance: the Virgin Mary, the
women of ancient Rome, the Golden Age, John the Baptist.

Già era l'angel dietro a noi rimaso,
l'angel che n'avea vòlti al sesto giro,
avendomi dal viso un colpo raso;

e quei c'hanno a giustizia lor disiro   4
detto n'avea beati, e le sue voci
con *"sitiunt,"* sanz' altro, ciò forniro.

E io più lieve che per l'altre foci   7
m'andava, sì che sanz' alcun labore
seguiva in sù li spiriti veloci;

quando Virgilio incominciò: "Amore,   10
acceso di virtù, sempre altro accese,
pur che la fiamma sua paresse fore;

onde da l'ora che tra noi discese   13
nel limbo de lo 'nferno Giovenale,
che la tua affezion mi fé palese,

mia benvoglienza inverso te fu quale   16
più strinse mai di non vista persona,
sì ch'or mi parran corte queste scale.

Ma dimmi, e come amico mi perdona   19
se troppa sicurtà m'allarga il freno,
e come amico omai meco ragiona:

come poté trovar dentro al tuo seno   22
loco avarizia, tra cotanto senno
di quanto per tua cura fosti pieno?"

Queste parole Stazio mover fenno   25
un poco a riso pria; poscia rispuose:
"Ogne tuo dir d'amor m'è caro cenno.

Veramente più volte appaion cose   28
che danno a dubitar falsa matera
per le vere ragion che son nascose.

La tua dimanda tuo creder m'avvera   31
esser ch'i' fossi avaro in l'altra vita,
forse per quella cerchia dov' io era.

had been my sin. Know then that I was far 34
from avarice—it was my lack of measure
thousands of months have punished. And if I

had not corrected my assessment by 37
my understanding what your verses meant
when you, as if enraged by human nature,

exclaimed: 'Why cannot you, o holy hunger 40
for gold, restrain the appetite of mortals?'—
I'd now, while rolling weights, know sorry jousts.

Then I became aware that hands might open 43
too wide, like wings, in spending; and of this,
as of my other sins, I did repent.

How many are to rise again with heads 46
cropped close, whom ignorance prevents from reaching
repentance in—and at the end of—life!

And know that when a sin is countered by 49
another fault—directly opposite
to it—then, here, both sins see their green wither.

Thus, I join those who pay for avarice 52
in my purgation, though what brought me here
was prodigality—its opposite."

"Now, when you sang the savage wars of those 55
twin sorrows of Jocasta," said the singer
of the bucolic poems, "it does not seem—

from those notes struck by you and Clio there— 58
that you had yet turned faithful to the faith
without which righteous works do not suffice.

If that is so, then what sun or what candles 61
drew you from darkness so that, in their wake,
you set your sails behind the fisherman?"

And he to him: "You were the first to send me 64
to drink within Parnassus' caves and you,
the first who, after God, enlightened me.

You did as he who goes by night and carries 67
the lamp behind him—he is of no help
to his own self but teaches those who follow—

when you declared: 'The ages are renewed; 70
justice and man's first time on earth return;
from Heaven a new progeny descends.'

Through you I was a poet and, through you, 73
a Christian; but that you may see more plainly,
I'll set my hand to color what I sketch.

Or sappi ch'avarizia fu partita   34
troppo da me, e questa dismisura
migliaia di lunari hanno punita.

  E se non fosse ch'io drizzai mia cura,   37
quand' io intesi là dove tu chiame,
crucciato quasi a l'umana natura:

  'Per che non reggi tu, o sacra fame   40
de l'oro, l'appetito de' mortali?'
voltando sentirei le giostre grame.

  Allor m'accorsi che troppo aprir l'ali   43
potean le mani a spendere, e pente'mi
così di quel come de li altri mali.

  Quanti risurgeran coi crini scemi   46
per ignoranza, che di questa pecca
toglie 'l penter vivendo e ne li stremi!

  E sappie che la colpa che rimbecca   49
per dritta opposizione alcun peccato,
con esso insieme qui suo verde secca;

  però, s'io son tra quella gente stato   52
che piange l'avarizia, per purgarmi,
per lo contrario suo m'è incontrato."

  "Or quando tu cantasti le crude armi   55
de la doppia trestizia di Giocasta,"
disse 'l cantor de' buccolici carmi,

  "per quello che Cliò teco lì tasta,   58
non par che ti facesse ancor fedele
la fede, sanza qual ben far non basta.

  Se così è, qual sole quai candele   61
ti stenebraron sì, che tu drizzasti
poscia di retro al pescator le vele?"

  Ed elli a lui: "Tu prima m'invïasti   64
verso Parnaso a ber ne le sue grotte,
e prima appresso Dio m'alluminasti.

  Facesti come quei che va di notte,   67
che porta il lume dietro e sé non giova,
ma dopo sé fa le persone dotte,

  quando dicesti: 'Secol si rinova;   70
torna giustizia e primo tempo umano,
e progenïe scende da ciel nova.'

  Per te poeta fui, per te cristiano: 73
ma perché veggi mei ciò ch'io disegno,
a colorare stenderò la mano.

Disseminated by the messengers   76
of the eternal kingdom, the true faith
by then had penetrated all the world,

and the new preachers preached in such accord   79
with what you'd said (and I have just repeated),
that I was drawn into frequenting them.

Then they appeared to me to be so saintly   82
that, when Domitian persecuted them,
my own laments accompanied their grief;

and while I could—as long as I had life—   85
I helped them, and their honest practices
made me disdainful of all other sects.

Before—within my poem—I'd led the Greeks   88
unto the streams of Thebes, I was baptized;
but out of fear, I was a secret Christian

and, for a long time, showed myself as pagan;   91
for this halfheartedness, for more than four
centuries, I circled the fourth circle.

And now may you, who lifted up the lid   94
that hid from me the good of which I speak,
while time is left us as we climb, tell me

where is our ancient Terence, and Caecilius   97
and Plautus, where is Varius, if you know;
tell me if they are damned, and in what quarter."

"All these and Persius, I, and many others,"   100
my guide replied, "are with that Greek to whom
the Muses gave their gifts in greatest measure.

Our place is the blind prison, its first circle;   103
and there we often talk about the mountain
where those who were our nurses always dwell.

Euripides is with us, Antiphon,   106
Simonides, and Agathon, as well
as many other Greeks who once wore laurel

upon their brow; and there—of your own people—   109
one sees Antigone, Deiphyle,
Ismene, sad still, Argia as she was.

There one can see the woman who showed Langia,   112
and there, Tiresias' daughter; there is Thetis;
and, with her sisters, there, Deidamia."

Both poets now were silent, once again   115
intent on their surroundings—they were free
of stairs and walls; with day's first four handmaidens

Già era 'l mondo tutto quanto pregno
de la vera credenza, seminata
per li messaggi de l'etterno regno;

   e la parola tua sopra toccata   79
si consonava a' nuovi predicanti;
ond' io a visitarli presi usata.

   Vennermi poi parendo tanto santi,   82
che, quando Domizian li perseguette,
sanza mio lagrimar non fur lor pianti;

   e mentre che di là per me si stette,   85
io li sovvenni, e i lor dritti costumi
fer dispregiare a me tutte altre sette.

   E pria ch'io conducessi i Greci a' fiumi   88
di Tebe poetando, ebb' io battesmo;
ma per paura chiuso cristian fu'mi,

   lungamente mostrando paganesmo;   91
e questa tepidezza il quarto cerchio
cerchiar mi fé più che 'l quarto centesmo.

   Tu dunque, che levato hai il coperchio   94
che m'ascondeva quanto bene io dico,
mentre che del salire avem soverchio,

   dimmi dov' è Terrenzio nostro antico,   97
Cecilio e Plauto e Varro, se lo sai:
dimmi se son dannati, e in qual vico."

   "Costoro e Persio e io e altri assai,"   100
rispuose il duca mio, "siam con quel Greco
che le Muse lattar più ch'altri mai,

   nel primo cinghio del carcere cieco;   103
spesse fïate ragioniam del monte
che sempre ha le nutrice nostre seco.

   Euripide v'è nosco e Antifonte,   106
Simonide, Agatone e altri piùe
Greci che già di lauro ornar la fronte.

   Quivi si veggion de le genti tue   109
Antigone, Deïfile e Argia,
e Ismene sì trista come fue.

   Védeisi quella che mostrò Langia;   112
èvvi la figlia di Tiresia, e Teti,
e con le suore sue Deïdamia."

   Tacevansi ambedue già li poeti,   115
di novo attenti a riguardar dintorno,
liberi da saliri e da pareti;

already left behind, and with the fifth   118
guiding the chariot-pole and lifting it,
so that its horn of flame rose always higher,

    my master said: "I think it's time that we   121
turn our right shoulders toward the terrace edge,
circling the mountain in the way we're used to."

    In this way habit served us as a banner;   124
and when we chose that path, our fear was less
because that worthy soul gave his assent.

    Those two were in the lead; I walked alone,   127
behind them, listening to their colloquy,
which taught me much concerning poetry.

    But their delightful conversation soon   130
was interrupted by a tree that blocked
our path; its fruits were fine, their scent was sweet,

    and even as a fir-tree tapers upward
from branch to branch, that tree there tapered downward,
so as—I think—to ward off any climber.

    Upon our left, where wall enclosed our path,   136
bright running water fell from the high rock
and spread itself upon the leaves above.

    When the two poets had approached the tree,   139
a voice emerging from within the leaves
cried out: "This food shall be denied to you."

    Then it cried: "Mary's care was for the marriage-   142
feast's being seemly and complete, not for
her mouth (which now would intercede for you).

    And when they drank, of old, the Roman women   145
were satisfied with water; and young Daniel,
through his disdain of food, acquired wisdom.

    The first age was as fair as gold: when hungry,   148
men found the taste of acorns good; when thirsty,
they found that every little stream was nectar.

    When he was in the wilderness, the Baptist   151
had fed on nothing more than honey, locusts:
for this he was made great, as glorious

    as, in the Gospel, is made plain to you."   154

e già le quattro ancelle eran del giorno 118
rimase a dietro, e la quinta era al temo,
drizzando pur in sù l'ardente corno,

    quando il mio duca: "Io credo ch'a lo stremo 121
le destre spalle volger ne convegna,
girando il monte come far solemo."

    Così l'usanza fu lì nostra insegna, 124
e prendemmo la via con men sospetto
per l'assentir di quell' anima degna.

    Elli givan dinanzi, e io soletto 127
di retro, e ascoltava i lor sermoni,
ch'a poetar mi davano intelletto.

    Ma tosto ruppe le dolci ragioni 130
un alber che trovammo in mezza strada,
con pomi a odorar soavi e buoni;

    e come abete in alto si digrada 133
di ramo in ramo, così quello in giuso,
cred' io, perché persona sù non vada.

    Dal lato onde 'l cammin nostro era chiuso, 136
cadea de l'alta roccia un liquor chiaro
e si spandeva per le foglie suso.

    Li due poeti a l'alber s'appressaro; 139
e una voce per entro le fronde
gridò: "Di questo cibo avrete caro."

    Poi disse: "Più pensava Maria onde 142
fosser le nozze orrevoli e intere,
ch'a la sua bocca, ch'or per voi risponde.

    E le Romane antiche, per lor bere, 145
contente furon d'acqua; e Daniello
dispregiò cibo e acquistò savere.

    Lo secol primo quant' oro fu bello, 148
fé savorose con fame le ghiande,
e nettare con sete ogne ruscello.

    Mele e locuste furon le vivande 151
che nodriro il Batista nel diserto;
per ch'elli è glorïoso e tanto grande

    quanto per lo Vangelio v'è aperto." 154

CANTO XXIII

While I was peering so intently through
the green boughs, like a hunter who, so used,
would waste his life in chasing after birds,

my more than father said to me: "Now come,   4
son, for the time our journey can permit
is to be used more fruitfully than this."

I turned my eyes, and I was no less quick   7
to turn my steps; I followed those two sages,
whose talk was such, my going brought no loss.

And—there!—"Labïa mëa, Domine"   10
was wept and sung and heard in such a manner
that it gave birth to both delight and sorrow.

"O gentle father, what is this I hear?"   13
I asked. And he: "Perhaps they're shades who go
loosening the knot of what they owe."

Even as pensive pilgrims do, who when   16
they've overtaken folk unknown to them
along the way, will turn but will not stop,

so, overtaking us—they had come from   19
behind but were more swift—a crowd of souls,
devout and silent, looked at us in wonder.

Each shade had dark and hollow eyes; their faces   22
were pale and so emaciated that
their taut skin took its shape from bones beneath.

I don't believe that even Erysichthon   25
had been so dried, down to his very hide,
by hunger, when his fast made him fear most.

Thinking, I told myself: "I see the people   28
who lost Jerusalem, when Mary plunged
her beak into her son." The orbits of

their eyes seemed like a ring that's lost its gems;   31
and he who, in the face of man, would read
OMO would here have recognized the *M*.

Still the Sixth Terrace: the Gluttonous. Encounter with Forese
Donati, Dante's friend, who explains the punishment of the
Gluttonous, condemned to emaciating hunger and thirst; praises
his widow, Nella; and rebukes the shameless women of Florence.
Dante's presentation of Virgil and Statius.

CANTO XXIII 201

Mentre che li occhi per la fronda verde
ficcava ïo sì come far suole
chi dietro a li uccellin sua vita perde,

    lo più che padre mi dicea: "Figliuole,   4
vienne oramai, ché 'l tempo che n'è imposto
più utilmente compartir si vuole."

    Io volsi 'l viso, e 'l passo non men tosto,   7
appresso i savi, che parlavan sìe,
che l'andar mi facean di nullo costo.

    Ed ecco piangere e cantar s'udìe   10
"*Labïa mëa, Domine*" per modo
tal, che diletto e doglia parturìe.

    "O dolce padre, che è quel ch'i' odo?"   13
comincia' io; ed elli: "Ombre che vanno
forse di lor dover solvendo il nodo."

    Sì come i peregrin pensosi fanno,   16
giugnendo per cammin gente non nota,
che si volgono ad essa e non restanno,

    così di retro a noi, più tosto mota,   19
venendo e trapassando ci ammirava
d'anime turba tacita e devota.

    Ne li occhi era ciascuna oscura e cava,   22
palida ne la faccia, e tanto scema
che da l'ossa la pelle s'informava.

    Non credo che così a buccia strema   25
Erisittone fosse fatto secco,
per digiunar, quando più n'ebbe tema.

    Io dicea fra stesso pensando: "Ecco   28
la gente che perdé Ierusalemme,
quando Maria nel figlio diè di becco!"

    Parean l'occhiaie anella sanza gemme: 31
chi nel viso de li uomini legge "omo"
ben avria quivi conosciuta l'emme.

Who—if he knew not how—would have believed   34
that longing born from odor of a tree,
odor of water, could reduce souls so?
    I was already wondering what had   37
so famished them (for I had not yet learned
the reason for their leanness and sad scurf),
    when—there!—a shade, his eyes deep in his head,   40
turned toward me, staring steadily; and then
he cried aloud: "What grace is granted me!"
    I never would have recognized him by   43
his face; and yet his voice made plain to me
what his appearance had obliterated.
    This spark rekindled in me everything   46
I knew about those altered features; thus,
I realized it was Forese's face.
    "Ah, don't reproach me for the dried-out scabs   49
that stain my skin," he begged, "nor for the lack
of flesh on me; but do tell me the truth
    about yourself, do tell me who those two   52
souls there are, those who are escorting you;
may you not keep yourself from speaking to me!"
    "Your face, which I once wept on when you died,"   55
I answered him, "now gives me no less cause
for sad lament, seeing you so deformed.
    But tell me, for God's sake, what has unleaved   58
you so; don't make me speak while I'm amazed—
he who's distracted answers clumsily."
    And he to me: "From the eternal counsel,   61
the water and the tree you left behind
receive the power that makes me waste away.
    All of these souls who, grieving, sing because   64
their appetite was gluttonous, in thirst
and hunger here resanctify themselves.
    The fragrance of the fruit and of the water   67
that's sprayed through that green tree kindles in us
craving for food and drink; and not once only,
    as we go round this space, our pain's renewed—   70
I speak of pain but I should speak of solace,
for we are guided to those trees by that
    same longing that had guided Christ when He   73
had come to free us through the blood He shed
and, in His joyousness, called out: 'Eli.'"

Chi crederebbe che l'odor d'un pomo
sì governasse, generando brama,
e quel d'un'acqua, non sappiendo como?

Già era in ammirar che sì li affama,   37
per la cagione ancor non manifesta
di lor magrezza e di lor trista squama,

ed ecco del profondo de la testa   40
volse a me li occhi un'ombra e guardò fiso;
poi gridò forte: "Qual grazia m'è questa?"

Mai non l'avrei riconosciuto al viso;   43
ma ne la voce sua mi fu palese
ciò che l'aspetto in sé avea conquiso.

Questa favilla tutta mi raccese   46
mia conoscenza a la cangiata labbia,
e ravvisai la faccia di Forese.

"Deh, non contendere a l'asciutta scabbia   49
che mi scolora," pregava, "la pelle,
né a difetto di carne ch'io abbia;

ma dimmi il ver di te, dì chi son quelle   52
due anime che là ti fanno scorta;
non rimaner che tu non mi favelle!"

"La faccia tua, ch'io lagrimai già morta,   55
mi dà di pianger mo non minor doglia,"
rispuos' io lui, "veggendola sì torta.

Però mi dì, per Dio, che sì vi sfoglia;   58
non mi far dir mentr' io mi maraviglio,
ché mal può dir chi è pien d'altra voglia."

Ed elli a me: "De l'etterno consiglio   61
cade vertù ne l'acqua e ne la pianta
rimasa dietro, ond' io sì m'assottiglio.

Tutta esta gente che piangendo canta   64
per seguitar la gola oltra misura,
in fame e 'n sete qui si rifà santa.

Di bere e di mangiar n'accende cura   67
l'odor ch'esce del pomo e de lo sprazzo
che si distende su per sua verdura.

E non pur una volta, questo spazzo   70
girando, si rinfresca nostra pena:
io dico pena, e dovria dir sollazzo,

ché quella voglia a li alberi ci mena   73
che menò Cristo lieto a dire 'Elì,'
quando ne liberò con la sua vena."

And I to him: "Forese, from that day   76
when you exchanged the world for better life
until now, less than five years have revolved;
    and if you waited for the moment when   79
the power to sin was gone before you found
the hour of the good grief that succors us
    and weds us once again to God, how have   82
you come so quickly here? I thought to find
you down below, where time must pay for time."
    And he to me: "It is my Nella who,   85
with her abundant tears, has guided me
to drink the sweet wormwood of torments: she,
    with sighs and prayers devout has set me free   88
of that slope where one waits and has freed me
from circles underneath this circle. She—
    my gentle widow, whom I loved most dearly—   91
was all the more beloved and prized by God
as she is more alone in her good works.
    For even the Barbagia of Sardinia   94
is far more modest in its women than
is that Barbagia where I left her. O
    sweet brother, what would you have had me say?   97
A future time's already visible
to me—a time not too far-off from now—
    when, from the pulpit, it shall be forbidden   100
to those immodest ones—Florentine women—
to go displaying bosoms with bare paps.
    What ordinances—spiritual, civil—   103
were ever needed by barbarian or
Saracen women to make them go covered?
    But if those shameless ones had certain knowledge   106
of what swift Heaven's readying for them,
then they would have mouths open now to howl,
    for if our foresight here does not deceive me,   109
they will be sad before the cheeks of those
whom lullabies can now appease grow beards.
    Ah, brother, do not hide things any longer!   112
You see that I am not alone, for all
these people stare at where you veil the sun."
    At this I said to him: "If you should call   115
to mind what you have been with me and I
with you, remembering now will still be heavy.

E io a lui: "Forese, da quel dì
nel qual mutasti mondo a miglior vita,
cinqu' anni non son vòlti infino a qui.

Se prima fu la possa in te finita   79
di peccar più, che sovvenisse l'ora
del buon dolor ch'a Dio ne rimarita,

come se' tu qua sù venuto ancora?   82
Io ti credea trovar là giù di sotto,
dove tempo per tempo si ristora."

Ond' elli a me: "Sì tosto m'ha condotto   85
a ber lo dolce assenzo d'i martìri
la Nella mia con suo pianger dirotto.

Con suoi prieghi devoti e con sospiri   88
tratto m'ha de la costa ove s'aspetta,
e liberato m'ha de li altri giri.

Tanto è a Dio più cara e più diletta   91
la vedovella mia, che molto amai,
quanto in bene operare è più soletta;

ché la Barbagia di Sardigna assai   94
ne le femmine sue più è pudica
che la Barbagia dov' io la lasciai.

O dolce frate, che vuo' tu ch'io dica?   97
Tempo futuro m'è già nel cospetto,
cui non sarà quest' ora molto antica,

nel qual sarà in pergamo interdetto   100
a le sfacciate donne fiorentine
l'andar mostrando con le poppe il petto.

Quai barbare fuor mai, quai saracine,   103
cui bisognasse, par farle ir coperte,
o spiritali o altre discipline?

Ma se le svergognate fosser certe   106
di quel che 'l ciel veloce loro ammanna,
già per urlare avrian le bocche aperte;

ché, se l'antiveder qui non m'inganna,   109
prima fien triste che le guance impeli
colui che mo si consola con nanna.

Deh, frate, or fa che più non mi ti celi!   112
vedi che non pur io, ma questa gente
tutta rimira là dove 'l sol veli."

Per ch'io a lui: "Se tu riduci a mente   115
qual fosti meco, e qual io teco fui,
ancor fia grave il memorar presente.

He who precedes me turned me from that life   118
some days ago, when she who is the sister
of him," I pointed to the sun, "was showing

    her roundness to you. It is he who's led   121
me through the deep night of the truly dead
with this true flesh that follows after him.

    His help has drawn me up from there, climbing   124
and circling round this mountain, which makes straight
you whom the world made crooked. And he says

    that he will bear me company until   127
I reach the place where Beatrice is; there
I must remain without him. It is Virgil

    who speaks to me in this way," and I pointed   130
to him; "this other is the shade for whom
just now, your kingdom caused its every slope

    to tremble as it freed him from itself."   133

Di quella vita mi volse costui
che mi va innanzi, l'altr' ier, quando tonda
vi si mostrò la suora di colui,"

    e 'l sol mostrai; "costui per la profonda   121
notte menato m'ha d'i veri morti
con questa vera carne che 'l seconda.

    Indi m'han tratto sù li suoi conforti,   124
salendo e rigirando la montagna
che drizza voi che 'l mondo fece torti.

    Tanto dice di farmi sua compagna   127
che io sarò là dove fia Beatrice;
quivi convien che sanza lui rimagna.

    Virgilio è questi che così mi dice,"   130
e addita'lo; "e quest' altro è quell' ombra
per cuï scosse dianzi ogne pendice

    lo vostro regno, che da sé lo sgombra."   133

XXIV·123

CANTO XXIV

Our talking did not slow our pace, our pace
not slow our talking; but conversing, we
moved quickly, like a boat a fair wind drives.
    And recognizing that I was alive,   4
the shades—they seemed to be things twice dead—drew
amazement from the hollows of their eyes.
    And I, continuing my telling, added: 7
"Perhaps he is more slow in his ascent
than he would be had he not met the other.
    But tell me, if you can: where is Piccarda?   10
And tell me if, among those staring at me,
I can see any person I should note."
    "My sister—and I know not whether she   13
was greater in her goodness or her beauty—
on high Olympus is in triumph; she
    rejoices in her crown already." He   16
began, then added: "It is not forbidden
to name each shade here—abstinence has eaten
    away our faces." And he pointed: "This   19
is Bonagiunta, Bonagiunta da
Lucca; the one beyond him, even more
    emaciated than the rest, had clasped   22
the Holy Church; he was from Tours; his fast
purges Bolsena's eels, Vernaccia's wine."
    And he named many others, one by one   25
and, at their naming, they all seemed content;
so that—for this—no face was overcast.
    I saw—their teeth were biting emptiness—   28
both Ubaldin da la Pila and Boniface,
who shepherded so many with his staff.
    I saw Messer Marchese, who once had   31
more ease, less dryness, drinking at Forlì
and yet could never satisfy his thirst.

Still the Sixth Terrace: the Gluttonous. Forese on his sister   CANTO XXIV 211
Piccarda. The poet Bonagiunta da Lucca's praise of Gentucca and
discourse on poetry. Forese on Florence and on the death of Corso
Donati. The second tree. Voices reciting examples of gluttony:
the Centaurs and those Hebrews rejected by Gideon. The angel of
temperance. The last part of the Fourth Beatitude.

Né 'l dir l'andar, né l'andar lui più lento
facea, ma ragionando andavam forte,
sì come nave pinta da buon vento;

   e l'ombre, che parean cose rimorte,   4
per le fosse de li occhi ammirazione
traean di me, di mio vivere accorte.

   E io, continüando al mio sermone,   7
disse: "Ella sen va sù forse più tarda
che non farebbe, per altrui cagione.

   Ma dimmi, se tu sai, dov' è Piccarda;   10
dimmi s'io veggio da notar persona
tra questa gente che sì mi riguarda."

   "La mia sorella, che tra bella e buona   13
non so qual fosse più, trïunfa lieta
ne l'alto Olimpo già di sua corona."

   Sì disse prima; e poi: "Qui non si vieta   16
di nominar ciascun, da ch'è sì munta
nostra sembianza via per la dïeta.

   "Questi," e mostrò col dito, "è Bonagiunta,   19
Bonagiunta da Lucca; e quella faccia
di là da lui più che l'altre trapunta

   ebbe la Santa Chiesa in le sue braccia: 22
dal Torso fu, e purga per digiuno
l'anguille di Bolsena e la vernaccia."

   Molti altri mi nomò ad uno ad uno;   25
e del nomar parean tutti contenti,
sì ch'io però non vidi un atto bruno.

   Vidi per fame a vòto usar li denti   28
Ubaldin da la Pila e Bonifazio
che pasturò col rocco molte genti.

   Vidi messer Marchese, ch'ebbe spazio   31
già di bere a Forlì con men secchezza,
e sì fu tal, che non si sentì sazio.

But just as he who looks and then esteems   34
one more than others, so did I prize him
of Lucca, for he seemed to know me better.

He murmured; something like "Gentucca" was   37
what I heard from the place where he could feel
the wound of justice that denudes them so.

"O soul," I said, "who seems so eager to   40
converse with me, do speak so that I hear you,
for speech may satisfy both you and me."

He answered: "Although men condemn my city,   43
there is a woman born—she wears no veil
as yet—because of whom you'll find it pleasing.

You are to journey with this prophecy;   46
and if there's something in my murmuring
you doubt, events themselves will bear me out.

But tell me if the man whom I see here   49
is he who brought the new rhymes forth, beginning:
'Ladies who have intelligence of love.'"

I answered: "I am one who, when Love breathes   52
in me, takes note; what he, within, dictates,
I, in that way, without, would speak and shape."

"O brother, now I see," he said, "the knot   55
that kept the Notary, Guittone, and me
short of the sweet new manner that I hear.

I clearly see how your pens follow closely   58
behind him who dictates, and certainly
that did not happen with our pens; and he

who sets himself to ferreting profoundly   61
can find no other difference between
the two styles." He fell still, contentedly.

Even as birds that winter on the Nile   64
at times will slow and form a flock in air,
then speed their flight and form a file, so all

the people who were there moved much more swiftly,
turning away their faces, hurrying
their pace because of leanness and desire.

And just as he who's tired of running lets   70
his comrades go ahead and slows his steps
until he's eased the panting of his chest,

so did Forese let the holy flock   73
pass by and move, behind, with me, saying:
"How long before I shall see you again?"

Ma come fa chi guarda e poi s'apprezza
più d'un che d'altro, fei a quel da Lucca,
che più parea di me aver contezza.

El mormorava; e non so che "Gentucca"   37
sentiv' io là, ov' el sentia la piaga
de la giustizia che sì li pilucca.

"O anima," diss' io, "che par sì vaga   40
di parlar meco, fa sì ch'io t'intenda,
e te e me col tuo parlare appaga."

"Femmina è nata, e non porta ancor benda,"   43
cominciò el, "che ti farà piacere
la mia città, come ch'om la riprenda.

Tu te n'andrai con questo antivedere: 46
se nel mio mormorar prendesti errore,
dichiareranti ancor le cose vere.

Ma dì s'i' veggio qui colui che fore   49
trasse le nove rime, cominciando
'Donne ch'avete intelletto d'amore.'"

E io a lui: "I' mi son un che, quando   52
Amor mi spira, noto, e a quel modo
ch'e' ditta dentro vo significando."

"O frate, issa vegg' io," diss' elli, "il nodo   55
che 'l Notaro e Guittone e me ritenne
di qua dal dolce stil novo ch'i' odo

Io veggio ben come le vostre penne   58
di retro al dittator sen vanno strette,
che de le nostre certo non avvenne;

e qual più a gradire oltre si mette,   61
non vede più da l'uno a l'altro stilo";
e, quasi contentato, si tacette.

Come li augei che vernan lungo 'l Nilo,   64
alcuna volta in aere fanno schiera,
poi volan più a fretta e vanno in filo,

così tutta la gente che lì era,   67
volgendo 'l viso, raffrettò suo passo,
e per magrezza e per voler leggera.

E come l'uom che di trottare è lasso,   70
lascia andar li compagni, e sì passeggia
fin che si sfoghi l'affollar del casso,

sì lasciò trapassar la santa greggia   73
Forese, e dietro meco sen veniva,
dicendo: "Quando fia ch'io ti riveggia?"

"I do not know," I said, "how long I'll live; 76
and yet, however quick is my return,
my longing for these shores would have me here

sooner—because the place where I was set 79
to live is day by day deprived of good
and seems along the way to wretched ruin."

"Do not be vexed," he said, "for I can see 82
the guiltiest of all dragged by a beast's
tail to the valley where no sin is purged.

At every step the beast moves faster, always 85
gaining momentum, till it smashes him
and leaves his body squalidly undone.

Those wheels," and here he looked up at the sky, 88
"do not have long to turn before you see
plainly what I can't tell more openly.

Now you remain behind, for time is costly 91
here in this kingdom; I should lose too much
by moving with you thus, at equal pace."

Just as a horseman sometimes gallops out, 94
leaving behind his troop of riders, so
that he may gain the honor of the first

clash—so, with longer strides, did he leave us; 97
and I remained along my path with those
two who were such great marshals of the world.

And when he'd gone so far ahead of us 100
that my eyes strained to follow him, just as
my mind was straining after what he'd said,

the branches of another tree, heavy 103
with fruit, alive with green, appeared to me
nearby, just past a curve where I had turned.

Beneath the tree I saw shades lifting hands, 106
crying I know not what up toward the branches,
like little eager, empty-headed children

who beg—but he of whom they beg does not 109
reply, but to provoke their longing, he
holds high, and does not hide, the thing they want.

Then they departed as if disabused; 112
and we—immediately—reached that great tree,
which turns aside so many prayers and tears.

"Continue on, but don't draw close to it; 115
there is a tree above from which Eve ate,
and from that tree above, this plant was raised."

"Non so," rispuos' io lui, "quant' io mi viva;   76
ma già non fïa il tornar mio tantosto,
ch'io non sia col voler prima a la riva;

    però che 'l loco u' fui a viver posto,   79
di giorno in giorno più di ben si spolpa,
e a trista ruina par disposto."

    "Or va," diss' el; "che quei che più n'ha colpa,   82
vegg' ïo a coda d'una bestia tratto
inver' la valle ove mai non si scolpa.

    La bestia ad ogne passo va più ratto,   85
crescendo sempre, fin ch'ella il percuote,
e lascia il corpo vilmente disfatto.

    Non hanno molto a volger quelle ruote,"   88
e drizzò li occhi al ciel, "che ti fia chiaro
ciò che 'l mio dir più dichiarar non puote.

    Tu ti rimani omai; ché 'l tempo è caro   91
in questo regno, sì ch'io perdo troppo
venendo teco sì a paro a paro."

    Qual esce alcuna volta di gualoppo   94
lo cavalier di schiera che cavalchi,
e va per farsi onor del primo intoppo,

    tal si partì da noi con maggior valchi;   97
e io rimasi in via con esso i due
che fuor del mondo sì gran marescalchi.

    E quando innanzi a noi intrato fue,   100
che li occhi miei si fero a lui seguaci,
come la mente a le parole sue,

    parvermi i rami gravidi e vivaci   103
d'un altro pomo, e non molto lontani
per esser pur allora vòlto in laci.

    Vidi gente sott' esso alzar le mani   106
e gridar non so che verso le fronde,
quasi bramosi fantolini e vani

    che pregano, e 'l pregato non risponde,   109
ma, per fare esser ben la voglia acuta,
tien alto lor disio e nol nasconde.

    Poi si partì sì come ricreduta;   112
e noi venimmo al grande arbore adesso,
che tanti prieghi e lagrime rifiuta.

    "Trapassate oltre sanza farvi presso: 115
legno è più sù che fu morso da Eva,
e questa pianta si levò da esso."

Among the boughs, a voice—I know not whose—   118
spoke so; thus, drawing closer, Virgil, Statius,
and I edged on, along the side that rises.

It said: "Remember those with double chests,   121
the miserable ones, born of the clouds,
whom Theseus battled when they'd gorged themselves;

and those whom Gideon refused as comrades—   124
those Hebrews who had drunk too avidly—
when he came down the hills to Midian."

So, keeping close to one of that road's margins,   127
we moved ahead, hearing of gluttony—
its sins repaid by sorry penalties.

Then, with more space along the lonely path,   130
a thousand steps and more had brought us forward,
each of us meditating wordlessly.

"What are you thinking of, you three who walk   133
alone?" a sudden voice called out; at which
I started—like a scared young animal.

I raised my head to see who it might be;   136
no glass or metal ever seen within
a furnace was so glowing or so red

as one I saw, who said: "If you'd ascend,   139
then you must turn at this point; for whoever
would journey unto peace must pass this way."

But his appearance had deprived me of   142
my sight, so that—as one who uses hearing
as guide—I turned and followed my two teachers.

And like the breeze of May that—heralding   145
the dawning of the day—when it is steeped
in flowers and in grass, stirs fragrantly,

so did I feel the wind that blew against   148
the center of my brow, and clearly sensed
the movement of his wings, the air's ambrosia.

And then I heard: "Blessed are those whom grace   151
illumines so, that, in their breasts, the love
of taste does not awake too much desire—

whose hungering is always in just measure."   154

Sì tra le frasche non so chi diceva;
per che Virgilio e Stazio e io, ristretti,
oltre andavam dal lato che si leva.

 "Ricordivi," dicea, "d'i maladetti   121
nei nuvoli formati, che, satolli,
Tesëo combatter co' doppi petti;

 e de li Ebrei ch'al ber si mostrar molli, 124
per che no i volle Gedeon compagni,
quando inver' Madïan discese i colli."

 Sì accostati a l'un d'i due vivagni   127
passammo, udendo colpe de la gola
seguite già da miseri guadagni.

 Poi, rallargati per la strada sola,   130
ben mille passi e più ci portar oltre,
contemplando ciascun sanza parola.

 "Che andate pensando sì voi sol tre?" 133
sùbita voce disse; ond' io mi scossi
come fan bestie spaventate e poltre.

 Drizzai la testa per veder chi fossi; 136
e già mai non si videro in fornace
vetri o metalli sì lucenti e rossi,

 com' io vidi un che dicea: "S'a voi piace 139
montare in sù, qui si convien dar volta;
quinci si va chi vuole andar per pace."

 L'aspetto suo m'avea la vista tolta; 142
per ch'io mi volsi dietro a' miei dottori,
com' om che va secondo ch'elli ascolta.

 E quale, annunziatrice de li albori, 145
l'aura di maggio movesi e olezza,
tutta impregnata da l'erba e da' fiori;

 tal mi senti' un vento dar per mezza 148
la fronte, e ben senti' mover la piuma,
che fé sentir d'ambrosïa l'orezza.

 E senti' dir: "Beati cui alluma   151
tanto di grazia, che l'amor del gusto
nel petto lor troppo disir non fuma,

 esurïendo sempre quanto è giusto!" 154

CANTO XXV

The hour when climbers cannot pause had come:
the sun had left to Taurus the meridian,
and night had left it to the Scorpion.

Therefore, like one who will not stop but moves   4
along his path, no matter what he sees,
if he is goaded by necessity,

we made our way into the narrow gap   7
and, one behind the other, took the stairs
so strait that climbers there must separate.

And as the fledgling stork will lift its wing   10
because it wants to fly, but dares not try
to leave the nest, and lets its wing drop back,

so I, with my desire to question kindled   13
then spent, arrived as far as making ready
to speak. But my dear father, though our steps

were hurrying, did not stop talking, for   16
he said: "The iron of the arrow's touched
the bowstring; let the shaft of speech fly off."

Then I had confidence enough to open   19
my mouth and ask him: "How can one grow lean
where there is never need for nourishment?"

"If you recall how Meleager was   22
consumed," he said, "just when the firebrand
was spent, this won't be hard to understand;

and if you think how, though your body's swift,   25
your image in the mirror captures it,
then what perplexed will seem to you transparent.

But that your will to know may be appeased,   28
here's Statius, and I call on him and ask
that he now be the healer of your doubts."

"If I explain eternal ways to him,"   31
Statius replied, "while you are present here,
let my excuse be: I cannot refuse you."

From the Sixth to the Seventh Terrace: the Lustful. Hour and
mode of ascent to the Seventh Terrace. Dante's queries about the
leanness of bodiless shades. Statius' explanation of generation,
souls after death, and aerial bodies. The punishment of the
Lustful, purification through fire. The Lustful shouting examples
of chastity: the Virgin Mary and Diana.

Ora era onde 'l salir non volea storpio;
ché 'l sole avëa il cerchio di merigge
lasciato al Tauro e la notte a lo Scorpio:

  per che, come fa l'uom che non s'affigge   4
ma vassi a la via sua, che che li appaia,
se di bisogno stimolo il trafigge,

  così intrammo noi per la callaia,   7
uno innanzi altro prendendo la scala
che per artezza i salitor dispaia.

  E quale il cicognin che leva l'ala   10
per voglia di volare, e non s'attenta
d'abbandonar lo nido, e giù la cala;

  tal era io con voglia accesa e spenta   13
di dimandar, venendo infino a l'atto
che fa colui ch'a dicer s'argomenta.

  Non lasciò, per l'andar che fosse ratto,   16
lo dolce padre mio, ma disse: "Scocca
l'arco del dir, che 'nfino al ferro hai tratto."

  Allor sicuramente apri' la bocca   19
e cominciai: "Come si può far magro
là dove l'uopo di nodrir non tocca?"

  "Se t'ammentassi come Meleagro   22
si consumò al consumar d'un stizzo,
non fora," disse, "a te questo sì agro;

  e se pensassi come, al vostro guizzo,   25
guizza dentro a lo specchio vostra image,
ciò che par duro ti parrebbe vizzo.

  Ma perché dentro a tuo voler t'adage,   28
ecco qui Stazio; e io lui chiamo e prego
che sia or sanator de le tue piage."

  "Se la veduta etterna li dislego,"   31
rispuose Stazio, "là dove tu sie,
discolpi me non potert' io far nego."

Then he began: "If, son, your mind receives   34
and keeps my words, then what I say will serve
as light upon the *how* that you have asked.

The thirsty veins drink up the perfect blood—   37
but not all of that blood: a portion's left,
like leavings that are taken from the table.

Within the heart, that part acquires power   40
to form all of another's human limbs,
as blood that flows through veins feeds one's own limbs.

Digested yet again, that part descends   43
to what is best not named; from there it drips
into the natural receptacle,

upon another's blood; the two bloods mingle,   46
one ready to be passive and one active
because a perfect place, the heart, prepared them.

The active, having reached the passive, starts   49
to work: first it coagulates—and then
quickens—the matter it has made more dense.

Having become a soul (much like a plant,   52
though with this difference—a plant's complete,
whereas a fetus still is journeying),

the active virtue labors, so the fetus   55
may move and feel, like a sea-sponge; and then
it starts to organize the powers it's seeded.

At this point, son, the power that had come   58
from the begetter's heart unfolds and spreads,
that nature may see every limb perfected.

But how the animal becomes a speaking   61
being, you've not yet seen; this point's so hard,
it led one wiser than you are to err

in separating from the possible   64
intellect the soul, since he could see
no organ for the mind—so did he teach.

Open your heart to truth we now have reached   67
and know that, once the brain's articulation
within the fetus has attained perfection,

then the First Mover turns toward it with joy   70
on seeing so much art in nature and
breathes into it new spirit—vigorous—

which draws all that is active in the fetus   73
into its substance and becomes one soul
that lives and feels and has self-consciousness.

Poi cominciò: "Se le parole mie,   34
figlio, la mente tua guarda e riceve,
lume ti fiero al come che tu die.

   Sangue perfetto, che poi non si beve   37
da l'assetate vene, e si rimane
quasi alimento che di mensa leve,

   prende nel core a tutte membra umane   40
virtute informativa, come quello
ch'a farsi quelle per le vene vane.

   Ancor digesto, scende ov' è più bello   43
tacer che dire; e quindi poscia geme
sovr' altrui sangue in natural vasello.

   Ivi s'accoglie l'uno e l'altro insieme,   46
l'un disposto a patire, e l'altro a fare
per lo perfetto loco onde si preme;

   e, giunto lui, comincia ad operare   49
coagulando prima, e poi avviva
ciò che per sua matera fé constare.

   Anima fatta la virtute attiva   52
qual d'una pianta, in tanto differente,
che questa è in via e quella è già a riva,

   tanto ovra poi, che già si move e sente,   55
come spungo marino; e indi imprende
ad organar le posse ond' è semente.

   Or si spiega, figliuolo, or si distende   58
la virtù ch'è dal cor del generante,
dove natura a tutte membra intende.

   Ma come d'animal divegna fante,   61
non vedi tu ancor: quest' è tal punto,
che più savio di te fé già errante,

   sì che per sua dottrina fé disgiunto   64
da l'anima il possibile intelletto,
perché da lui non vide organo assunto.

   Apri a la verità che viene il petto;   67
e sappi che, sì tosto come al feto
l'articular del cerebro è perfetto,

   lo motor primo a lui si volge lieto   70
sovra tant' arte di natura, e spira
spirito novo, di vertù repleto,

   che ciò che trova attivo quivi, tira   73
in sua sustanzia, e fassi un'alma sola,
che vive e sente e sé in sé rigira.

That what I say may leave you less perplexed,   76
consider the sun's heat that, when combined
with sap that flows from vines, is then made wine.

And when Lachesis lacks more thread, then soul's   79
divided from the flesh; potentially,
it bears with it the human and divine;

but with the human powers mute, the rest—   82
intelligence and memory and will—
are more acute in action than they were.

With no delay, the soul falls of itself—   85
astonishingly—on one of two shores;
there it learns—early—what way it will journey.

There, once the soul is circumscribed by space,   88
the power that gives form irradiates
as—and as much as—once it formed live limbs.

And even as the saturated air,   91
since it reflects the rays the sun has sent,
takes rainbow colors as its ornament,

so there, where the soul stopped, the nearby air   94
takes on the form that soul impressed on it,
a shape that is, potentially, real body;

and then, just as a flame will follow after   97
the fire whenever fire moves, so that
new form becomes the spirit's follower.

Since from that airy body it takes on   100
its semblance, that soul is called 'shade': that shape
forms organs for each sense, even for sight.

This airy body lets us speak and laugh;   103
with it we form the tears and sigh the sighs
that you, perhaps, have heard around this mountain.

Just as we are held fast by longings and   106
by other sentiments, our shade takes form:
this is the cause of your astonishment.''

By now we'd reached the final turning we   109
would meet and took the pathway right, at which
we were preoccupied with other cares.

There, from the wall, the mountain hurls its flames;   112
but, from the terrace side, there whirls a wind
that pushes back the fire and limits it;

thus, on the open side, proceeding one   115
by one, we went; I feared the fire on
the left and, on the right, the precipice.

E perché meno ammiri la parola,
guarda il calor del sol che si fa vino,
giunto a l'omor che de la vite cola.

 Quando Làchesis non ha più del lino,   79
solvesi da la carne, e in virtute
ne porta seco e l'umano e 'l divino:

 l'altre potenze tutte quante mute;   82
memoria, intelligenza e volontade
in atto molto più che prima agute.

 Sanza restarsi, per sé stessa cade   85
mirabilmente a l'una de le rive;
quivi conosce prima le sue strade.

 Tosto che loco lì la circunscrive,   88
la virtù formativa raggia intorno
così e quanto ne le membra vive.

 E come l'aere, quand' è ben pïorno,   91
per l'altrui raggio che 'n sé si reflette,
di diversi color diventa addorno;

 così l'aere vicin quivi si mette   94
e in quella forma ch'è in lui suggella
virtüalmente l'alma che ristette;

 e simigliante poi a la fiammella   97
che segue il foco là 'vunque si muta,
segue lo spirto sua forma novella.

 Però che quindi ha poscia sua paruta,   100
è chiamata ombra; e quindi organa poi
ciascun sentire infino a la veduta.

 Quindi parliamo e quindi ridiam noi;   103
quindi facciam le lagrime e ' sospiri
che per lo monte aver sentiti puoi.

 Secondo che ci affliggono i disiri   106
e li altri affetti, l'ombra si figura;
e quest' è la cagion di che tu miri."

 E già venuto a l'ultima tortura   109
s'era per noi, e vòlto a la man destra,
ed eravamo attenti ad altra cura.

 Quivi la ripa fiamma in fuor balestra,   112
e la cornice spira fiato in suso
che la reflette e via da lei sequestra;

 ond' ir ne convenia dal lato schiuso   115
ad uno ad uno; e io temëa 'l foco
quinci, e quindi temeva cader giuso.

My guide said: "On this terrace, it is best   118
to curb your eyes: the least distraction—left
or right—can mean a step you will regret."

Then, from the heart of that great conflagration,   121
I heard *"Summae Deus clementiae"*
sung—and was not less keen to turn my eyes;

and I saw spirits walking in the flames,   124
so that I looked at them and at my steps,
sharing the time I had to look at each.

After they'd reached that hymn's end, *"Virum non*   127
cognosco" were the words they cried aloud;
then they began the hymn in a low voice

again, and, done again, they cried: "Diana   130
kept to the woods and banished Helice
after she'd felt the force of Venus' poison."

Then they returned to singing; and they praised   133
aloud those wives and husbands who were chaste,
as virtue and as matrimony mandate.

This is—I think—the way these spirits act   136
as long as they are burned by fire: this is
the care and this the nourishment with which

one has to heal the final wound of all.   139

Lo duca mio dicea: "Per questo loco 118
si vuol tenere a li occhi stretto il freno,
però ch'errar potrebbesi per poco."

"*Summae Deus clementïae*" nel seno 121
al grande ardore allora udi' cantando,
che di volger mi fé caler non meno;

e vidi spirti per la fiamma andando; 124
per ch'io guardava a loro e a' miei passi,
compartendo la vista a quando a quando.

Appresso il fine ch'a quell' inno fassi, 127
gridavano alto: "*Virum non cognosco*";
indi ricominciavan l'inno bassi.

Finitolo anco, gridavano: "Al bosco 130
si tenne Diana, ed Elice caccionne
che di Venere avea sentito il tòsco."

Indi al cantar tornavano; indi donne 133
gridavano e mariti che fuor casti
come virtute e matrimonio imponne.

E questo modo credo che lor basti 136
per tutto il tempo che 'l foco li abbruscia:
con tal cura conviene e con tai pasti

che la piaga da sezzo si ricuscia. 139

XXV · 127-133

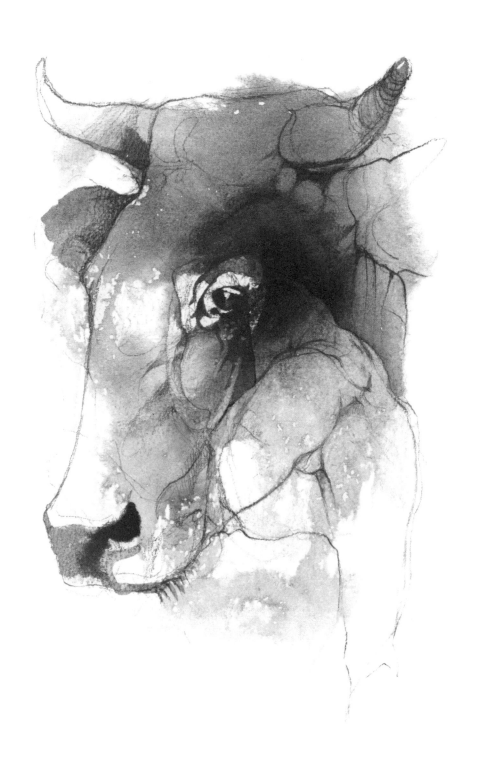

XXVI · 42

CANTO XXVI

While we moved at the edge, one first, one after,
and I could often hear my gentle master
saying: "Take care—and do not waste my warning,"

the sun, its rays already altering   4
the coloring of all the west to azure
from white, was striking me on my right shoulder.

And where my shadow fell, it made the flames   7
seem more inflamed; and I saw many shades
walking, intent upon a sight so strange.

This was the reason that first prompted them   10
to speak to me. Among themselves they said:
"He does not seem to have a fictive body."

Then certain of them came as close to me   13
as they were able to while, cautiously,
they never left the boundaries of their burning.

"O you who move behind the others not   16
because of sloth but reverence perhaps,
give me who burn in thirst and fire your answer.

I'm not alone in needing your response;   19
for all these shades thirst so for it—more than
an Indian or Ethiopian

thirsts for cool water. Tell us how you can—   22
as if you're not yet caught within death's net—
make of yourself a wall against the sun."

Thus one of them had spoken to me; I   25
should now have answered clearly, had I not
been fixed on something strangely evident;

for in the middle of the burning path,   28
came people moving opposite to these—
and I, since they moved left, stared in suspense.

There, on all sides, I can see every shade   31
move quickly to embrace another shade,
content—they did not pause—with their brief greeting,

Mentre che sì per l'orlo, uno innanzi altro,
ce n'andavamo, e spesso il buon maestro
diceami: "Guarda: giovi ch'io ti scaltro";

feriami il sole in su l'omero destro,   4
che già, raggiando, tutto l'occidente
mutava in bianco aspetto di cilestro;

e io facea con l'ombra più rovente   7
parer la fiamma; e pur a tanto indizio
vidi molt' ombre, andando, poner mente.

Questa fu la cagion che diede inizio   10
loro a parlar di me; e cominciarsi
a dir: "Colui non par corpo fittizio";

poi verso me, quanto potëan farsi,   13
certi si fero, sempre con riguardo
di non uscir dove non fosser arsi.

"O tu che vai, non per esser più tardo,   16
ma forse reverente, a li altri dopo,
rispondi a me che 'n sete e 'n foco ardo.

Né solo a me la tua risposta è uopo;   19
ché tutti questi n'hanno maggior sete
che d'acqua fredda Indo o Etïopo.

Dinne com' è che fai di te parete   22
al sol, pur come tu non fossi ancora
di morte intrato dentro da la rete."

Sì mi parlava un d'essi; e io mi fora   25
già manifesto, s'io non fossi atteso
ad altra novità ch'apparve allora;

ché per lo mezzo del cammino acceso   28
venne gente col viso incontro a questa,
la qual mi fece a rimirar sospeso.

Lì veggio d'ogne parte farsi presta   31
ciascun' ombra e basciarsi una con una
sanza restar, contente a brieve festa;

as ants, in their dark company, will touch 34
their muzzles, each to each, perhaps to seek
news of their fortunes and their journeyings.

No sooner is their friendly greeting done 37
than each shade tries to outcry all the rest
even before he starts to move ahead,

the new group shouting: "Sodom and Gomorrah"; 40
the other: "That the bull may hurry toward
her lust, Pasiphaë hides in the cow."

Then, just like cranes, of whom a part, to flee 43
the sun, fly north to Riphean mountains, while
the rest, to flee the frost, fly toward the sands,

one group moves with—the other opposite—us; 46
and they return with tears to their first chants
and to the shout appropriate to each.

And those who had entreated me came close 49
again, in the same way they'd done before;
their faces showed how keen they were to listen.

I, seeing their desire once again, 52
began: "O souls who can be sure of gaining
the state of peace, whenever that may be,

my limbs—mature or green—have not been left 55
within the world beyond; they're here with me,
together with their blood and with their bones.

That I be blind no longer, through this place 58
I pass; above, a lady has gained grace
for me; therefore, I bear my mortal body

across your world. So may your deepest longing 61
soon be appeased and you be lodged within
the heaven that's most full of love, most spacious,

please tell me, so that I may yet transcribe it 64
upon my pages, who you are, and what
crowd moves in the direction opposite."

Each shade displayed no less astonishment 67
or less confusion than a mountaineer,
who, even as he stares about, falls silent

when, rough and rustic, he comes to the city; 70
but when they'd set aside astonishment—
that's soon subdued in noble hearts—he who

had questioned me before, began again: 73
"Blessed are you who would, in order to
die better, store experience of our lands!

così per entro loro schiera bruna   34
s'ammusa l'una con l'altra formica,
forse a spïar lor via e lor fortuna.

    Tosto che parton l'accoglienza amica,   37
prima che 'l primo passo lì trascorra,
sopragridar ciascuna s'affatica:

    la nova gente: "Soddoma e Gomorra";   40
e l'altra: "Ne la vacca entra Pasife,
perché 'l torello a sua lussuria corra."

    Poi, come grue ch'a le montagne Rife   43
volasser parte, e parte inver' l'arene,
queste del gel, quelle del sole schife,

    l'una gente sen va, l'altra sen vene;   46
e tornan, lagrimando, a' primi canti
e al gridar che più lor si convene;

    e raccostansi a me, come davanti,   49
essi medesmi che m'avean pregato,
attenti ad ascoltar ne' lor sembianti.

    Io, che due volte avea visto lor grato,   52
incominciai: "O anime sicure
d'aver, quando che sia, di pace stato,

    non son rimase acerbe né mature   55
le membra mie di là, ma son qui meco
col sangue suo e con le sue giunture.

    Quinci sù vo per non esser più cieco;   58
donna è di sopra che m'acquista grazia,
per che 'l mortal per vostro mondo reco.

    Ma se la vostra maggior voglia sazia   61
tosto divegna, sì che 'l ciel v'alberghi
ch'è pien d'amore e più ampio si spazia,

    ditemi, acciò ch'ancor carte ne verghi,   64
chi siete voi, e chi è quella turba
che se ne va di retro a' vostri terghi."

    Non altrimenti stupido si turba   67
lo montanaro, e rimirando ammuta,
quando rozzo e salvatico s'inurba,

    che ciascun' ombra fece in sua paruta;   70
ma poi che furon di stupore scarche,
lo qual ne li alti cuor tosto s'attuta,

    "Beato te, che de le nostre marche,"   73
ricominciò colei che pria m'inchiese,
"per morir meglio, esperïenza imbarche!

The people moving opposite us shared   76
the sin for which once, while in triumph, Caesar
heard 'Queen' called out against him; that is why,
    as they move off from us, they cry out 'Sodom,'   79
reproaching their own selves, as you have heard,
and through their shame abet the fire's work.
    Our sin was with the other sex; but since   82
we did not keep the bounds of human law,
but served our appetites like beasts, when we
    part from the other ranks, we then repeat,   85
to our disgrace, the name of one who, in
the bestial planks, became herself a beast.
    You now know why we act so, and you know   88
what our sins were; if you would know our names,
time is too short, and I don't know them all.
    But with regard to me, I'll satisfy   91
your wish to know: I'm Guido Guinizzelli,
purged here because I grieved before my end."
    As, after the sad raging of Lycurgus,   94
two sons, finding their mother, had embraced her,
so I desired to do—but dared not to—
    when I heard him declare his name: the father   97
of me and of the others—those, my betters—
who ever used sweet, gracious rhymes of love.
    And without hearing, speaking, pensive, I   100
walked on, still gazing at him, a long time,
prevented by the fire from drawing closer.
    When I had fed my sight on him, I offered   103
myself—with such a pledge that others must
believe—completely ready for his service.
    And he to me: "Because of what I hear,   106
you leave a trace within me—one so clear,
Lethe itself can't blur or cancel it.
    But if your words have now sworn truthfully,   109
do tell me why it is that you have shown
in speech and gaze that I am dear to you."
    And I to him: "It's your sweet lines that, for   112
as long as modern usage lasts, will still
make dear their very inks." "Brother," he said,
    "he there, whom I point out to you"—he showed   115
us one who walked ahead—"he was a better
artisan of the mother tongue, surpassing

La gente che non vien con noi, offese
di ciò per che già Cesar, trïunfando,
'Regina' contra sé chiamar s'intese:

   però si parton 'Soddoma' gridando,   79
rimproverando a sé com' hai udito,
e aiutan l'arsura vergognando.

   Nostro peccato fu ermafrodito;   82
ma perché non servammo umana legge,
seguendo come bestie l'appetito,

   in obbrobrio di noi, per noi si legge,   85
quando partinci, il nome di colei
che s'imbestiò ne le 'mbestiate schegge.

   Or sai nostri atti e di che fummo rei: 88
se forse a nome vuo' saper chi semo,
tempo non è di dire, e non saprei.

   Farotti ben di me volere scemo: 91
son Guido Guinizzelli, e già mi purgo
per ben dolermi prima ch'a lo stremo."

   Quali ne la tristizia di Ligurgo   94
si fer due figli a riveder la madre,
tal mi fec' io, ma non a tanto insurgo,

   quand' io odo nomar sé stesso il padre   97
mio e de li altri miei miglior che mai
rime d'amor usar dolci e leggiadre;

   e sanza udire e dir pensoso andai   100
lunga fïata rimirando lui,
né, per lo foco, in là più m'appressai.

   Poi che di riguardar pasciuto fui,   103
tutto m'offersi pronto al suo servigio
con l'affermar che fa credere altrui.

   Ed elli a me: "Tu lasci tal vestigio,   106
per quel ch'i' odo, in me, e tanto chiaro,
che Letè nol può tòrre né far bigio.

   Ma se le tue parole or ver giuraro,   109
dimmi che è cagion per che dimostri
nel dire e nel guardar d'avermi caro."

   E io a lui: "Li dolci detti vostri,   112
che, quanto durerà l'uso moderno,
faranno cari ancora i loro incostri."

   "O frate," disse, "questi ch'io ti cerno   115
col dito," e additò un spirto innanzi,
"fu miglior fabbro del parlar materno.

all those who wrote their poems of love or prose   118
romances—let the stupid ones contend,
who think that from Limoges there came the best.

    They credit rumor rather than the truth,   121
allowing their opinion to be set
before they hear what art or reason says.

    So, many of our fathers once persisted,   124
voice after voice, in giving to Guittone
the prize—but then, with most, the truth prevailed.

    Now if you are so amply privileged   127
that you will be admitted to the cloister
where Christ is abbot of the college, then

    pray say, for me, to Him, a Paternoster—   130
that is, as much of it as those in this
place need, since we have lost the power to sin.''

    Then, to make place, perhaps, for those behind him,   133
he disappeared into the fire, just as
a fish, through water, plunges toward the bottom.

    Saying that my desire was making ready   136
a place of welcome for his name, I moved
ahead a little, toward the one who had

    been pointed out to me. And he spoke freely: 139
"So does your courteous request please me—
I neither could nor would conceal myself

    from you. I am Arnaut, who, going, weep   142
and sing; with grief, I see my former folly;
with joy, I see the hoped-for day draw near.

    Now, by the Power that conducts you to   145
the summit of the stairway, I pray you:
remember, at time opportune, my pain!''

    Then, in the fire that refines, he hid.   148

Versi d'amore e prose di romanzi

soverchiò tutti; e lascia dir li stolti

che quel di Lemosì credon ch'avanzi.

    A voce più ch'al ver drizzan li volti,

e così ferman sua oppinïone

prima ch'arte o ragion per lor s'ascolti.

    Così fer molti antichi di Guittone,

di grido in grido pur lui dando pregio,

fin che l'ha vinto il ver con più persone.

    Or se tu hai sì ampio privilegio,

che licito ti sia l'andare al chiostro

nel quale è Cristo abate del collegio,

    falli per me un dir d'un paternostro,

quanto bisogna a noi di questo mondo,

dove poter peccar non è più nostro."

    Poi, forse per dar luogo altrui secondo

che presso avea, disparve per lo foco,

come per l'acqua il pesce andando al fondo.

    Io mi fei al mostrato innanzi un poco,

e dissi ch'al suo nome il mio disire

apparecchiava grazïoso loco.

    El cominciò liberamente a dire:

"*Tan m'abellis vostre cortes deman,*

qu'ieu no me puesc ni voill a vos cobrire.

    Ieu sui Arnaut, que plor e vau cantan;

consiros vei la passada folor,

e vei jausen lo joi qu'esper, denan.

    Ara vos prec, per aquella valor

que vos guida al som de l'escalina,

sovenha vos a temps de ma dolor!"

    Poi s'ascose nel foco che li affina.

CANTO XXVII

Just as, there where its Maker shed His blood,
the sun shed its first rays, and Ebro lay
beneath high Libra, and the ninth hour's rays

were scorching Ganges' waves; so here, the sun   4
stood at the point of day's departure when
God's angel—happy—showed himself to us.

He stood along the edge, beyond the flames,   7
singing "*Beati mundo corde*" in
a voice that had more life than ours can claim.

Then: "Holy souls, you cannot move ahead   10
unless the fire has stung you first: enter
the flames and don't be deaf to song you'll hear

beyond," he said when we were close to him;   13
and when I heard him say this, I became
like one who has been laid within the grave.

I joined my hands and stretched them out to fend   16
the flames, watching the fire, imagining
clearly the human bodies I'd once seen

burning. My gentle escorts turned to me,   19
and Virgil said: "My son, though there may be
suffering here, there is no death. Remember,

remember! If I guided you to safety   22
even upon the back of Geryon,
then now, closer to God, what shall I do?

Be sure: although you were to spend a full   25
one thousand years within this fire's center,
your head would not be balder by one hair.

And if you think I am deceiving you,   28
draw closer to the flames, let your own hands
try out, within the fire, your clothing's hem—

put down, by now put down, your every fear;   31
turn toward the fire, and enter, confident!"
But I was stubborn, set against my conscience.

From the Seventh Terrace to the threshold of the Earthly Paradise.
Sunset. The angel of chastity. The Sixth Beatitude. Dante's fear of
entering the flames. Virgil's exhortation. The passage through
fire. Dante's sleep and dream of Leah, exemplar of the active
life, and Rachel, exemplar of the contemplative life. Dante's
waking. Virgil's last words to him.

Sì come quando i primi raggi vibra
là dove il suo fattor lo sangue sparse,
cadendo Ibero sotto l'alta Libra,

e l'onde in Gange da nona rïarse,   4
sì stava il sole; onde 'l giorno sen giva,
come l'angel di Dio lieto ci apparse.

Fuor de la fiamma stava in su la riva,   7
e cantava *"Beati mundo corde!"*
in voce assai più che la nostra viva.

Poscia "Più non si va, se pria non morde,   10
anime sante, il foco: intrate in esso,
e al cantar di là non siate sorde,"

ci disse come noi li fummo presso;   13
per ch'io divenni tal, quando lo 'ntesi,
qual è colui che ne la fossa è messo.

In su le man commesse mi protesi,   16
guardando il foco e imaginando forte
umani corpi già veduti accesi.

Volsersi verso me le buone scorte;   19
e Virgilio mi disse: "Figliuol mio,
qui può esser tormento, ma non morte.

Ricorditi, ricorditi! E se io   22
sovresso Gerïon ti guidai salvo,
che farò ora presso più a Dio?

Credi per certo che se dentro a l'alvo   25
di questa fiamma stessi ben mille anni,
non ti potrebbe far d'un capel calvo.

E se tu forse credi ch'io t'inganni,   28
fatti ver' lei, e fatti far credenza
con le tue mani al lembo d'i tuoi panni.

Pon giù omai, pon giù ogne temenza;   31
volgiti in qua e vieni: entra sicuro!"
E io pur fermo e contra coscïenza.

When he saw me still halting, obstinate,   34
he said, somewhat perplexed: "Now see, son: this
wall stands between you and your Beatrice."

As, at the name of Thisbe, Pyramus,   37
about to die, opened his eyes, and saw her
(when then the mulberry became bloodred),

so, when my stubbornness had softened, I,   40
hearing the name that's always flowering
within my mind, turned to my knowing guide.

At which he shook his head and said: "And would   43
you have us stay along this side?"—then smiled
as one smiles at a child fruit has beguiled.

Then he, ahead of me, entered the fire;   46
and he asked Statius, who had walked between us
before, dividing us, to go behind.

No sooner was I in that fire than I'd   49
have thrown myself in molten glass to find
coolness—because those flames were so intense.

My gentle father, who would comfort me,   52
kept talking, as we walked, of Beatrice,
saying: "I seem to see her eyes already."

A voice that sang beyond us was our guide;   55
and we, attentive to that voice, emerged
just at the point where it began to climb.

"*Venite, benedicti Patris mei*,"   58
it sang within a light that overcame me:
I could not look at such intensity.

"The sun departs," it added; "evening comes;   61
don't stay your steps, but hurry on before
the west grows dark." The path we took climbed straight

within the rock, and its direction was   64
such that, in front of me, my body blocked
the rays of sun, already low behind us.

And we had only tried a few steps when   67
I and my sages sensed the sun had set
because the shadow I had cast was spent.

Before one color came to occupy   70
that sky in all of its immensity
and night was free to summon all its darkness,

each of us made one of those stairs his bed: 73
the nature of the mountain had so weakened
our power and desire to climb ahead.

Quando mi vide star pur fermo e duro,   34
turbato un poco disse: "Or vedi, figlio:
tra Bëatrice e te è questo muro."

Come al nome di Tisbe aperse il ciglio   37
Piramo in su la morte, e riguardolla,
allor che 'l gelso diventò vermiglio;

così, la mia durezza fatta solla,   40
mi volsi al savio duca, udendo il nome
che ne la mente sempre mi rampolla.

Ond' ei crollò la fronte e disse: "Come!   43
volenci star di qua?"; indi sorrise
come al fanciul si fa ch'è vinto al pome.

Poi dentro al foco innanzi mi si mise,   46
pregando Stazio che venisse retro,
che pria per lunga strada ci divise.

Sì com' fui dentro, in un bogliente vetro   49
gittato mi sarei per rinfrescarmi,
tant' era ivi lo 'ncendio sanza metro.

Lo dolce padre mio, per confortarmi,   52
pur di Beatrice ragionando andava,
dicendo: "Li occhi suoi già veder parmi."

Guidavaci una voce che cantava   55
di là; e noi, attenti pur a lei,
venimmo fuor là ove si montava.

"Venite, benedicti Patris mei,"   58
sonò dentro a un lume che lì era,
tal che mi vinse e guardar nol potei.

"Lo sol sen va," soggiunse, "e vien la sera;   61
non v'arrestate, ma studiate il passo,
mentre che l'occidente non si annera."

Dritta salia la via per entro 'l sasso   64
verso tal parte ch'io toglieva i raggi
dinanzi a me del sol ch'era già basso.

E di pochi scaglion levammo i saggi,   67
che 'l sol corcar, per l'ombra che si spense,
sentimmo dietro e io e li miei saggi.

E pria che 'n tutte le sue parti immense   70
fosse orizzonte fatto d'uno aspetto,
e notte avesse tutte sue dispense,

ciascun di noi d'un grado fece letto;   73
ché la natura del monte ci affranse
la possa del salir più e 'l diletto.

Like goats that, when they grazed, were swift and tameless
along the mountain peaks, but now are sated,
and rest and ruminate—while the sun blazes—

untroubled, in the shadows, silently,   79
watched over by the herdsman as he leans
upon his staff and oversees their peace;

or like the herdsman in the open fields,   82
spending the night beside his quiet flock,
watching to see that no beast drives them off;

such were all three of us at that point—they   85
were like the herdsmen, I was like the goat;
upon each side of us, high rock walls rose.

From there, one saw but little of the sky,   88
but in that little, I could see the stars
brighter and larger than they usually are.

But while I watched the stars, in reverie,   91
sleep overcame me—sleep, which often sees,
before it happens, what is yet to be.

It was the hour, I think, when Cytherea,   94
who always seems aflame with fires of love,
first shines upon the mountains from the east,

that, in my dream, I seemed to see a woman   97
both young and fair; along a plain she gathered
flowers, and even as she sang, she said:

"Whoever asks my name, know that I'm Leah,   100
and I apply my lovely hands to fashion
a garland of the flowers I have gathered.

To find delight within this mirror I   103
adorn myself; whereas my sister Rachel
never deserts her mirror; there she sits

all day; she longs to see her fair eyes gazing,   106
as I, to see my hands adorning, long:
she is content with seeing, I with labor."

And now, with the reflected lights that glow   109
before the dawn and, rising, are most welcome
to pilgrims as, returning, they near home,

the shadows fled upon all sides; my sleep   112
fled with them; and at this, I woke and saw
that the great teachers had already risen.

"Today your hungerings will find their peace   115
through that sweet fruit the care of mortals seeks
among so many branches." This, the speech,

Quali si stanno ruminando manse   76
le capre, state rapide e proterve
sovra le cime avante che sien pranse,

 tacite a l'ombra, mentre che 'l sol ferve, 79
guardate dal pastor, che 'n su la verga
poggiato s'è e lor di posa serve;

 e quale il mandrïan che fori alberga, 82
lungo il peculio suo queto pernotta,
guardando perché fiera non lo sperga;

 tali eravamo tutti e tre allotta, 85
io come capra, ed ei come pastori,
fasciati quinci e quindi d'alta grotta.

 Poco parer potea lì del di fori; 88
ma, per quel poco, vedea io le stelle
di lor solere e più chiare e maggiori.

 Sì ruminando e sì mirando in quelle, 91
mi prese il sonno; il sonno che sovente,
anzi che 'l fatto sia, sa le novelle.

 Ne l'ora, credo, che de l'orïente 94
prima raggiò nel monte Citerea,
che di foco d'amor par sempre ardente,

 giovane e bella in sogno mi parea 97
donna vedere andar per una landa
cogliendo fiori; e cantando dicea:

 "Sappia qualunque il mio nome dimanda 100
ch'i' mi son Lia, e vo movendo intorno
le belle mani a farmi una ghirlanda.

 Per piacermi a lo specchio, qui m'addorno; 103
ma mia suora Rachel mai non si smaga
dal suo miraglio, e siede tutto giorno.

 Ell' è d'i suoi belli occhi veder vaga 106
com' io de l'addornarmi con le mani;
lei lo vedere, e me l'ovrare appaga."

 E già per li splendori antelucani, 109
che tanto a' pellegrin surgon più grati,
quanto, tornando, albergan men lontani,

 le tenebre fuggian da tutti lati, 112
e 'l sonno mio con esse; ond' io leva'mi,
veggendo i gran maestri già levati.

 "Quel dolce pome che per tanti rami 115
cercando va la cura de' mortali,
oggi porrà in pace le tue fami."

the solemn words, that Virgil spoke to me; 118
and there were never tidings to compare,
in offering delight to me, with these.

My will on will to climb above was such 121
that at each step I took I felt the force
within my wings was growing for the flight.

When all the staircase lay beneath us and 124
we'd reached the highest step, then Virgil set
his eyes insistently on me and said:

"My son, you've seen the temporary fire 127
and the eternal fire; you have reached
the place past which my powers cannot see.

I've brought you here through intellect and art; 130
from now on, let your pleasure be your guide;
you're past the steep and past the narrow paths.

Look at the sun that shines upon your brow; 133
look at the grasses, flowers, and the shrubs
born here, spontaneously, of the earth.

Among them, you can rest or walk until 136
the coming of the glad and lovely eyes—
those eyes that, weeping, sent me to your side.

Await no further word or sign from me: 139
your will is free, erect, and whole—to act
against that will would be to err: therefore

I crown and miter you over yourself." 142

Virgilio inverso me queste cotali
parole usò; e mai non furo strenne
che fosser di piacere a queste iguali.

Tanto voler sopra voler mi venne   121
de l'esser sù, ch'ad ogne passo poi
al volo mi sentia crescer le penne.

Come la scala tutta sotto noi   124
fu corsa e fummo in su 'l grado superno,
in me ficcò Virgilio li occhi suoi,

e disse: "Il temporal foco e l'etterno   127
veduto hai, figlio; e se' venuto in parte
dov' io per me più oltre non discerno.

Tratto t'ho qui con ingegno e con arte;   130
lo tuo piacere omai prendi per duce;
fuor se' de l'erte vie, fuor se' de l'arte.

Vedi lo sol che 'n fronte ti riluce;   133
vedi l'erbette, i fiori e li arbuscelli
che qui la terra sol da sé produce.

Mentre che vegnan lieti li occhi belli   136
che, lagrimando, a te venir mi fenno,
seder ti puoi e puoi andar tra elli.

Non aspettar mio dir più né mio cenno;   139
libero, dritto e sano è tuo arbitrio,
e fallo fora non fare a suo senno:

per ch'io te sovra te corono e mitrio."   142

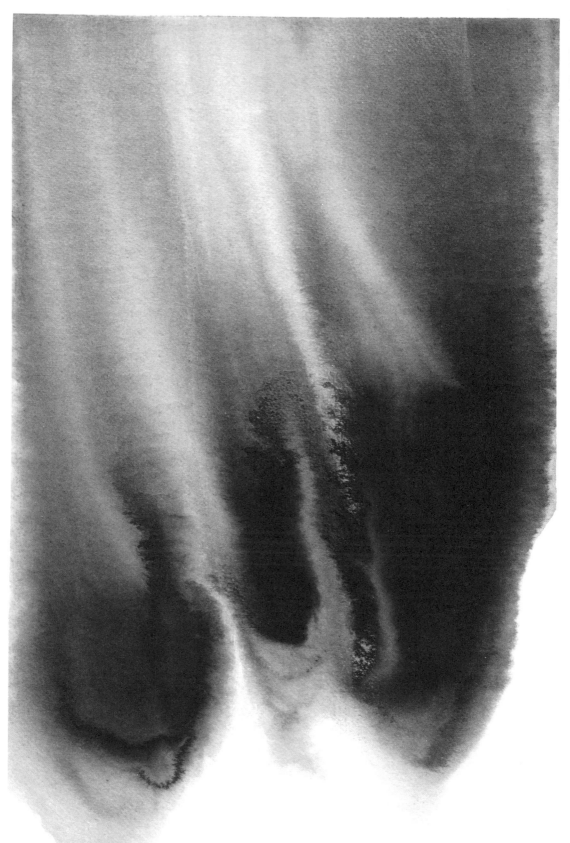

XXVII · 51

XXVIII · 40

CANTO XXVIII

Now keen to search within, to search around
that forest—dense, alive with green, divine—
which tempered the new day before my eyes,

without delay, I left behind the rise   4
and took the plain, advancing slowly, slowly
across the ground where every part was fragrant.

A gentle breeze, which did not seem to vary   7
within itself, was striking at my brow
but with no greater force than a kind wind's,

a wind that made the trembling boughs—they all   10
bent eagerly—incline in the direction
of morning shadows from the holy mountain;

but they were not deflected with such force   13
as to disturb the little birds upon
the branches in the practice of their arts;

for to the leaves, with song, birds welcomed those   16
first hours of the morning joyously,
and leaves supplied the burden to their rhymes—

just like the wind that sounds from branch to branch   19
along the shore of Classe, through the pines
when Aeolus has set Sirocco loose.

Now, though my steps were slow, I'd gone so far   22
into the ancient forest that I could
no longer see where I had made my entry;

and there I came upon a stream that blocked   25
the path of my advance; its little waves
bent to the left the grass along its banks.

All of the purest waters here on earth,   28
when matched against that stream, would seem to be
touched by impurity; it hides no thing—

that stream—although it moves, dark, dark, beneath   31
the never-ending shadows, which allow
no ray of sun or moon to reach those waters.

The Earthly Paradise. The divine forest. Arrival at the stream of Lethe. Apparition of a woman (Matilda). Her explanation of the origin of winds and water in the forest. The ancient poets and the golden age.

CANTO XXVIII 247

Vago già di cercar dentro e dintorno
la divina foresta spessa e viva,
ch'a li occhi temperava il novo giorno,

sanza più aspettar, lasciai la riva,   4
prendendo la campagna lento lento
su per lo suol che d'ogne parte auliva.

Un'aura dolce, sanza mutamento   7
avere in sé, mi feria per la fronte
non di più colpo che soave vento;

per cui le fronde, tremolando, pronte   10
tutte quante piegavano a la parte
u' la prim' ombra gitta il santo monte;

non però dal loro esser dritto sparte   13
tanto, che li augelletti per le cime
lasciasser d'operare ogne lor arte;

ma con piena letizia l'ore prime,   16
cantando, ricevieno intra le foglie,
che tenevan bordone a le sue rime,

tal qual di ramo in ramo si raccoglie   19
per la pineta in su 'l lito di Chiassi,
quand' Eolo scilocco fuor discioglie.

Già m'avean trasportato i lenti passi   22
dentro a la selva antica tanto, ch'io
non potea rivedere ond' io mi 'ntrassi;

ed ecco più andar mi tolse un rio,   25
che 'nver' sinistra con sue picciole onde
piegava l'erba che 'n sua ripa uscìo.

Tutte l'acque che son di qua più monde,   28
parrieno avere in sé mistura alcuna
verso di quella, che nulla nasconde,

avvegna che si mova bruna bruna   31
sotto l'ombra perpetüa, che mai
raggiar non lascia sole ivi né luna.

I halted, and I set my eyes upon   34
the farther bank, to look at the abundant
variety of newly-flowered boughs;

   and there, just like a thing that, in appearing   37
most suddenly, repels all other thoughts,
so great is the astonishment it brings,

   I saw a solitary woman moving,   40
singing, and gathering up flower on flower—
the flowers that colored all of her pathway.

   "I pray you, lovely lady, you who warm   43
yourself with rays of love, if I may trust
your looks—which often evidence the heart—

   may it please you," I asked of her, "to move   46
ahead and closer to this river, so
that I may understand what you are singing.

   You have reminded me of where and what—   49
just when her mother was deprived of her
and she deprived of spring—Proserpina was."

   As, when she turns, a woman, dancing, keeps   52
her soles close to the ground and to each other
and scarcely lets one foot precede the other,

   so did she turn, upon the little red   55
and yellow flowers, to me, no differently
than would a virgin, lowering chaste eyes.

   I had beseeched, and I was satisfied,   58
for she approached so close that the sweet sound
that reached me then became intelligible.

   No sooner had she reached the point where that   61
fair river's waves could barely bathe the grass,
than she gave me this gift: lifting her eyes.

   I do not think a light so bright had shone   64
beneath the lids of Venus when her son
pierced her in extraordinary fashion.

   Erect, along the farther bank, she smiled,   67
her hands entwining varicolored flowers,
which that high land, needing no seed, engenders.

   The river kept us just three steps apart;   70
but even Hellespont, where Xerxes crossed—
a case that still curbs all men's arrogance—

   did not provoke more hatred in Leander   73
when rough seas ran from Abydos to Sestos,
than hatred I bestowed upon that river

Coi piè ristetti e con li occhi passai
di là dal fiumicello, per mirare
la gran varïazion d'i freschi mai;

e là m'apparve, sì com' elli appare
subitamente cosa che disvia
per maraviglia tutto altro pensare,

una donna soletta che si gia
e cantando e scegliendo fior da fiore
ond' era pinta tutta la sua via.

"Deh, bella donna, che a' raggi d'amore
ti scaldi, s'i' vo' credere a' sembianti
che soglion esser testimon del core,

vegnati in voglia di trarreti avanti,"
diss' io a lei, "verso questa rivera,
tanto ch'io possa intender che tu canti.

Tu mi fai rimembrar dove e qual era
Proserpina nel tempo che perdette
la madre lei, ed ella primavera."

Come si volge, con le piante strette
a terra e intra sé, donna che balli,
e piede innanzi piede a pena mette,

volsesi in su i vermigli e in su i gialli
fioretti verso me, non altrimenti
che vergine che li occhi onesti avvalli;

e fece i prieghi miei esser contenti,
sì appressando sé, che 'l dolce suono
veniva a me co' suoi intendimenti.

Tosto che fu là dove l'erbe sono
bagnate già da l'onde del bel fiume,
di levar li occhi suoi mi fece dono.

Non credo che splendesse tanto lume
sotto le ciglia a Venere, trafitta
dal figlio fuor di tutto suo costume.

Ella ridea da l'altra riva dritta,
trattando più color con le sue mani,
che l'alta terra sanza seme gitta.

Tre passi ci facea il fiume lontani;
ma Elesponto, là 've passò Serse,
ancora freno a tutti orgogli umani,

più odio da Leandro non sofferse
per mareggiare intra Sesto e Abido,
che quel da me perch' allor non s'aperse.

when it refused to open. She began: 76
"You are new here and may—because I smile
in this place, chosen to be mankind's nest—
   wonder, perplexed, unable to detect   79
the cause; but light to clear your intellect
is in the psalm beginning 'Delectasti.'
   And you, who have stepped forward, who beseeched me,
tell me if you'd hear more; I have come ready
for all your questions till you're satisfied."
   I said: "The water and the murmuring forest   85
contend, in me, against the recent credence
I gave to words denying their existence."
   At this she said: "I'll tell you how the source   88
of your amazement has its special cause;
I'll clear the cloud that's left you so distraught.
   The Highest Good, whose sole joy is Himself,   91
made man to be—and to enact—good; He
gave man this place as pledge of endless peace.
   Man's fault made brief his stay here; and man's fault   94
made him exchange frank laughter and sweet sport
for lamentation and for anxiousness.
   Below this mountain, land and water vapors,   97
which follow heat as far as they are able,
produce their perturbations; to prevent
   them from molesting man placed here, this mountain
rose up this close to Heaven; from the point
where its gate locks, it's free of such disturbance.
   Now, since all of the atmosphere revolves   103
within a circle, moved by the first circling,
unless its round is broken at some point,
   against this height, which stands completely free   106
within the living air, that motion strikes;
and since these woods are dense, they echo it.
   And when a plant is struck, its power is such   109
that it impregnates air with seeding force;
the air, revolving, casts this seed abroad;
   the other hemisphere, depending on   112
the nature of its land and sky, conceives
and bears, from diverse powers, diverse trees.
   If what I've said were known, you would not need   115
to be amazed on earth when growing things
take root but have no seed that can be seen.

"Voi siete nuovi, e forse perch' io rido,"
cominciò ella, "in questo luogo eletto
a l'umana natura per suo nido,

     maravigliando tienvi alcun sospetto;   79
ma luce rende il salmo *Delectasti*,
che puote disnebbiar vostro intelletto.

     E tu che se' dinanzi e mi pregasti,   82
dì s'altro vuoli udir; ch'i' venni presta
ad ogne tua question tanto che basti."

     "L'acqua," diss' io, "e 'l suon de la foresta   85
impugnan dentro a me novella fede
di cosa ch'io udi' contraria a questa."

     Ond' ella: "Io dicerò come procede   88
per sua cagion ciò ch'ammirar ti face,
e purgherò la nebbia che ti fiede.

     Lo sommo Ben, che solo esso a sé piace,   91
fé l'uom buono e a bene, e questo loco
diede per arr' a lui d'etterna pace.

     Per sua difalta qui dimorò poco;   94
per sua difalta in pianto e in affanno
cambiò onesto riso e dolce gioco.

     Perché 'l turbar che sotto da sé fanno   97
l'essalazion de l'acqua e de la terra,
che quanto posson dietro al calor vanno,

     a l'uomo non facesse alcuna guerra,   100
questo monte salìo verso 'l ciel tanto,
e libero n'è d'indi ove si serra.

     Or perché in circuito tutto quanto   103
l'aere si volge con la prima volta,
se non li è rotto il cerchio d'alcun canto,

     in questa altezza ch'è tutta disciolta   106
ne l'aere vivo, tal moto percuote,
e fa sonar la selva perch' è folta;

     e la percossa pianta tanto puote,   109
che de la sua virtute l'aura impregna
e quella poi, girando, intorno scuote;

     e l'altra terra, secondo ch'è degna   112
per sé e per suo ciel, concepe e figlia
di diverse virtù diverse legna.

     Non parrebbe di là poi maraviglia,   115
udito questo, quando alcuna pianta
sanza seme palese vi s'appiglia.

And you must know: the holy plain on which 118
you find yourself is full of every seed;
and it has fruit that—there—cannot be gathered.

The water that you see does not spring from 121
a vein that vapor—cold-condensed—restores,
like rivers that acquire or lose their force;

it issues from a pure and changeless fountain, 124
which by the will of God regains as much
as, on two sides, it pours and it divides.

On this side it descends with power to end 127
one's memory of sin; and on the other,
it can restore recall of each good deed.

To one side, it is Lethe; on the other, 130
Eunoe; neither stream is efficacious
unless the other's waters have been tasted:

their savor is above all other sweetness. 133
Although your thirst might well be satisfied
even if I revealed no more to you,

I'll give you freely, too, a corollary; 136
nor do I think my words will be less welcome
to you if they extend beyond my promise.

Those ancients who in poetry presented 139
the golden age, who sang its happy state,
perhaps, in their Parnassus, dreamt this place.

Here, mankind's root was innocent; and here 142
were every fruit and never-ending spring;
these streams—the nectar of which poets sing."

Then I turned round completely, and I faced 145
my poets; I could see that they had heard
with smiles this final corollary spoken;

that done, my eyes returned to the fair woman. 148

E saper dei che la campagna santa
dove tu se', d'ogne semenza è piena,
e frutto ha in sé che di là non si schianta.

L'acqua che vedi non surge di vena   121
che ristori vapor che gel converta,
come fiume ch'acquista e perde lena;

ma esce di fontana salda e certa,   124
che tanto dal voler di Dio riprende,
quant' ella versa da due parti aperta.

Da questa parte con virtù discende   127
che toglie altrui memoria del peccato;
da l'altra d'ogne ben fatto la rende.

Quinci Letè; così da l'altro lato   130
Eünoè si chiama, e non adopra
se quinci e quindi pria non è gustato:

a tutti altri sapori esto è di sopra.   133
E avvegna ch'assai possa esser sazia
la sete tua perch' io più non ti scuopra,

darotti un corollario ancor per grazia;   136
né credo che 'l mio dir ti sia men caro,
se oltre promession teco si spazia.

Quelli ch'anticamente poetaro   139
l'età de l'oro e suo stato felice,
forse in Parnaso esto loco sognaro.

Qui fu innocente l'umana radice;   142
qui primavera sempre e ogne frutto;
nettare è questo di che ciascun dice.''

Io mi rivolsi 'n dietro allora tutto   145
a' miei poeti, e vidi che con riso
udito avëan l'ultimo costrutto;

poi a la bella donna torna' il viso.   148

CANTO XXIX

Her words were done, but without interruption
she sang—like an enamored woman—thus:
"Beati quorum tecta sunt peccata!"

And just as nymphs who used to walk alone   4
among the woodland shadows, some desiring
to see and some to flee the sun, so she

moved countercurrent as she walked along   7
the riverbank; and following her short
footsteps with my own steps, I matched her pace.

Her steps and mine together did not sum   10
one hundred when the banks, still parallel,
so curved about that I was facing east.

Nor had we gone much farther on that path   13
when she turned fully round toward me and said:
"My brother, look and listen"; and I saw

a sudden radiance that swept across   16
the mighty forest on all sides—and I
was wondering if lightning had not struck.

But since, when lightning strikes, it stops at once,   19
while that light, lingering, increased its force,
within my mind I asked: "What thing is this?"

And through the incandescent air there ran   22
sweet melody; at which, just indignation
made me rebuke the arrogance of Eve

because, where earth and heaven were obedient,   25
a solitary woman, just created,
found any veil at all beyond endurance;

if she had been devout beneath her veil,   28
I should have savored those ineffable
delights before, and for a longer time.

While I moved on, completely rapt, among   31
so many first fruits of eternal pleasure,
and longing for still greater joys, the air

The Earthly Paradise. The banks of the Lethe. Sudden light and melody. Invocation to the Muses. The extraordinary procession. The seven candelabra. The seven pennants. The twenty-four elders. The four animals. The chariot drawn by a griffin. The seven women. Seven more elders. The sudden halt.

CANTO XXIX 255

Cantando come donna innamorata,
continüò col fin di sue parole:
"*Beati quorum tecta sunt peccata!*"

E come ninfe che si givan sole   4
per le salvatiche ombre, disïando
qual di veder, qual di fuggir lo sole,

allor si mosse contra 'l fiume, andando   7
su per la riva; e io pari di lei,
picciol passo con picciol seguitando.

Non eran cento tra ' suoi passi e ' miei,   10
quando le ripe igualmente dier volta,
per modo ch'a levante mi rendei.

Né ancor fu così nostra via molta,   13
quando la donna tutta a me si torse,
dicendo: "Frate mio, guarda e ascolta."

Ed ecco un lustro sùbito trascorse   16
da tutte parti per la gran foresta,
tal che di balenar mi mise in forse.

Ma perché 'l balenar, come vien, resta,   19
e quel, durando, più e più splendeva,
nel mio pensier dicea: "Che cosa è questa?"

E una melodia dolce correva   22
per l'aere luminoso; onde buon zelo
mi fé riprender l'ardimento d'Eva,

che là dove ubidia la terra e 'l cielo,   25
femmina, sola e pur testé formata,
non sofferse di star sotto alcun velo;

sotto 'l qual se divota fosse stata,   28
avrei quelle ineffabili delizie
sentite prima e più lunga fïata.

Mentr' io m'andava tra tante primizie   31
de l'etterno piacer tutto sospeso,
e disïoso ancora a più letizie,

before us altered underneath the green   34
branches, becoming like an ardent fire,
and now the sweet sound was distinctly song.

O Virgins, sacrosanct, if I have ever,   37
for your sake, suffered vigils, cold, and hunger,
great need makes me entreat my recompense.

Now Helicon must pour its fountains for me,   40
Urania must help me with her choir
to put in verses things hard to conceive.

Not far beyond, we made out seven trees   43
of gold, though the long stretch of air between
those trees and us had falsified their semblance;

but when I'd drawn so close that things perceived   46
through mingled senses, which delude, did not,
now they were nearer, lose their real features,

the power that offers reason matter judged   49
those trees to be—what they were—candelabra,
and what those voices sang to be "Hosanna."

The upper part of those fair candles flamed   52
more radiantly than the midmonth moon
shines at midnight in an untroubled sky.

Full of astonishment, I turned to my   55
good Virgil; but he only answered me
with eyes that were no less amazed than mine.

Then I looked at the extraordinary   58
things that were moving toward us—but so slowly
that even brides just wed would move more quickly.

The woman chided me: "Why are you only   61
so eager to behold the living lights
and not in seeing what comes after them?"

Then I saw people following those candles,   64
as if behind their guides, and they wore white—
whiteness that, in this world, has never been.

The water, to my left, reflected flames,   67
and it reflected, too, my left-hand side
if I gazed into it, as in a mirror.

When I was at a point along my shore   70
where all that sundered me from them was water,
I stayed my steps in order to see better,

and I could see the candle flames move forward,   73
leaving the air behind them colored like
the strokes a painter's brush might have described,

dinanzi a noi, tal quale un foco acceso,
ci si fé l'aere sotto i verdi rami;
e 'l dolce suon per canti era già inteso.

O sacrosante Vergini, se fami,   37
freddi o vigilie mai per voi soffersi,
cagion mi sprona ch'io mercé vi chiami.

Or convien che Elicona per me versi,   40
e Uranìe m'aiuti col suo coro
forti cose a pensar mettere in versi.

Poco più oltre, sette alberi d'oro   43
falsava nel parere il lungo tratto
del mezzo ch'era ancor tra noi e loro;

ma quand' i' fui sì presso di lor fatto,   46
che l'obietto comun, che 'l senso inganna,
non perdea per distanza alcun suo atto,

la virtù ch'a ragion discorso ammanna,   49
sì com' elli eran candelabri apprese,
e ne le voci del cantare "Osanna."

Di sopra fiammeggiava il bello arnese   52
più chiaro assai che luna per sereno
di mezza notte nel suo mezzo mese.

Io mi rivolsi d'ammirazion pieno   55
al buon Virgilio, ed esso mi rispuose
con vista carca di stupor non meno.

Indi rendei l'aspetto a l'alte cose   58
che si movieno incontr' a noi sì tardi,
che foran vinte da novelle spose.

La donna mi sgridò: "Perché pur ardi   61
sì ne l'affetto de le vive luci,
e ciò che vien di retro a lor non guardi?"

Genti vid' io allor, come a lor duci,   64
venire appresso, vestite di bianco;
e tal candor di qua già mai non fuci.

L'acqua imprendëa dal sinistro fianco,   67
e rendea me la mia sinistra costa,
s'io riguardava in lei, come specchio anco.

Quand' io da la mia riva ebbi tal posta,   70
che solo il fiume mi facea distante,
per veder meglio ai passi diedi sosta,

e vidi le fiammelle andar davante,   73
lasciando dietro a sé l'aere dipinto,
e di tratti pennelli avean sembiante;

so that the air above that retinue   76
was streaked with seven bands in every hue
of which the rainbow's made and Delia's girdle.

    These pennants stretched far back, beyond my vision;   79
as for the width they filled, I judged the distance
between the outer ones to be ten paces.

    Beneath the handsome sky I have described,   82
twenty-four elders moved on, two by two,
and they had wreaths of lilies on their heads.

    And all were singing: "You, among the daughters   85
of Adam, *benedicta* are; and may
your beauties blessed be eternally."

    After the flowers and the other fresh   88
plants facing me, along the farther shore,
had seen those chosen people disappear,

    then—as in heaven, star will follow star—   91
the elders gone, four animals came on;
and each of them had green leaves as his crown;

    each had six wings as plumage, and those plumes   94
were full of eyes; they would be very like
the eyes of Argus, were his eyes alive.

    Reader, I am not squandering more rhymes   97
in order to describe their forms; since I
must spend elsewhere, I can't be lavish here;

    but read Ezekiel, for he has drawn   100
those animals approaching from the north;
with wings and cloud and fire, he painted them.

    And just as you will find them in his pages,   103
such were they here, except that John's with me
as to their wings; with him, John disagrees.

    The space between the four of them contained   106
a chariot—triumphal—on two wheels,
tied to a griffin's neck and drawn by him.

    His wings, stretched upward, framed the middle band
with three bands on each outer side, so that,
though he cleaved air, he left the bands intact.

    His wings—so high that they were lost to sight;   112
his limbs were gold as far as he was bird;
the rest of him was white mixed with bloodred.

    Not only did no chariot so handsome   115
gladden Rome's Africanus or Augustus
himself—even the Sun's own cannot match it;

sì che lì sopra rimanea distinto
di sette liste, tutte in quei colori
onde fa l'arco il Sole e Delia il cinto.

Questi ostendali in dietro eran maggiori   79
che la mia vista; e, quanto a mio avviso,
diece passi distavan quei di fori.

Sotto così bel ciel com' io diviso   82
ventiquattro seniori, a due a due,
coronati venien di fiordaliso.

Tutti cantavan: "*Benedicta* tue   85
ne le figlie d'Adamo, e benedette
sieno in etterno le bellezze tue!"

Poscia che i fiori e l'altre fresche erbette   88
a rimpetto di me da l'altra sponda
libere fuor da quelle genti elette,

sì come luce luce in ciel seconda,   91
vennero appresso lor quattro animali,
coronati ciascun di verde fronda.

Ognuno era pennuto di sei ali;   94
le penne piene d'occhi; e li occhi d'Argo,
se fosser vivi, sarebber cotali.

A descriver lor forme più non spargo   97
rime, lettor; ch'altra spesa mi strigne,
tanto ch'a questa non posso esser largo;

ma leggi Ezechïel, che li dipigne   100
come li vide da la fredda parte
venir con vento e con nube e con igne;

e quali i troverai ne le sue carte,   103
tali eran quivi, salvo ch'a le penne
Giovanni è meco e da lui si diparte.

Lo spazio dentro a lor quattro contenne   106
un carro, in su due rote, trïunfale,
ch'al collo d'un grifon tirato venne.

Esso tendeva in sù l'una e l'altra ale   109
tra la mezzana e le tre e tre liste,
sì ch'a nulla, fendendo, facea male.

Tanto salivan che non eran viste;   112
le membra d'oro avea quant' era uccello,
e bianche l'altre, di vermiglio miste.

Non che Roma di carro così bello   115
rallegrasse Affricano, o vero Augusto,
ma quel del Sol saria pover con ello;

the Sun's—which, gone astray, was burnt to cinders   118
because Earth offered up her pious prayers,
when Jove, in ways not known to us, was just.

   Three circling women, then advancing, danced   121
at the right wheel; the first of them, so red
that even in a flame she'd not be noted;

   the other seemed as if her flesh and bone   124
were fashioned out of emerald; the third
seemed to be newly fallen snow. And now

   the white one seemed to lead them, now the red;   127
and from the way in which the leader chanted,
the others took their pace, now slow, now rapid.

   Upon the left, four other women, dressed   130
in crimson, danced, depending on the cadence
of one of them, with three eyes in her head.

   Behind all of the group I have described   133
I saw two elders, different in their dress
but like in manner—grave and decorous.

   The first seemed to be one of the disciples   136
of great Hippocrates, whom nature made
for those who are her dearest living beings;

   the other showed an opposite concern—   139
his sword was bright and sharp, and even on
this near side of the river, I felt fear.

   Then I saw four of humble aspect; and,   142
when all the rest had passed, a lone old man,
his features keen, advanced, as if in sleep.

   The clothes these seven wore were like the elders'   145
in the first file, except that these had no
garlands of lilies round their brow; instead,

   roses and other red flowers wreathed their heads;   148
one seeing them less closely would have sworn
that all of them had flames above their eyebrows.

   And when the chariot stood facing me,   151
I heard a bolt of thunder; and it seemed
to block the path of that good company,

   which halted there, its emblems in the lead.   154

quel del Sol che, svïando, fu combusto   118
per l'orazion de la Terra devota,
quando fu Giove arcanamente giusto.

   Tre donne in giro da la destra rota   121
venian danzando; l'una tanto rossa
ch'a pena fora dentro al foco nota;

   l'altr' era come se le carni e l'ossa   124
fossero state di smeraldo fatte;
la terza parea neve testé mossa;

   e or parëan da la bianca tratte,   127
or da la rossa; e dal canto di questa
l'altre toglien l'andare e tarde e ratte.

   Da la sinistra quattro facean festa,   130
in porpore vestite, dietro al modo
d'una di lor ch'avea tre occhi in testa.

   Appresso tutto il pertrattato nodo   133
vidi due vecchi in abito dispari,
ma pari in atto e onesto e sodo.

   L'un si mostrava alcun de' famigliari   136
di quel sommo Ipocràte che natura
a li animali fé ch'ell' ha più cari;

   mostrava l'altro la contraria cura   139
con una spada lucida e aguta,
tal che di qua dal rio mi fé paura.

   Poi vidi quattro in umile paruta;   142
e di retro da tutti un vecchio solo
venir, dormendo, con la faccia arguta.

   E questi sette col primaio stuolo   145
erano abitüati, ma di gigli
dintorno al capo non facëan brolo,

   anzi di rose e d'altri fior vermigli;   148
giurato avria poco lontano aspetto
che tutti ardesser di sopra da' cigli.

   E quando il carro a me fu a rimpetto,   151
un tuon s'udì, e quelle genti degne
parvero aver l'andar più interdetto,

   fermandosi ivi con le prime insegne.   154

XXIX

106~154

CANTO XXX

When the first heaven's Seven-Stars had halted
(those stars that never rise or set, that are
not veiled except when sin beclouds our vision;
    those stars that, there, made everyone aware   4
of what his duty was, just as the Bear
below brings helmsmen home to harbor), then
    the truthful band that had come first between   7
the griffin and the Seven-Stars turned toward
that chariot as toward their peace, and one
    of them, as if sent down from Heaven, hymned   10
aloud, "*Veni, sponsa, de Libano*,"
three times, and all the others echoed him.
    Just as the blessed, at the Final Summons,   13
will rise up—ready—each out of his grave,
singing, with new-clothed voices, Alleluia,
    so did, *ad vocem tanti senis*, one   16
hundred of life's eternal ministers
and messengers rise from the godly chariot.
    All of them cried: "*Benedictus qui venis*,"   19
and, scattering flowers upward and around,
"*Manibus, oh, date lilia plenis.*"
    I have at times seen all the eastern sky   22
becoming rose as day began and seen,
adorned in lovely blue, the rest of heaven;
    and seen the sun's face rise so veiled that it   25
was tempered by the mist and could permit
the eye to look at length upon it; so,
    within a cloud of flowers that were cast   28
by the angelic hands and then rose up
and then fell back, outside and in the chariot,
    a woman showed herself to me; above   31
a white veil, she was crowned with olive boughs;
her cape was green; her dress beneath, flame-red.

The Earthly Paradise. The seven candelabra likened to seven stars (as if a Great Bear) of the Empyrean. The disappearance of Virgil. Beatrice's rebuke of Dante. The angels' compassion for Dante. Beatrice's accusations.

CANTO XXX 265

Quando il settentrïon del primo cielo,
che né occaso mai seppe né orto
né d'altra nebbia che di colpa velo,

e che faceva lì ciascuno accorto   4
di suo dover, come 'l più basso face
qual temon gira per venire a porto,

fermo s'affisse: la gente verace,   7
venuta prima tra 'l grifone ed esso,
al carro volse sé come a sua pace;

e un di loro, quasi da ciel messo,   10
"*Veni, sponsa, de Libano*" cantando
gridò tre volte, e tutti li altri appresso.

Quali i beati al novissimo bando   13
surgeran presti ognun di sua caverna,
la revestita voce alleluiando,

cotali in su la divina basterna   16
si levar cento, *ad vocem tanti senis*,
ministri e messaggier di vita etterna.

Tutti dicean: "*Benedictus qui venis!*"   19
e fior gittando e di sopra e dintorno,
"*Manibus, oh, date lilïa plenis!*"

Io vidi già nel cominciar del giorno   22
la parte orïental tutta rosata,
e l'altro ciel di bel sereno addorno;

e la faccia del sol nascere ombrata,   25
sì che per temperanza di vapori
l'occhio la sostenea lunga fïata:

così dentro una nuvola di fiori   28
che da le mani angeliche saliva
e ricadeva in giù dentro e di fori,

sovra candido vel cinta d'uliva   31
donna m'apparve, sotto verde manto
vestita di color di fiamma viva.

Within her presence, I had once been used   34
to feeling—trembling—wonder, dissolution;
but that was long ago. Still, though my soul,
        now she was veiled, could not see her directly,   37
by way of hidden force that she could move,
I felt the mighty power of old love.
        As soon as that deep force had struck my vision   40
(the power that, when I had not yet left
my boyhood, had already transfixed me),
        I turned around and to my left—just as   43
a little child, afraid or in distress,
will hurry to his mother—anxiously,
        to say to Virgil: "I am left with less   46
than one drop of my blood that does not tremble:
I recognize the signs of the old flame."
        But Virgil had deprived us of himself,   49
Virgil, the gentlest father, Virgil, he
to whom I gave my self for my salvation;
        and even all our ancient mother lost   52
was not enough to keep my cheeks, though washed
with dew, from darkening again with tears.
        "Dante, though Virgil's leaving you, do not   55
yet weep, do not weep yet; you'll need your tears
for what another sword must yet inflict."
        Just like an admiral who goes to stern   58
and prow to see the officers who guide
the other ships, encouraging their tasks;
        so, on the left side of the chariot   61
(I'd turned around when I had heard my name—
which, of necessity, I transcribe here),
        I saw the lady who had first appeared   64
to me beneath the veils of the angelic
flowers look at me across the stream.
        Although the veil she wore—down from her head,   67
which was encircled by Minerva's leaves—
did not allow her to be seen distinctly,
        her stance still regal and disdainful, she   70
continued, just as one who speaks but keeps
until the end the fiercest parts of speech:
        "Look here! For I am Beatrice, I am!   73
How were you able to ascend the mountain?
Did you not know that man is happy here?"

E lo spirito mio, che già cotanto
tempo era stato ch'a la sua presenza
non era di stupor, tremando, affranto,

     sanza de li occhi aver più conoscenza,   37
per occulta virtù che da lei mosse,
d'antico amor sentì la gran potenza.

     Tosto che ne la vista mi percosse   40
l'alta virtù che già m'avea trafitto
prima ch'io fuor di püerizia fosse,

     volsimi a la sinistra col respitto   43
col quale il fantolin corre a la mamma
quando ha paura o quando elli è afflitto,

     per dicere a Virgilio: "Men che dramma   46
di sangue m'è rimaso che non tremi:
conosco i segni de l'antica fiamma."

     Ma Virgilio n'avea lasciati scemi   49
di sé, Virgilio dolcissimo patre,
Virgilio a cui per mia salute die'mi;

     né quantunque perdeo l'antica matre,   52
valse a le guance nette di rugiada
che, lagrimando, non tornasser atre.

     "Dante, perché Virgilio se ne vada,   55
non pianger anco, non piangere ancora;
ché pianger ti conven per altra spada."

     Quasi ammiraglio che in poppa e in prora   58
viene a veder la gente che ministra
per li altri legni, e a ben far l'incora;

     in su la sponda del carro sinistra,   61
quando mi volsi al suon del nome mio,
che di necessità qui si registra,

     vidi la donna che pria m'appario   64
velata sotto l'angelica festa,
drizzar li occhi ver' me di qua dal rio.

     Tutto che 'l vel che le scendea di testa,   67
cerchiato de le fronde di Minerva,
non la lasciasse parer manifesta,

     regalmente ne l'atto ancor proterva   70
continüò come colui che dice
e 'l più caldo parlar dietro reserva:

     "Guardaci ben! Ben son, ben son Beatrice.   73
Come degnasti d'accedere al monte?
non sapei tu che qui è l'uom felice?"

My lowered eyes caught sight of the clear stream,　　76
but when I saw myself reflected there,
such shame weighed on my brow, my eyes drew back

　　and toward the grass; just as a mother seems　　79
harsh to her child, so did she seem to me—
how bitter is the savor of stern pity!

　　Her words were done. The angels—suddenly—　　82
sang, "*In te, Domine, speravi*"; but
their singing did not go past "*pedes meos.*"

　　Even as snow among the sap-filled trees　　85
along the spine of Italy will freeze
when gripped by gusts of the Slavonian winds,

　　then, as it melts, will trickle through itself—　　88
that is, if winds breathe north from shade-less lands—
just as, beneath the flame, the candle melts;

　　so I, before I'd heard the song of those　　91
whose notes always accompany the notes
of the eternal spheres, was without tears

　　and sighs; but when I heard the sympathy　　94
for me within their gentle harmonies,
as if they'd said: "Lady, why shame him so?"—

　　then did the ice that had restrained my heart　　97
become water and breath; and from my breast
and through my lips and eyes they issued—anguished.

　　Still standing motionless upon the left　　100
side of the chariot, she then addressed
the angels who had been compassionate:

"You oversee the never-ending day,　　103
and neither night nor sleep can steal from you
one step the world would take along its way;

　　therefore, I'm more concerned that my reply　　106
be understood by him who weeps beyond,
so that his sorrow's measure match his sin.

　　Not only through the work of the great spheres—　　109
which guide each seed to a determined end,
depending on what stars are its companions—

　　but through the bounty of the godly graces,　　112
which shower down from clouds so high that we
cannot approach them with our vision, he,

　　when young, was such—potentially—that any　　115
propensity innate in him would have
prodigiously succeeded, had he acted.

Li occhi mi cadder giù nel chiaro fonte; 76
ma veggendomi in esso, i trassi a l'erba,
tanta vergogna mi gravò la fronte.

Così la madre al figlio par superba, 79
com' ella parve a me; perché d'amaro
sente il sapor de la pietade acerba.

Ella si tacque; e li angeli cantaro 82
di sùbito *"In te, Domine, speravi"*;
ma oltre *"pedes meos"* non passaro.

Sì come neve tra le vive travi 85
per lo dosso d'Italia si congela,
soffiata e stretta da li venti schiavi,

poi, liquefatta, in sé stessa trapela, 88
pur che la terra che perde ombra spiri,
sì che par foco fonder la candela;

così fui sanza lagrime e sospiri 91
anzi 'l cantar di quei che notan sempre
dietro a le note de li etterni giri;

ma poi che 'ntesi ne le dolci tempre 94
lor compartire a me, par che se detto
avesser: "Donna, perché sì lo stempre?"

lo gel che m'era intorno al cor ristretto, 97
spirito e acqua fessi, e con angoscia
de la bocca e de li occhi uscì del petto.

Ella, pur ferma in su la detta coscia 100
del carro stando, a le sustanze pie
volse le sue parole così poscia:

"Voi vigilate ne l'etterno die, 103
sì che notte né sonno a voi non fura
passo che faccia il secol per sue vie;

onde la mia risposta è con più cura 106
che m'intenda colui che di là piagne,
perché sia colpa e duol d'una misura.

Non pur per ovra de le rote magne, 109
che drizzan ciascun seme ad alcun fine
secondo che le stelle son compagne,

ma per larghezza di grazie divine, 112
che sì alti vapori hanno a lor piova,
che nostre viste là non van vicine,

questi fu tal ne la sua vita nova 115
virtüalmente, ch'ogne abito destro
fatto averebbe in lui mirabil prova.

But where the soil has finer vigor, there 118
precisely—when untilled or badly seeded—
will that terrain grow wilder and more noxious.

My countenance sustained him for a while; 121
showing my youthful eyes to him, I led
him with me toward the way of righteousness.

As soon as I, upon the threshold of 124
my second age, had changed my life, he took
himself away from me and followed after

another; when, from flesh to spirit, I 127
had risen, and my goodness and my beauty
had grown, I was less dear to him, less welcome:

he turned his footsteps toward an untrue path; 130
he followed counterfeits of goodness, which
will never pay in full what they have promised.

Nor did the inspirations I received— 133
with which, in dream and otherwise, I called
him back—help me; he paid so little heed!

He fell so far there were no other means 136
to lead him to salvation, except this:
to let him see the people who were lost.

For this I visited the gateway of 139
the dead; to him who guided him above
my prayers were offered even as I wept.

The deep design of God would have been broken 142
if Lethe had been crossed and he had drunk
such waters but had not discharged the debt

of penitence that's paid when tears are shed." 145

Ma tanto più maligno e più silvestro 118
si fa 'l terren col mal seme e non cólto,
quant' elli ha più di buon vigor terrestre.

Alcun tempo il sostenni col mio volto: 121
mostrando li occhi giovanetti a lui,
meco il menava in dritta parte vòlto.

Sì tosto come in su la soglia fui 124
di mia seconda etade e mutai vita,
questi si tolse a me, e diessi altrui.

Quando di carne a spirto era salita, 127
e bellezza e virtù cresciuta m'era,
fu' io a lui men cara e men gradita;

e volse i passi suoi per via non vera, 130
imagini di ben seguendo false,
che nulla promession rendono intera.

Né l'impetrare ispirazion mi valse, 133
con le quali e in sogno e altrimenti
lo rivocai: sì poco a lui ne calse!

Tanto giù cadde, che tutti argomenti 136
a la salute sua eran già corti,
fuor che mostrarli le perdute genti.

Per questo visitai l'uscio d'i morti, 139
e a colui che l'ha qua sù condotto,
li preghi miei, piangendo, furon porti.

Alto fato di Dio sarebbe rotto, 142
se Letè si passasse e tal vivanda
fosse gustata sanza alcuno scotto

di pentimento che lagrime spanda." 145

CANTO XXXI

"O you upon the holy stream's far shore,"
so she, turning her speech's point against me—
even its edge had seemed too sharp—began

 again, without allowing interruption,   4
"tell, tell if this is true; for your confession
must be entwined with such self-accusation."

 My power of speech was so confounded that   7
my voice would move and yet was spent before
its organs had released it. She forbore

 a moment, then she said: "What are you thinking?   10
Reply to me, the water has not yet
obliterated your sad memories."

 Confusion mixed with fear compelled a *Yes*   13
out of my mouth, and yet that *Yes* was such—
one needed eyes to make out what it was.

 Just as a crossbow that is drawn too taut   16
snaps both its cord and bow when it is shot,
and arrow meets its mark with feeble force,

 so, caught beneath that heavy weight, I burst;   19
and I let tears and sighs pour forth; my voice
had lost its life along its passage out.

 At this she said: "In the desire for me   22
that was directing you to love the Good
beyond which there's no thing to draw our longing,

 what chains were strung, what ditches dug across   25
your path that, once you'd come upon them, caused
your loss of any hope of moving forward?

 What benefits and what allurements were   28
so evident upon the brow of others
that you had need to promenade before them?"

 After I had withheld a bitter sigh,   31
I scarcely had the voice for my reply,
but, laboring, my lips gave my words form.

*The Earthly Paradise. Dante's confession and new rebukes by
Beatrice. Dante's repentance and loss of his senses. Matilda's
immersion of Dante in Lethe. The four handmaids of Beatrice.
The mystery of the griffin. The other three women beseeching
Beatrice. Beatrice unveiled.*

"O tu che se' di là dal fiume sacro,"
volgendo suo parlare a me per punta,
che pur per taglio m'era paruto acro,

  ricominciò, seguendo sanza cunta,   4
"dì, dì se questo è vero; a tanta accusa
tua confession conviene esser congiunta."

  Era la mia virtù tanto confusa,   7
che la voce si mosse, e pria si spense
che da li organi suoi fosse dischiusa.

  Poco sofferse; poi disse: "Che pense?   10
Rispondi a me; ché le memorie triste
in te non sono ancor da l'acqua offense."

  Confusione e paura insieme miste   13
mi pinsero un tal "sì" fuor de la bocca,
al quale intender fuor mestier le viste.

  Come balestro frange, quando scocca   16
da troppa tesa, la sua corda e l'arco,
e con men foga l'asta il segno tocca,

  sì scoppia' io sottesso grave carco,   19
fuori sgorgando lagrime e sospiri,
e la voce allentò per lo suo varco.

  Ond' ella a me: "Per entro i mie' disiri, 22
che ti menavano ad amar lo bene
di là dal qual non è a che s'aspiri,

  quai fossi attraversati o quai catene   25
trovasti, per che del passare innanzi
dovessiti così spogliar la spene?

  E quali agevolezze o quali avanzi   28
ne la fronte de li altri si mostraro,
per che dovessi lor passeggiare anzi?"

  Dopo la tratta d'un sospiro amaro,   31
a pena ebbi la voce che rispuose,
e le labbra a fatica la formaro.

Weeping, I answered: "Mere appearances   34
turned me aside with their false loveliness,
as soon as I had lost your countenance."

And she: "Had you been silent or denied   37
what you confess, your guilt would not be less
in evidence: it's known by such a Judge!

But when the charge of sinfulness has burst   40
from one's own cheek, then in our court the whet-
stone turns and blunts our blade's own cutting edge.

Nevertheless, that you may feel more shame   43
for your mistake, and that—in time to come—
hearing the Sirens, you may be more strong,

have done with all the tears you sowed, and listen: 46
so shall you hear how, unto other ends,
my buried flesh should have directed you.

Nature or art had never showed you any   49
beauty that matched the lovely limbs in which
I was enclosed—limbs scattered now in dust;

and if the highest beauty failed you through   52
my death, what mortal thing could then induce
you to desire it? For when the first

arrow of things deceptive struck you, then   55
you surely should have lifted up your wings
to follow me, no longer such a thing.

No green young girl or other novelty—
such brief delight—should have weighed down your wings,
awaiting further shafts. The fledgling bird

must meet two or three blows before he learns,   61
but any full-fledged bird is proof against
the net that has been spread or arrow, aimed."

Even as children stand when they're ashamed,   64
eyes to the ground—they listen, silently
acknowledging their fault repentantly—

so did I stand; and she enjoined me: "Since   67
hearing alone makes you grieve so, lift up
your beard, and sight will bring you greater tears."

There's less resistance in the sturdy oak   70
to its uprooting by a wind from lands
of ours or lands of Iarbas than I showed

in lifting up my chin at her command;   73
I knew quite well—when she said "beard" but meant
my face—the poison in her argument.

Piangendo dissi: "Le presenti cose   34
col falso lor piacer volser miei passi,
tosto che 'l vostro viso si nascose."

Ed ella: "Se tacessi o se negassi   37
ciò che confessi, non fora men nota
la colpa tua: da tal giudice sassi!

Ma quando scoppia de la propria gota   40
l'accusa del peccato, in nostra corte
rivolge sé contra 'l taglio la rota.

Tuttavia, perché mo vergogna porte   43
del tuo errore, e perché altra volta,
udendo le serene, sie più forte,

pon giù il seme del piangere e ascolta: 46
sì udirai come in contraria parte
mover dovieti mia carne sepolta.

Mai non t'appresentò natura o arte   49
piacer, quanto le belle membra in ch'io
rinchiusa fui, e che so' 'n terra sparte;

e se 'l sommo piacer sì ti fallio   52
per la mia morte, qual cosa mortale
dovea poi trarre te nel suo disio?

Ben ti dovevi, per lo primo strale   55
de le cose fallaci, levar suso
di retro a me che non era più tale.

Non ti dovea gravar le penne in giuso,   58
ad aspettar più colpo, o pargoletta
o altra novità con sì breve uso.

Novo augelletto due o tre aspetta;   61
ma dinanzi da li occhi d'i pennuti
rete si spiega indarno o si saetta."

Quali fanciulli, vergognando, muti   64
con li occhi a terra stannosi, ascoltando
e sé riconoscendo e ripentuti,

tal mi stav' io; ed ella disse: "Quando   67
per udir se' dolente, alza la barba,
e prenderai più doglia riguardando."

Con men di resistenza si dibarba   70
robusto cerro, o vero al nostral vento
o vero a quel de la terra di Iarba,

ch'io non levai al suo comando il mento;   73
e quando per la barba il viso chiese,
ben conobbi il velen de l'argomento.

When I had raised my face upright, my eyes 76
were able to perceive that the first creatures
had paused and were no longer scattering flowers;

and still uncertain of itself, my vision 79
saw Beatrice turned toward the animal
that is, with its two natures, but one person.

Beneath her veil, beyond the stream, she seemed 82
so to surpass her former self in beauty
as, here on earth, she had surpassed all others.

The nettle of remorse so stung me then, 85
that those—among all other—things that once
most lured my love, became most hateful to me.

Such self-indictment seized my heart that I 88
collapsed, my senses slack; what I became
is known to her who was the cause of it.

Then, when my heart restored my outer sense, 91
I saw the woman whom I'd found alone,
standing above me, saying: "Hold, hold me!"

She'd plunged me, up to my throat, in the river, 94
and, drawing me behind her, she now crossed,
light as a gondola, along the surface.

When I was near the blessed shore, I heard 97
"*Asperges me*" so sweetly sung that I
cannot remember or, much less, transcribe it.

The lovely woman opened wide her arms; 100
she clasped my head, and then she thrust me under
to that point where I had to swallow water.

That done, she drew me out and led me, bathed, 103
into the dance of the four lovely women;
and each one placed her arm above my head.

"Here we are nymphs; in heaven, stars; before 106
she had descended to the world, we were
assigned, as her handmaids, to Beatrice;

we'll be your guides unto her eyes; but it 109
will be the three beyond, who see more deeply,
who'll help you penetrate her joyous light."

So, singing, they began; then, leading me 112
together with them to the griffin's breast,
where Beatrice, turned toward us, stood, they said:

"See that you are not sparing of your gaze: 115
before you we have set those emeralds
from which Love once had aimed his shafts at you."

E come la mia faccia si distese,
posarsi quelle prime creature
da loro aspersïon l'occhio comprese;

 e le mie luci, ancor poco sicure,   79
vider Beatrice volta in su la fiera
ch'è sola una persona in due nature.

 Sotto 'l suo velo e oltre la rivera   82
vincer pariemi più sé stessa antica,
vincer che l'altre qui, quand' ella c'era.

 Di penter sì mi punse ivi l'ortica,   85
che di tutte altre cose qual mi torse
più nel suo amor, più mi si fé nemica.

 Tanta riconoscenza il cor mi morse,   88
ch'io caddi vinto; e quale allora femmi,
salsi colei che la cagion mi porse.

 Poi, quando il cor virtù di fuor rendemmi,   91
la donna ch'io avea trovata sola
sopra me vidi, e dicea: "Tiemmi, tiemmi!"

 Tratto m'avea nel fiume infin la gola,   94
e tirandosi me dietro sen giva
sovresso l'acqua lieve come scola.

 Quando fui presso a la beata riva,   97
"*Asperges me*" sì dolcemente udissi,
che nol so rimembrar, non ch'io lo scriva.

 La bella donna ne le braccia aprissi;   100
abbracciommi la testa e mi sommerse
ove convenne ch'io l'acqua inghiottissi.

 Indi mi tolse, e bagnato m'offerse   103
dentro a la danza de le quattro belle;
e ciascuna del braccio mi coperse.

 "Noi siam qui ninfe e nel ciel siamo stelle;   106
pria che Beatrice discendesse al mondo,
fummo ordinate a lei per sue ancelle.

 Merrenti a li occhi suoi; ma nel giocondo   109
lume ch'è dentro aguzzeranno i tuoi
le tre di là, che miran più profondo."

 Così cantando cominciaro; e poi   112
al petto del grifon seco menarmi,
ove Beatrice stava volta a noi.

 Disser: "Fa che le viste non risparmi;   115
posto t'avem dinanzi a li smeraldi
ond' Amor già ti trasse le sue armi."

A thousand longings burning more than flames   118
compelled my eyes to watch the radiant eyes
that, motionless, were still fixed on the griffin.

Just like the sun within a mirror, so   121
the double-natured creature gleamed within,
now showing one, and now the other guise.

Consider, reader, if I did not wonder   124
when I saw something that displayed no movement
though its reflected image kept on changing.

And while, full of astonishment and gladness,   127
my soul tasted that food which, even as
it quenches hunger, spurs the appetite,

the other three, whose stance showed them to be   130
the members of a higher troop, advanced—
and, to their chant, they danced angelically.

"Turn, Beatrice, o turn your holy eyes   133
upon your faithful one," their song beseeched,
"who, that he might see you, has come so far.

Out of your grace, do us this grace; unveil   136
your lips to him, so that he may discern
the second beauty you have kept concealed."

O splendor of eternal living light,   139
who's ever grown so pale beneath Parnassus'
shade or has drunk so deeply from its fountain,

that he'd not seem to have his mind confounded,   142
trying to render you as you appeared
where heaven's harmony was your pale likeness—

your face, seen through the air, unveiled completely?   145

Mille disiri più che fiamma caldi   118
strinsermi li occhi a li occhi rilucenti,
che pur sopra 'l grifone stavan saldi.
    Come in lo specchio il sol, non altrimenti   121
la doppia fiera dentro vi raggiava,
or con altri, or con altri reggimenti.
    Pensa, lettor, s'io mi maravigliava,   124
quando vedea la cosa in sé star queta,
e ne l'idolo suo si trasmutava.
    Mentre che piena di stupore e lieta   127
l'anima mia gustava di quel cibo
che, saziando di sé, di sé asseta,
    sé dimostrando di più alto tribo   130
ne li atti, l'altre tre si fero avanti,
danzando al loro angelico caribo.
    "Volgi, Beatrice, volgi li occhi santi,"   133
era la sua canzone, "al tuo fedele
che, per vederti, ha mossi passi tanti!
    Per grazia fa noi grazia che disvele   136
a lui la bocca tua, sì che discerna
la seconda bellezza che tu cele."
    O isplendor di viva luce etterna,   139
chi palido si fece sotto l'ombra
sì di Parnaso, o bevve in sua cisterna,
    che non paresse aver la mente ingombra,   142
tentando a render te qual tu paresti
là dove armonizzando il ciel t'adombra,
    quando ne l'aere aperto ti solvesti?   145

XXXII · 148~160

BEATRICE

CANTO XXXII

My eyes were so insistent, so intent
on finding satisfaction for their ten-
year thirst that every other sense was spent.

And to each side, my eyes were walled in by   4
indifference to all else (with its old net,
the holy smile so drew them to itself),

when I was forced to turn my eyes leftward   7
by those three goddesses because I heard
them warning me: "You stare too fixedly."

And the condition that afflicts the sight   10
when eyes have just been struck by the sun's force
left me without my vision for a time.

But when my sight became accustomed to   13
lesser sensations (that is, lesser than
the mighty force that made my eyes retreat),

I saw the glorious army: it had wheeled   16
around and to the right; it had turned east;
it faced the seven flames and faced the sun.

Just as, protected by its shields, a squadron   19
will wheel, to save itself, around its standard
until all of its men have changed direction;

so here all troops of the celestial kingdom   22
within the vanguard passed in front of us
before the chariot swung around the pole-shaft.

Back to the wheels the ladies then returned;   25
and though the griffin moved the blessed burden,
when he did that, none of his feathers stirred.

The lovely lady who'd helped me ford Lethe,   28
and I and Statius, following the wheel
that turned right, round the inner, smaller arc,

were slowly passing through the tall woods—empty   31
because of one who had believed the serpent;
our pace was measured by angelic song.

The Earthly Paradise. The eastward path of the procession.
Adam's tree. The griffin, the chariot, and the reflowering tree.
The sleep and waking of Dante. Beatrice's words on Dante's
mission. The eagle, the fox, the dragon, and the transfigured
chariot. The giant and the whore.

CANTO XXXII 283

Tant' eran li occhi miei fissi e attenti
a disbramarsi la decenne sete,
che li altri sensi m'eran tutti spenti.

Ed essi quinci e quindi avien parete   4
di non caler—così lo santo riso
a sé traéli con l'antica rete!—

quando per forza mi fu vòlto il viso   7
ver' la sinistra mia da quelle dee,
perch' io udi' da loro un "Troppo fiso!"

e la disposizion ch'a veder èe   10
ne li occhi pur testé dal sol percossi,
sanza la vista alquanto esser mi fée.

Ma poi ch'al poco il viso riformossi   13
(e dico "al poco" per rispetto al molto
sensibile onde a forza mi rimossi),

vidi 'n sul braccio destro esser rivolto   16
lo glorïoso essercito, e tornarsi
col sole e con le sette fiamme al volto.

Come sotto li scudi per salvarsi   19
volgesi schiera, e sé gira col segno,
prima che possa tutta in sé mutarsi;

quella milizia del celeste regno   22
che procedeva, tutta trapassonne
pria che piegasse il carro il primo legno.

Indi a le rote si tornar le donne,   25
e 'l grifon mosse il benedetto carco
sì, che però nulla penna crollonne.

La bella donna che mi trasse al varco   28
e Stazio e io seguitavam la rota
che fé l'orbita sua con minore arco.

Sì passeggiando l'alta selva vòta,   31
colpa di quella ch'al serpente crese,
temprava i passi un'angelica nota.

The space we covered could be matched perhaps   34
by three flights of an unleashed arrow's shafts,
when Beatrice descended from the chariot.

"Adam," I heard all of them murmuring,   37
and then they drew around a tree whose every
branch had been stripped of flowers and of leaves.

As it grows higher, so its branches spread   40
wider; it reached a height that even in
their forests would amaze the Indians.

"Blessed are you, whose beak does not, o griffin,   43
pluck the sweet-tasting fruit that is forbidden
and then afflicts the belly that has eaten!"

So, round the robust tree, the others shouted;   46
and the two-natured animal: "Thus is
the seed of every righteous man preserved."

And turning to the pole-shaft he had pulled,   49
he drew it to the foot of the stripped tree
and, with a branch of that tree, tied the two.

Just like our plants that, when the great light falls 52
on earth, mixed with the light that shines behind
the stars of the celestial Fishes, swell

with buds—each plant renews its coloring   55
before the sun has yoked its steeds beneath
another constellation—so the tree,

whose boughs—before—had been so solitary,   58
was now renewed, showing a tint that was
less than the rose, more than the violet.

I did not understand the hymn that they   61
then sang—it is not sung here on this earth—
nor, drowsy, did I listen to the end.

Could I describe just how the ruthless eyes   64
(eyes whose long wakefulness cost them so dear),
hearing the tale of Syrinx, fell asleep,

then like a painter painting from a model,   67
I'd draw the way in which I fell asleep;
but I refrain—let one more skillful paint.

I move, therefore, straight to my waking time;   70
I say that radiance rent the veil of sleep,
as did a voice: "Rise up: what are you doing?"

Even as Peter, John, and James, when brought   73
to see the blossoms of the apple tree—
whose fruit abets the angels' hungering,

Forse in tre voli tanto spazio prese 34
disfrenata saetta, quanto eramo
rimossi, quando Bëatrice scese.

Io senti' mormorare a tutti "Adamo"; 37
poi cerchiaro una pianta dispogliata
di foglie e d'altra fronda in ciascun ramo.

La coma sua, che tanto si dilata 40
più quanto più è sù, fora da l'Indi
ne' boschi lor per altezza ammirata.

"Beato se', grifon, che non discindi 43
col becco d'esto legno dolce al gusto,
poscia che mal si torce il ventre quindi."

Così dintorno a l'albero robusto 46
gridaron li altri; e l'animal binato:
"Sì si conserva il seme d'ogne giusto."

E vòlto al temo ch'elli avea tirato, 49
trasselo al piè de la vedova frasca,
e quel di lei a lei lasciò legato.

Come le nostre piante, quando casca 52
giù la gran luce mischiata con quella
che raggia dietro a la celeste lasca,

turgide fansi, e poi si rinovella 55
di suo color ciascuna, pria che 'l sole
giunga li suoi corsier sotto altra stella;

men che di rose e più che di vïole 58
colore aprendo, s'innovò la pianta,
che prima avea le ramora sì sole.

Io non lo 'ntesi, né qui non si canta 61
l'inno che quella gente allor cantaro,
né la nota soffersi tutta quanta.

S'io potessi ritrar come assonnaro 64
li occhi spietati udendo di Siringa,
li occhi a cui pur vegghiar costò sì caro;

come pintor che con essempro pinga, 67
disegnerei com' io m'addormentai;
ma qual vuol sia che l'assonnar ben finga.

Però trascorro a quando mi svegliai, 70
e dico ch'un splendor mi squarciò 'l velo
del sonno, e un chiamar: "Surgi: che fai?"

Quali a veder de' fioretti del melo 73
che del suo pome li angeli fa ghiotti
e perpetüe nozze fa nel cielo,

providing endless wedding-feasts in Heaven— 76
were overwhelmed by what they saw, but then,
hearing the word that shattered deeper sleeps,

arose and saw their fellowship was smaller— 79
since Moses and Elijah now had left—
and saw a difference in their Teacher's dress;

so I awoke and saw, standing above me, 82
she who before—compassionate—had guided
my steps along the riverbank. Completely

bewildered, I asked: "Where is Beatrice?" 85
And she: "Beneath the boughs that were renewed,
she's seated on the root of that tree; see

the company surrounding her; the rest 88
have left; behind the griffin they have climbed
on high with song that is more sweet, more deep."

I do not know if she said more than that, 91
because, by now, I had in sight one who
excluded all things other from my view.

She sat alone upon the simple ground, 94
left there as guardian of the chariot
I'd seen the two-form animal tie fast.

The seven nymphs encircled her as garland, 97
and in their hands they held the lamps that can
not be extinguished by the north or south winds.

"Here you shall be—awhile—a visitor; 100
but you shall be with me—and without end—
Rome's citizen, the Rome in which Christ is

Roman; and thus, to profit that world which 103
lives badly, watch the chariot steadfastly
and, when you have returned beyond, transcribe

what you have seen." Thus, Beatrice; and I, 106
devoutly, at the feet of her commandments,
set mind and eyes where she had wished me to.

Never has lightning fallen with such swift 109
motion from a thick cloud, when it descends
from the most distant limit in the heavens,

as did the bird of Jove that I saw swoop 112
down through the tree, tearing the bark as well
as the new leaves and the new flowering.

It struck the chariot with all its force; 115
the chariot twisted, like a ship that's crossed
by seas that now storm starboard and now port.

Pietro e Giovanni e Iacopo condotti 76
e vinti, ritornaro a la parola
da la qual furon maggior sonni rotti,

    e videro scemata loro scuola 79
così di Moïsè come d'Elia,
e al maestro suo cangiata stola;

    tal torna' io, e vidi quella pia 82
sovra me starsi che conducitrice
fu de' miei passi lungo 'l fiume pria.

    E tutto in dubbio dissi: "Ov' è Beatrice?" 85
Ond' ella: "Vedi lei sotto la fronda
nova sedere in su la sua radice.

    Vedi la compagnia che la circonda: 88
li altri dopo 'l grifon sen vanno suso
con più dolce canzone e più profonda."

    E se più fu lo suo parlar diffuso, 91
non so, però che già ne li occhi m'era
quella ch'ad altro intender m'avea chiuso.

    Sola sedeasi in su la terra mera, 94
come guardia lasciata lì del plaustro
che legar vidi a la biforme fera.

    In cerchio le facevan di sé claustro 97
le sette ninfe, con quei lumi in mano
che son sicuri d'Aquilone e d'Austro.

    "Qui sarai tu poco tempo silvano; 100
e sarai meco sanza fine cive
di quella Roma onde Cristo è romano.

    Però, in pro del mondo che mal vive, 103
al carro tieni or li occhi, e quel che vedi,
ritornato di là, fa che tu scrive."

    Così Beatrice; e io, che tutto ai piedi 106
d'i suoi comandamenti era divoto,
la mente e li occhi ov' ella volle diedi.

    Non scese mai con sì veloce moto 109
foco di spessa nube, quando piove
da quel confine che più va remoto,

    com' io vidi calar l'uccel di Giove 112
per l'alber giù, rompendo de la scorza,
non che d'i fiori e de le foglie nove;

    e ferì 'l carro di tutta sua forza; 115
ond' el piegò come nave in fortuna,
vinta da l'onda, or da poggia, or da orza.

I then saw, as it leaped into the body   118
of that triumphal chariot, a fox
that seemed to lack all honest nourishment:
    but, as she railed against its squalid sins,   121
my lady forced that fox to flight as quick
as, stripped of flesh, its bones permitted it.
    Then I could see the eagle plunge—again   124
down through the tree—into the chariot
and leave it feathered with its plumage; and,
    just like a voice from an embittered heart,   127
a voice issued from Heaven, saying this:
"O my small bark, your freight is wickedness!"
    Then did the ground between the two wheels seem   130
to me to open; from the earth, a dragon
emerged; it drove its tail up through the chariot;
    and like a wasp when it retracts its sting,   133
drawing its venomed tail back to itself,
it dragged part of the bottom off, and went
    its way, undulating. And what was left   136
was covered with the eagle's plumes—perhaps
offered with sound and kind intent—much as
    grass covers fertile ground; and the pole-shaft   139
and both wheels were re-covered in less time
than mouth must be kept open when one sighs.
    Transfigured so, the saintly instrument   142
grew heads, which sprouted from its parts; three grew
upon the pole-shaft, and one at each corner.
    The three were horned like oxen, but the four   145
had just a single horn upon their foreheads:
such monsters never have been seen before.
    Just like a fortress set on a steep slope,   148
securely seated there, ungirt, a whore,
whose eyes were quick to rove, appeared to me;
    and I saw at her side, erect, a giant,   151
who seemed to serve as her custodian;
and they—again, again—embraced each other.
    But when she turned her wandering, wanton eyes   154
to me, then that ferocious amador
beat her from head to foot; then, swollen with
    suspicion, fierce with anger, he untied   157
the chariot-made-monster, dragging it
into the wood, so that I could not see
    either the whore or the strange chariot-beast.   160

Poscia vidi avventarsi ne la cuna   118
del trïunfal veiculo una volpe
che d'ogne pasto buon parea digiuna;

    ma, riprendendo lei di laide colpe,   121
la donna mia la volse in tanta futa
quanto sofferser l'ossa sanza polpe.

    Poscia per indi ond' era pria venuta,   124
l'aguglia vidi scender giù ne l'arca
del carro e lasciar lei di sé pennuta;

    e qual esce di cuor che si rammarca,   127
tal voce uscì del cielo e cotal disse:
"O navicella mia, com' mal se' carca!"

    Poi parve a me che la terra s'aprisse   130
tr'ambo le ruote, e vidi uscirne un drago
che per lo carro sù la coda fisse;

    e come vespa che ritragge l'ago,   133
a sé traendo la coda maligna,
trasse del fondo, e gissen vago vago.

    Quel che rimase, come da gramigna   136
vivace terra, da la piuma, offerta
forse con intenzion sana e benigna,

    si ricoperse, e funne ricoperta   139
e l'una e l'altra rota e 'l temo, in tanto
che più tiene un sospir la bocca aperta.

    Trasformato così 'l dificio santo   142
mise fuor teste per le parti sue,
tre sovra 'l temo e una in ciascun canto.

    Le prime eran cornute come bue,   145
ma le quattro un sol corno avean per fronte:
simile mostro visto ancor non fue.

    Sicura, quasi rocca in alto monte,   148
seder sovresso una puttana sciolta
m'apparve con le ciglia intorno pronte;

    e come perché non li fosse tolta,   151
vidi di costa a lei dritto un gigante;
e basciavansi insieme alcuna volta.

    Ma perché l'occhio cupido e vagante   154
a me rivolse, quel feroce drudo
la flagellò dal capo infin le piante;

    poi, di sospetto pieno e d'ira crudo,   157
disciolse il mostro, e trassel per la selva,
tanto che sol di lei mi fece scudo

    a la puttana e a la nova belva.   160

CANTO XXXIII

Weeping, the women then began—now three,
now four, alternately—to psalm gently,
"*Deus venerunt gentes*"; and at this,
    sighing and full of pity, Beatrice   4
was changed; she listened, grieving little less
than Mary when, beneath the Cross, she wept.
    But when the seven virgins had completed   7
their psalm, and she was free to speak, erect,
her coloring like ardent fire, she answered:
    "*Modicum, et non videbitis me*   10
et iterum, sisters delightful to me,
modicum, et vos videbitis me."
    Then she set all the seven nymphs in front   13
of her and signaled me, the lady, and
the sage who had remained, to move behind her.
    So she advanced; and I do not believe   16
that she had taken her tenth step upon
the ground before her eyes had struck my eyes;
    and gazing tranquilly, "Pray come more quickly," 19
she said to me, "so that you are more ready
to listen to me should I speak to you."
    As soon as I, responding to my duty,   22
had joined her, she said: "Brother, why not try,
since now you're at my side, to query me?"
    Like those who, speaking to superiors   25
too reverently do not speak distinctly,
not drawing their clear voice up to their teeth—
    so did I speak with sound too incomplete   28
when I began: "Lady, you know my need
to know, and know how it can be appeased."
    And she to me: "I'd have you disentangle   31
yourself, from this point on, from fear and shame,
that you no longer speak like one who dreams.

The Earthly Paradise. The lament of the seven women and the compassion of Beatrice. Beatrice's prophecy: God's vengeance against the dragon, the whore, and the giant. Her words on Adam's tree. Her last rebuke of Dante. Dante led to Eunoe by Matilda. The sweet draught. Readiness for Paradise.

CANTO XXXIII 291

"*Deus, venerunt gentes,*" alternando
or tre or quattro dolce salmodia,
le donne incominciaro, e lagrimando;
  e Bëatrice, sospirosa e pia,   4
quelle ascoltava sì fatta, che poco
più a la croce si cambiò Maria.
  Ma poi che l'altre vergini dier loco   7
a lei di dir, levata dritta in pè,
rispuose, colorata come foco:
  "*Modicum, et non videbitis me*;   10
et iterum, sorelle mie dilette,
modicum, et vos videbitis me."
  Poi le si mise innanzi tutte e sette,   13
e dopo sé, solo accennando, mosse
me e la donna e 'l savio che ristette.
  Così sen giva; e non credo che fosse   16
lo decimo suo passo in terra posto,
quando con li occhi li occhi mi percosse;
  e con tranquillo aspetto "Vien più tosto,"   19
mi disse, "tanto che, s'io parlo teco,
ad ascoltarmi tu sie ben disposto."
  Sì com' io fui, com' io dovëa, seco,   22
dissemi: "Frate, perché non t'attenti
a domandarmi omai venendo meco?"
  Come a color che troppo reverenti   25
dinanzi a suo maggior parlando sono,
che non traggon la voce viva ai denti,
  avvenne a me, che sanza intero suono   28
incominciai: "Madonna, mia bisogna
voi conoscete, e ciò ch'ad essa è buono."
  Ed ella a me: "Da tema e da vergogna   31
voglio che tu omai ti disviluppe,
sì che non parli più com' om che sogna.

Know that the vessel which the serpent broke   34
was and is not; but he whose fault it is
may rest assured—God's vengeance fears no hindrance.

The eagle that had left its plumes within   37
the chariot, which then became a monster
and then a prey, will not forever be

without an heir; for I can plainly see,   40
and thus I tell it: stars already close
at hand, which can't be blocked or checked, will bring

a time in which, dispatched by God, a Five   43
Hundred and Ten and Five will slay the whore
together with that giant who sins with her.

And what I tell, as dark as Sphinx and Themis,   46
may leave you less convinced because—like these—
it tires the intellect with quandaries;

but soon events themselves will be the Naiads   49
that clarify this obstinate enigma—
but without injury to grain or herds.

Take note; and even as I speak these words,   52
do you transmit them in your turn to those
who live the life that is a race to death.

And when you write them, keep in mind that you   55
must not conceal what you've seen of the tree
that now has been despoiled twice over here.

Whoever robs or rends that tree offends,   58
with his blaspheming action, God; for He
created it for His sole use—holy.

For tasting of that tree, the first soul waited   61
five thousand years and more in grief and longing
for Him who on Himself avenged that taste.

Your intellect's asleep if it can't see   64
how singular's the cause that makes that tree
so tall and makes it grow invertedly.

And if, like waters of the Elsa, your   67
vain thoughts did not encrust your mind; if your
delight in them were not like Pyramus

staining the mulberry, you'd recognize   70
in that tree's form and height the moral sense
God's justice had when He forbade trespass.

But since I see your intellect is made   73
of stone and, petrified, grown so opaque—
the light of what I say has left you dazed—

Sappi che 'l vaso che 'l serpente ruppe,
fu e non è; ma chi n'ha colpa, creda
che vendetta di Dio non teme suppe.

Non sarà tutto tempo sanza reda   37
l'aguglia che lasciò le penne al carro,
per che divenne mostro e poscia preda;

ch'io veggio certamente, e però il narro,   40
a darne tempo già stelle propinque,
secure d'ogn' intoppo e d'ogne sbarro,

nel quale un cinquecento diece e cinque,   43
messo di Dio, anciderà la fuia
con quel gigante che con lei delinque.

E forse che la mia narrazion buia,   46
qual Temi e Sfinge, men ti persuade,
perch' a lor modo lo 'ntelletto attuia;

ma tosto fier li fatti le Naiade,   49
che solveranno questo enigma forte
sanza danno di pecore o di biade.

Tu nota; e sì come da me son porte,   52
così queste parole segna a' vivi
del viver ch'è un correre a la morte.

E aggi a mente, quando tu le scrivi,   55
di non celar qual hai vista la pianta
ch'è or due volte dirubata quivi.

Qualunque ruba quella o quella schianta,   58
con bestemmia di fatto offende a Dio,
che solo a l'uso suo la creò santa.

Per morder quella, in pena e in disio   61
cinquemilia anni e più l'anima prima
bramò colui che 'l morso in sé punio.

Dorme lo 'ngegno tuo, se non estima   64
per singular cagione essere eccelsa
lei tanto e sì travolta ne la cima.

E se stati non fossero acqua d'Elsa   67
li pensier vani intorno a la tua mente,
e 'l piacer loro un Piramo a la gelsa,

per tante circostanze solamente   70
la giustizia di Dio, ne l'interdetto,
conosceresti a l'arbor moralmente.

Ma perch' io veggio te ne lo 'ntelletto   73
fatto di pietra e, impetrato, tinto,
sì che t'abbaglia il lume del mio detto,

I'd also have you bear my words within you—   76
if not inscribed, at least outlined— just as
the pilgrim's staff is brought back wreathed with palm."

     And I: "Even as wax the seal's impressed,   79
where there's no alteration in the form,
so does my brain now bear what you have stamped.

     But why does your desired word ascend   82
so high above my understanding that
the more I try, the more am I denied?"

     "That you may recognize," she said, "the school   85
that you have followed and may see if what
it taught can comprehend what I have said—

     and see that, as the earth is distant from   88
the highest and the swiftest of the heavens,
so distant is your way from the divine."

     And I replied to her: "I don't remember   91
making myself a stranger to you, nor
does conscience gnaw at me because of that."

     "And if you can't remember that," she answered,   94
smiling, "then call to mind how you—today—
have drunk of Lethe; and if smoke is proof

     of fire, then it is clear: we can conclude   97
from this forgetfulness, that in your will
there was a fault—your will had turned elsewhere.

     But from now on the words I speak will be   100
naked; that is appropriate if they
would be laid bare before your still-crude sight."

     More incandescent now, with slower steps,   103
the sun was pacing the meridian,
which alters with the place from which it's seen,

     when, just as one who serves as escort for   106
a group will halt if he has come upon
things strange or even traces of strangeness,

     the seven ladies halted at the edge   109
of a dense shadow such as mountains cast,
beneath green leaves and black boughs, on cold banks.

     In front of them I seemed to see Euphrates   112
and Tigris issuing from one same spring
and then, as friends do, separating slowly.

     "O light, o glory of the human race,   115
what water is this, flowing from one source
and then becoming distant from itself?"

voglio anco, e se non scritto, almen dipinto,
che 'l te ne porti dentro a te per quello
che si reca il bordon di palma cinto."

E io: "Sì come cera da suggello,   79
che la figura impressa non trasmuta,
segnato è or da voi lo mio cervello.

Ma perchè tanto sovra mia veduta   82
vostra parola disïata vola,
che più la perde quanto più s'aiuta?"

"Perché conoschi," disse, "quella scuola   85
c'hai seguitata, e veggi sua dottrina
come può seguitar la mia parola;

e veggi vostra via da la divina   88
distar cotanto, quanto si discorda
da terra il ciel che più alto festina."

Ond' io rispuosi lei: "Non mi ricorda   91
ch'i' stranïasse me già mai da voi,
né honne coscïenza che rimorda."

"E se tu ricordar non te ne puoi,"   94
sorridendo rispuose, "or ti rammenta
come bevesti di Letè ancoi;

e se dal fummo foco s'argomenta,   97
cotesta oblivïon chiaro conchiude
colpa ne la tua voglia altrove attenta.

Veramente oramai saranno nude   100
le mie parole, quanto converrassi
quelle scovrire a la tua vista rude."

E più corusco e con più lenti passi   103
teneva il sole il cerchio di merigge,
che qua e là, come li aspetti, fassi,

quando s'affisser, sì come s'affigge   106
chi va dinanzi a gente per iscorta
se trova novitate o sue vestigge,

le sette donne al fin d'un'ombra smorta,   109
qual sotto foglie verdi e rami nigri
sovra suoi freddi rivi l'alpe porta.

Dinanzi ad esse Eufratès e Tigri   112
veder mi parve uscir d'una fontana,
e, quasi amici, dipartirsi pigri.

"O luce, o gloria de la gente umana,   115
che acqua è questa che qui si dispiega
da un principio e sé da sé lontana?"

Her answer to what I had asked was: "Ask   118
Matilda to explain this"; and the lovely
lady, as one who frees herself from blame,

replied: "He's heard of this and other matters   121
from me; and I am sure that Lethe's waters
have not obscured his memory of this."

And Beatrice:"Perhaps some greater care,   124
which often weakens memory, has made
his mind, in things regarding sight, grow dark.

But see Eunoe as it flows from there: 127
lead him to it and, as you're used to doing,
revive the power that is faint in him."

As would the noble soul, which offers no   130
excuse, but makes another's will its own
as soon as signs reveal that will; just so,

when she had taken me, the lovely lady   133
moved forward; and she said with womanly
courtesy to Statius: "Come with him."

If, reader, I had ampler space in which   136
to write, I'd sing—though incompletely—that
sweet draught for which my thirst was limitless;

but since all of the pages pre-disposed   139
for this, the second canticle, are full,
the curb of art will not let me continue.

From that most holy wave I now returned   142
to Beatrice; remade, as new trees are
renewed when they bring forth new boughs, I was

pure and prepared to climb unto the stars.   145

Per cotal priego detto mi fu: "Priega
Matelda che 'l ti dica." E qui rispuose,
come fa chi da colpa si dislega,

    la bella donna: "Questo e altre cose   121
dette li son per me; e son sicura
che l'acqua di Letè non gliel nascose."

    E Bëatrice: "Forse maggior cura,   124
che spesse volte la memoria priva,
fatt' ha la mente sua ne li occhi oscura.

    Ma vedi Eünoè che là diriva: 127
menalo ad esso, e come tu se' usa,
la tramortita sua virtù ravviva."

    Come anima gentil, che non fa scusa,   130
ma fa sua voglia de la voglia altrui
tosto che è per segno fuor dischiusa;

    così, poi che da essa preso fui,   133
la bella donna mossesi, e a Stazio
donnescamente disse: "Vien con lui."

    S'io avessi, lettor, più lungo spazio   136
da scrivere, i' pur cantere' in parte
lo dolce ber che mai non m'avria sazio;

    ma perché piene son tutte le carte   139
ordite a questa cantica seconda,
non mi lascia più ir lo fren de l'arte.

    Io ritornai da la santissima onda   142
rifatto sì come piante novelle
rinovellate di novella fronda,

    puro e disposto a salire a le stelle.   145

A NOTE ON THE DRAWINGS FOR THE CALIFORNIA DANTE

When I began work on *Inferno* in 1979, I was filled with apprehension and some fear of my predecessors. By the time the book was published in 1980, those fears and apprehensions had been, if not dispelled, at least quieted. The major problems of format, iconographic approach, and the style and technique of drawing had been solved, establishing as a fait accompli the format and technique for the remaining two volumes, *Purgatorio* and *Paradiso*. Consequently, I began the *Purgatorio* suite with a sense of ease and even a bit of daring.

Quiet meditations on my readings of the text and lively conversations with Allen Mandelbaum brought me to recognize passion and suffering as the primary wards of *my* key to *Purgatorio*'s illustration. Using the human face and figure, the most expressive vehicles available to an artist, I hoped to portray that passion and suffering reflected in a drumming procession of Purgatory's inhabitants and evocations—Manfred and St. Stephen; Buonconte and Omberto; Haman and Aglauros. Hope, of course, was also a presence—renewed in the angelic apparitions and in the stellar cross that preludes *Purgatorio*. The theme of close confrontation established in *Inferno* (there are twenty-nine pairs of eyes looking directly at the viewer) is continued in the *Purgatorio* suite, but with a passive rather than threatening character.

One hundred and fifty-seven drawings for *Purgatorio* were begun—thirty-four survived. Those thirty-four were culled, cajoled, and completed from amorphic beginnings, loose sketches, abstract gestures, and quick tracings.

The process of drawing described in the first volume of the *California Dante* was closely followed for this suite as well; quick, *urgent* slashes of pale washes laid over penciled gestures; mingling into that wetness, dark washes and dense inks; adding and subtracting, I explored many solutions simultaneously.

Often there is no clear premonition of a "final" drawing—drawings emerge through the act of drawing (e.g., Arachne,

The Isle of Purgatory, The Helmsman Angel). Conversely, images are also approached quite literally and deliberately, —a searching *through* drawing for a preconceived idea (e.g., Beatrice, Dante with the Seven *P's*, Virgil and Statius).

The *Purgatorio* drawings are generally simpler than the *Inferno* drawings, both in subject and in composition. There is, for instance, only one page in *Purgatorio* which has more than one autonomous image on it—the double portrait of The Virgin Mary and Diana. That drawing echoes the *six* multiple-image pages in *Inferno* (three of which are actually triple images). Likewise, in the *Purgatorio* suite, there is a single image which crosses over two pages—the diptych of Canto xxix. I leave it as suggestion that this cross-over image presages what may happen with the *Paradiso* suite.

As the *Purgatorio* drawings are *simpler* than the *Inferno* drawings, so also are they *darker*—another step in the procession towards *Paradiso*, from the frightening, complex cacophony and pain of precise—even minutely limned—images towards the great and profound quiet of mystery.

Northampton, Massachusetts   Barry Moser
September, 1981

ALLEN MANDELBAUM's verse volumes are: *Chelmaxioms: The Maxims, Axioms, Maxioms of Chelm*; *Leaves of Absence*; *A Lied of Letterpress*; *Journeyman*; and the forthcoming *The Savantasse of Montparnasse*. (The first two of these volumes are now being translated into Italian by A. Cima.) In addition to *The Aeneid of Virgil: A Verse Translation*, a University of California Press volume for which he won a National Book Award, his verse translations/editions include: *Life of a Man* by Giuseppe Ungaretti; *Selected Writings of Salvatore Quasimodo*; *Selected Poems of Giuseppe Ungaretti*; and the forthcoming *Mediterranean: Selected Poems of Eugenio Montale*. The general title of his selected verse translations will be *Targuman*, with the first three volumes devoted to modern Italian, Latin, and medieval Hebrew poetry, respectively. A recipient of the Order of Merit from the Republic of Italy, Mr. Mandelbaum was in the Society of Fellows at Harvard University, a Rockefeller Fellow in Humanities, and a Fulbright Research Scholar in Italy. On leaves away from the Graduate Center of the City University of New York, where he is Professor of English and Comparative Literature, he has been Hurst Professor at Washington University in St. Louis, Honors Professor of Humanities at the University of Houston, and Distinguished Professor of Humanities at the University of Colorado at Boulder.

BARRY MOSER was educated at Auburn University and the University of Tennessee at Chattanooga, and did graduate studies at the University of Massachusetts. His work, which includes the books of Pennyroyal Press, is represented in many collections, museums, and libraries in the United States and abroad, among them, The British Museum, The Library of Congress, The New York Public Library, The National Library of Australia, The London College of Printing, Harvard University, Cambridge University, Dartmouth College. Mr. Moser has exhibited internationally in both one-man and group exhibits. His illustrated books form a list of over fifty titles, including the Arion Press *Moby Dick*, The Pennyroyal *Alice*, and California's Bimillennial *Aeneid*. In addition to being a designer, printer, wood engraver, and draughtsman, he is a member of the faculty of The Williston-Northampton School in Easthampton, Massachusetts, and lectures and often acts as visiting artist at universities across the country.

This volume of *The California Dante* was designed by Barry Moser and Czeslaw Jan Grycz. The typeface, Monotype Dante, was designed in 1957 by the late Giovanni Mardersteig and first used by him at the Officina Bodoni, Verona. The type was set by Michael and Winifred Bixler, Boston, Massachusetts. The paper is Mohawk Superfine, manufactured by the Mohawk Paper Mills, Cohoes, New York. The illustrations were reproduced by the three-dot process under the supervision of Charles Wood and were printed with the text by the Southeastern Printing Company, Stuart, Florida. This trade edition will be followed by a Pennyroyal/California bibliophiles' edition in five hundred signed and numbered copies of which twenty are reserved for the Schlesinger Foundation and its publisher, Pieraldo Editore, Socio Benemerito.